Sell to Excel

Other Books by The Author

Happiness: A Way of Life

Face Time: Event Planning for Business Success

The Stuff of Life

Sell to Excel

The Art and Science *of* Personal Selling

ASIF ZAIDI

SELL TO EXCEL
THE ART AND SCIENCE OF PERSONAL SELLING

iUniverse books may be ordered through booksellers or by contacting:

iUniverse
1663 Liberty Drive
Bloomington, IN 47403
www.iuniverse.com
1-800-Authors (1-800-288-4677)

ISBN: 978-1-5320-7598-8 (sc)
ISBN: 978-1-5320-7599-5 (hc)
ISBN: 978-1-5320-7597-1 (e)

Library of Congress Control Number: 2019908531

Print information available on the last page.

iUniverse rev. date: 06/25/2019

Contents

Preface vii

Introduction... ix

I.   THE BASICS OF PERSONAL SELLING 1

    1.   Personal Selling... 3

    2.   Helping Buyers Buy.. 7

    3.   Identifying Customer Requirements................... 38

    4.   Handling Objections..51

    5.   In-Person Selling 60

    6.   Influencing... 67

    7.   Negotiating 113

    8.   Assertiveness...135

    9.   Being An Agent of Change.................................145

    10. Making A Presentation......................................147

II. THE ART OF PERSONAL SELLING 161

    11. Using Metaphors...163

    12. Asking Questions...169

    13. Anchoring..179

    14. Reframing..183

    15. Mirroring.. 187

    16. Storytelling 193

    17. Active Listening 197

    18. Likability.. 206

    19. Selling on Value 213

20. Selling to The Old Brain... 229
21. Networking... 234
22. Using Voicemail 257
23. Handling Rejection 261

Other Books by the Author.. 269

Preface

Selling is the art of persuasion at its finest. It is a way to willingly influence others' behavior, to develop relationships, to build credibility, and to let the world know what you have to offer. No one gets by without selling.

In fact, selling may be the single most important skill in human life. Whether you are a business person, a teacher, a prophet, or a parent, to get your point across you have to sell. The first skill we learn as babies is selling. We begin by crying and then move on to crowing, smiling, frowning, moaning, and beyond.

Selling is the second oldest profession in the world, after farming. Effective selling helps people make their decisions. A good business always thinks long-term and privileges building lasting relationships with its customers.

For the purposes of this book, we will limit our discussion to selling in business and the situations where face-to-face human interaction is warranted. In almost every situation where two people come together, there is an opportunity for someone to sell something. This book will help make you alert to selling situations and equip you with selling skills to use in such situations on a daily basis.

By the same token, this is not a book about when to use personal selling. Whether or not a company uses personal selling as part of its marketing mix depends on its industry and its business model.

Introduction

Many people do not see themselves as selling, whereas they are actually doing it all the time. But if you ask them professionally to sell a product, a service, an idea, or themselves, they feel awkward. Nothing sabotages business success more than viewing selling with trepidation or indifference. You can change that by seeing what you are selling as an instrument for other people to achieve their own goals. The shared economy powered by the digital revolution has shifted power from the seller to the buyer. More than ever, selling is about understanding the customer's needs and creating a solution to fulfill them. The value of a selling proposition is dictated by each customer's unique situation. If you cannot understand how your offering will benefit your prospects, then neither will they.

Digitalization is changing the way we buy and sell. Online channels are ubiquitous and getting cheaper. Customers like them for ease of use and because they make it convenient to compare information between products, competitors, and markets. In this situation it is easy to assume that personal selling can simply be transferred to online channels, or that customers are only interested in the transaction and see little value in interacting with a sales consultant.

However, we should not underestimate the human factor. It still plays an important role in a number of industries, especially in premium products. Surveys show that customers often remain open to being convinced, even after they have spent time researching a product. They find the human element reassuring. This offers salespeople the opportunity to be experts in their area and to provide value beyond the solution itself. Fortified with the right digital tools, process, and knowledge, salespeople can enable decision-making, improve the purchasing experience, and help customers build a relationship with the brand.

When your product or service has a high unit value, requires a demonstration of its benefits, and relies on differentiation, it is well suited for personal sales. Personal selling, though, needs a new approach; conventional sales strategies that rely on pushing customers into closing sales will no longer work in the digital age. Sales interactions must add value from the customer's perspective. Current data suggests that salespeople whose interactions include customized product configuration, product knowledge, a systematic approach to sales talks, and measurement of value are more successful at selling. They sell at higher premiums, are better at cross-selling, are more likely to secure a sale, and command greater customer satisfaction.

PART I

THE BASICS OF PERSONAL SELLING

Salespeople from different industries go through similar basic stages when making a sale. While they may carry different names in different businesses, these activities include the following:

- Identifying the target market
- Prospecting
- Qualifying
- Planning the approach
- Research
- Presentation
- Demonstration
- Handling objections
- Negotiation
- Closing
- Follow-up

In this section, we will discuss how you can address the buyer's needs and preferences and offer advice, information, and recommendations so that as a skilled salesperson, you can help buyers save money and time during the decision process.

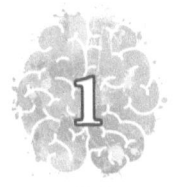

Personal Selling

"Salesmanship is limitless. Our very living is selling. We are all salespeople."
James Cash Penney

Personal selling is the process of interacting with prospects face-to-face with the intent of selling a product or service. What distinguishes personal selling from other methods of selling—online selling, advertising, sales promotion, public relations—is that the seller conducts business with the buyer in person. Most successful entrepreneurs and executives are highly skilled at personal selling. They are able to personally represent and promote their companies and products in the marketplace. Despite the increasing influence of technology in our interactions with others, personal selling remains alive, robust, and relevant. Personal interface with customers gives you the chance to build trust, create a stronger connection, and help in their decision-making process.

ADVANTAGES

Here are some of the advantages of personal selling.

1. It is focused: Unlike a mass-marketing message that reaches many people outside the target market, personal selling requires the sales force to pinpoint the target market, establish contacts, and make focused efforts, with a stronger probability of leading to a sale.

2. It helps build personal relationships: Personal selling is an effective means for building relationships with customers, which is important when a sale takes a considerable amount of time to complete. It also helps make international sales in cultures where personal relationships between the buyer and seller are often more important than seeking the best business deal.

3. It adapts solutions to customer requirements: Customers value being able to adapt products to their own needs. Customers generally appreciate the flexibility of being able to choose from a wide range of options, but they can be overwhelmed when faced with too many choices. Personal selling gives the salesperson an opportunity to reduce complexity and prevent choice overload. Customers are more satisfied with sales talks when they feel that the product or service configurations have been adjusted to best suit their needs.

4. It adds value through sales talk: The salesperson can add value at every interaction throughout the sales process by presenting pertinent, convincing content. For example, comparison with alternatives is a great tool to generate value. Personal selling also generates a focus on the content and not the price. The salesperson is also able to defend the price based on the benefits of the solution against those of the competition.

5. It offers flexibility: An important advantage of personal selling is its flexibility. Salespeople can customize their presentations to fit the needs, motives, and behavior of individual customers. You can gauge the customer's reaction to a sales approach and immediately adjust the message to foster better understanding.

6. It brings a systematic approach to sales: Personal selling enables you to follow a structured sales process with strategic elements—such as cost-benefit analysis, comparative scrutiny, cross-selling, and upselling. Salespeople who employ an organized sales approach with a specific sequence achieve better results.

7. It shows the productivity of each step: You can measure the value of each step in the sales process, not just the results at the end. This gives you the opportunity to identify best practices and areas for improvement and to re-engineer your sales interaction accordingly. Most businesses have heavily invested in digital technologies to streamline and optimize sales operations. The challenge is to innovate and add value to your offline sales consultations beyond what is available online in order to increase cross-selling, upselling, and customer loyalty.

8. It adds precision: Personal selling enables you to target your message precisely to the customer and obtain immediate feedback. In this way, it is more precise and often more persuasive than other forms of promotion. Personal selling makes it easy for the customer to determine their return on investment (ROI).

9. It is a valuable source of information: Personal selling can be an important source of market information. It allows salespeople to learn about customers' feedback, competitors' products, market trends, or emerging customer needs.

10. It builds customer loyalty: When you act as a problem solver and advisor for customers rather than merely pushing for a sale, personal selling can help a business build loyal, long-term relationships with customers.

11. It gives an opportunity to close: The most significant advantage of personal selling is that a salesperson can effectively respond to and overcome concerns and reservations. You are in an excellent position to encourage the customer to act.

12. It is complementary to other promotional tools: Personal selling is a great way to support advertising, promotion, and publicity. It can render sales promotion tools more real by adding a personal touch.

13. It gets immediate feedback: This is the only selling technique that delivers immediate feedback from customers.

14. It draws on the prospect's social drives: A salesperson can understand and draw on a buyer's social motives—fear, love, hate, envy, status, or prestige—to make the sale.

CHALLENGES

Personal selling comes with challenges as well.

1. High cost: Personal selling entails higher costs—salaries, perks, travel, lodging and so on—and therefore is not competitive in every industry. Companies can, however, reduce sales costs by complementing personal selling with other techniques such as telemarketing, direct mail, toll-free numbers, and online communication with qualified prospects. Technology can be used to convey sales messages, reply to questions, take payment, and follow up.

2. Need for the right people: Probably the biggest challenge in personal selling is finding and retaining good salespeople. This book is written for that purpose—to make you a good salesperson and meet that demand.

3. Message inconsistency: It is difficult to get all salespeople to adhere to a uniform sales culture, message, and ethics. Many salespeople view themselves as independent from the organization, so they may devise their own sales techniques and use their own message strategies.

Helping Buyers Buy

"Every sale has five obstacles: no need, no money, no hurry, no desire, no trust."
Zig Ziglar

The art of selling requires you to concentrate on the buyer to understand their needs and to attract, engage, and then empower them to buy. Selling in this age of information and accessibility revolves totally around the buyer. It is no longer difficult to reach the buyer; what matters is how you help them buy. For that you have to be focused on the buyer and not on your product or yourself. To help a buyer buy, you must relate to the buyer's top-of-mind concerns. Helping a buyer requires you to view every transaction as a win-win equation: you help a buyer with a solution to their need, and in the process help your business turn an idea into revenue.

Your competition is not just a competitor of your product or service; it can also be another priority in the buying organization. To help the buyer buy, you must often enable them to sell your solution within their organization. Once you have convinced a manager to buy, their work is only beginning. Many potential sales fail to materialize because the person you are dealing with is unable to justify their purchase decision to their colleagues.

There are four steps in a buying process: trust, needs, help, and hurry.

TRUST

Trust is the foundation of any successful relationship. People do business with people they like and trust, so let's start with that. Trust is invariably the first step in the journey of selling. We all need to feel understood by others and find it easier to trust people who we think understand us. From my years in business, I can tell you that one common failing of many salespeople is that they fail to gain their buyer's trust. Trust plays a greater role than ever because today's customers buy differently; they know there is no urgency because good deals, good salespeople, and good companies show up every day. If you do not work on building trust, then you are missing out on a decisive distinguisher.

WINNING THE TRUST OF A BUYER

Trust is the foundation to all customer experiences. It cannot be developed in a day, but it can be wrecked fast. Pay attention to each customer individually instead of rushing to get things done. That can help create a long-term relationship of trust. Be intentional and strategic about the way you relate to the buyer. Here are some suggestions for gaining the trust of a buyer:

1. Be passionate about what you are selling: "For every sale you miss because you're too enthusiastic, you will miss a hundred because you're not enthusiastic enough," said sales guru Zig Ziglar. And he was spot on.

Passion is when you view what you sell not as a job, but as your calling. Passion is contagious; deeply caring about what you sell attracts people to you. Tell your story of why you do what you do and what makes it special for you. Do not use bombast, but use your expertise to build credibility. A desire to share your story shows passion and builds bridges. Discover common ground with your customer to explore where your passions might intersect.

Your passion also motivates customers to recommend you to their peers; they will want to carry forth the message that both you and your offerings are worth the trust. Here are some suggestions for conveying passion for what you sell:

Build the right attitude. In sales, attitude and mindset are everything. If you lack enthusiasm for your offering and for how the buyer will benefit, you will not inspire their trust. Passion for what and how you are selling is essential for building trust with your customer.

Enjoy the process. Now that your journey has brought you face-to-face with the prospect, the next step is to arm them with knowledge and offer great advice, guiding them to their purchase decision. Enjoy demonstrating how your solution meets the prospect's needs. Your buyer will trust you when they feel that you have a strong belief in the value and effectiveness of what you are selling. The buyer then sees you as a trusted advisor. They feel secure in the knowledge that you stand behind your claims and that their needs rank highest in your mind.

Sell the idea. A drill-machine manufacturer sells a hole. A coffee shop sells its barista experience, its coffee aroma, and its ambience. A gym sells a healthier you. No matter what you are selling, you are selling ideas. When you see the big picture through your customer's eyes, you will feel more passionate about addressing their needs, hopes, wishes, desires, and fears. Be passionate about helping the customer make the best choice for them.

Listen well. Passion is not gauged by your rehearsed delivery of canned pitches; it comes through in how well you listen to your customer's requests. And next, through how well you explain your solution's fit with the customer's needs as you have heard and understood them.

Work for the customer. You cannot become a trusted advisor without passion for the customer's wellbeing. In wanting the best possible outcome for your customer, you create a happier, more fulfilled work life for yourself—one in which you are passionate about what you do. You also help your performance; the more customers trust you, the more they are likely to buy from you.

2. Do your research: Research your prospect so that you do not have to ask the obvious. Knowing your customer's industry and competition helps you ascertain their buying criteria and performance imperatives. Be able to provide case studies and testimonials of other relevant winning experiences. Tell how you helped someone achieve the results that your customer hopes to achieve. Social proof is a highly effective tool for building trust.

3. Inquire: When a doctor or a car mechanic asks you specific, relevant questions to find more about your situation, that builds trust. Doesn't it? The same holds true for your selling. Before they can trust your prescription, your customer has to feel that you understand their needs and their pain.

4. Build your ability: Do people see you as an authority in your profession? Can they count on your insights when they seek advice? Offering expertise that your customer can trust is a sure way to build trust. People have to be able to trust your ability, and not just your intent, to help them. Trust in a seller's capability means buyers believe you can do what you say you can. Be an expert; know your buyer's industry and business, competition, marketplace, full set of needs, and more. If you want to guide the way, you must be able to answer a buyer's questions about your offerings and the market, as well as about the buying process itself. Be prepared to discuss, in concrete terms, what results the buyer can expect to achieve.

5. Be ethical: The foundation for trust consists not in what you do but in how you do it. An authentic person is authentic in every aspect of their behavior, and that also extends into their work. Never try to manipulate your customer; manipulation kills trust. Handle every aspect of the sales process with a high degree of professionalism. Make sure what you sell is the right fit. Even if you forego the sale, you will have made a friend and a business contact.

Regardless of a company's reputation, customers choose to do business with people they trust. To build a group of customers who consider you a credible salesperson, you have to earn their trust by behaving ethically and conveying a commitment to customer needs. Here are some suggestions for ethical behavior:

Be transparent. Always present full and clear information. If you do not have the information a customer wants, be honest enough to admit it; let the customer know, and offer to find out. The customer must be confident that they can rely on the information you provide.

Be fair. Describe your competition and compare yourself with them fairly. Criticizing the competition unfairly is seen as unethical.

Give truthful advice. Your customer should be able to trust the advice and recommendations you give them. When your solution is not the right fit for them, say so and do not try to get a sale at all costs. Giving a customer untrue or biased information can quickly destroy trust.

Deal honestly with problems. When problems such as a quality issue, an unforeseen rise in costs, delays in delivery, or a change of specification arise, be upfront about them.

Accept responsibility. When something goes wrong, explain the reason and accept responsibility.

Be reliable. Be reliable in keeping every commitment you make—small or big.

6. Look to build relationships: Privilege developing long-term trust in customer relationships rather than simply making one-shot sales. Make it clear that you want to help, not just make a sale. Form a partnership in which your customer also plays an active part in finding the best solution.

7. Stay in touch: Stay in contact after the sale. Communicate regularly about delivery dates, installation, training, and other relevant matters. Make sure your customer is satisfied with their purchase. Help the customer track their results and analyze the efficacy of the solution.

8. Be dependable: Clarify expectations. Do what you promise and do it well. Make sure buyers are clear about how you operate and honor your commitments. In any business, customers expect the same standards. The last thing people want is to be surprised; they want dependability.

9. Offer social proof: When we see other people—especially those we hold in respect—endorsing something by using it, consuming it, or talking it up, it influences our opinion. Harness the bandwagon effect by using recommendations from similar customers or describing an instance when you helped a customer achieve stellar results. See if you share common connections with the prospect; check platforms such as LinkedIn and see if you can use any of your connections.

10. Maintain eye contact: Eye contact builds trust, whereas avoiding it carries negative connotations. Maintain healthy eye contact to communicate trustworthiness and confidence.

11. Show consistency: Being consistent is a significant factor in building trust. Show a behavior that is consistent with what you say. For example, if you say "This will only take five minutes" and stop promptly at the five-minute mark, the buyer knows that you mean what you say and will be more willing to trust you. Trust is built upon a foundation of consistency.

12. Trust the customer: When you find your prospect trustworthy, exhibiting your trust in them will reassure them to trust you back. This is a psychological phenomenon known as the "Pygmalion effect," which holds that we treat others in ways that match our expectations of them, causing the person to behave in a way that confirms those expectations.

13. Show that you care: Show interest in your prospect's welfare and person. When they divulge information about their lives, empathize. The best salespeople are concerned with helping their buyers above all else, and their sincere interest and empathy is rewarded with the buyer's trust.

You can have the most efficient experience in the industry, but if customers do not feel that you care about them, they will not trust you. Here are some suggestions for showing your customers that you care:

Align your feelings. Care comes through when a salesperson aligns their own personal feelings with those of their prospect's. You can do it by understanding the prospect's interpretation of a situation, accepting it as valid, and advocating for the best solution.

Do not assume, ask. Do not assume things about your potential buyers. Ask them to tell you what their pain point is, what is hampering their performance, or what the biggest hurdle they face is. Once you know this, it is much easier to put yourself in their shoes and suggest a solution.

Build your emotional intelligence. A great salesperson invariably has high emotional intelligence. Making a connection with people you sell to is key. When you know how to regulate your emotional experience, it is easier to build trust.

Ask good questions. To be of genuine help, you need to get to the root of the problem. Ask good questions to understand what the customer's pain is and how you can help. If you cannot help, say so. If you know someone (even a competitor) who can help, bring up their name.

Understand how your solution will improve the prospect's life. Good salespeople know their customers' needs. For example, if you are selling mattresses, experience sleeping on it so that you can explain to your customer how it will feel for them.

Send a handwritten note. A handwritten note is even more memorable in today's digital world. Writing short handwritten notes—thank you, appreciation, good wishes—will have a huge impact.

Address the customer by their name: You and everyone within your company who regularly interacts with customers must remember their names, whether in person or over the phone. This small gesture tells your customers that you care about them.

Seek their opinion. Customers are willing to give you their feedback, suggestions, and ideas. All you need to do is ask. Asking for their opinion shows you care by wanting to improve the product and the customer experience. They will feel included and know that their opinions and ideas are important to you.

Personalize your communications. Rather than sending general emails or wishes to a broad group of contacts, send personalized messages. Show how your business can meet their needs by sending targeted, relevant information.

NEED

The next step in the buying process is need. A customer need is the motive that prompts them to buy a product or service. Every sale you make must address a real customer need. As Steve Jobs explained, you have to start with the customer experience and work backwards to the solution you offer. Jobs understood that when you try to reverse-engineer the need from the product, it is easy to lose touch with reality. The customer need is your "why," the foundation of your entire business and what it offers. The more you know about your customers, the more you are likely to understand customer needs and expectations and to design outstanding solutions. The need is contextual; to understand it, you have to understand the customer's context. This enables you to understand their current priorities and goals and, thus, the functional, emotional aspects of their need. When your message addresses the customer's needs, they identify themselves with its every point. Only when the customer validates the need should you proceed to explain how you can address it.

ADDRESSING CUSTOMER NEEDS

Here are some suggestions to help you better address customer needs.

1. Put yourself in the customer's shoes: The first step involves putting yourself in your customer's shoes and thinking about the world from their perspective. When you know your customer's thought process, you can focus on the benefits of your offering for the customer instead of harping on its features. If you know the challenges your customer faces, it is much easier to offer solutions.

2. Build a customer-centric organization: Remember, it is your customers who are running the show. Create a customer-focused mindset across the entire company. The organizational structure should be aligned to the customer. A customer-centric organization is one where each post is staffed and every process is designed and executed with customer satisfaction in mind. It is a culture, not an event. The use of a Customer Relationship Management systems allows you to collect useful data on all contacts and transactions, purchasing and service history, product inquiries, complaints, communication channel preferences, and responses to marketing strategies. Here are some suggestions to create a customer-centric culture at your company:

Institutionalize customer focus. To inculcate customer focus as an organizational value, one that informs everything the organization does, leaders must lead the way. They should get employees to invest time in reading customer messages and observing customers to discern what they want and need. They should encourage people in support functions to research the customers they are helping and to create profiles. In support positions, the company must employ people who can express empathy through the written word.

Hire the right people. From the initial interface with probable employees, organizations should make thinking about customers and their needs a clear priority. Sales, marketing, and human resources executives need to collaborate to do this. During the interview process, candidates should be screened for their customer orientation. This not only assesses their alignment with customer-centric thinking, but also sends a clear message about the importance of customer experience at the company.

Provide exposure to customer experience. In order to practice a customer-centric approach, employees must understand the organization's customers. All employees should have some access to customer insights, rather than allowing the sales and marketing departments to hoard customer understanding and expecting other departments to focus solely on their functions. Company meetings must include updates by executives on the company's customer experience delivery.

Empower direct interaction with customers. The company should develop ways—such as focus groups, sales and support calls, customer visits, and participation in customer events—to allow employees to interact with customers, even in middle and back office functions. Every employee plays some role in the customer experience and will benefit from a better understanding of customers through interacting with them.

Connect compensation to the customer. The compensation structure should take into account performance on customer experience. This gives every employee skin in the game and lets them know that the business expects customer-oriented attitudes and behaviors from them. It produces organization-wide customer alignment.

Define the desired customer experience. Everyone in the organization should be clear on what the perfect customer experience means for the organization. Empower people to uphold those standards for customers.

Model the behavior. Leaders and managers should be role models for others, and everyone must step up. Only when employees are treated with respect and dignity will they treat customers in the same manner.

3. Seek and heed customer feedback: Great salespeople value customer feedback as an effective tool for learning and improvement. Communicate with your ideal customer in their preferred social media space to access questions, comments, and suggestions. The more you know about your customers, the more effective your sales and marketing efforts will be. It is well worth making the effort to find out who they are, what they buy, and why they buy it.

When you match customer feedback to what you see in your analytics, it gives you a much clearer picture of what is going on. You will then know how to fix problems and go after the right opportunities. When you actively seek customer feedback, keep it short to ensure quality answers, ask only questions that you will use the answers to, and start with open-ended questions. Where warranted, reach out to provide follow-up on customer feedback.

4. Build and maintain customer relationships: Nurture relationships with your customers to stay attuned with their future needs. Relationships can be cultivated with a combination of customer service structure and communication strategies.

Building strong relationships with existing customers can set you up for repeat business and will lead to getting referrals. Here are some suggestions for building enduring relationships with your customers:

Focus on quality communication. Communication must be prompt, efficient, and relevant. Your availability shows that your customer's needs are important to you. Make your customer feel comfortable being open and honest with you.

Respect your customer as an individual. A simple way of showing that a customer matters to you is to begin building a more personalized relationship with them. Show the customer that you consider them important as an individual—more than as a part of a company you are targeting.

Share knowledge. Be willing to share information that will help the customer understand what you do. This will build trust and confidence in the process, and help the customer feel knowledgeable and on the ball.

Be transparent. In order to build a lasting relationship, the customer must be able to trust you as an expert and an individual. When you confidently express your honest opinions, the customer will respect your initiative for excellence and your desire to be helpful.

Exceed expectations. Make realistic promises and do your best to surpass them. Do something extra that is valuable to the customer. It could be as simple as making a call after the sale to learn about their experience or to provide after-hours service. What matters is to find the opportunity to go above and beyond in a manner that your customer will appreciate.

Seek feedback. Asking customers for personal feedback shows that you listen to them. When you get feedback, respond promptly to compliments and complaints alike. Even negative feedback is valuable and can give you an opportunity to build or preserve a relationship.

5. Target the right fit: Understand whose needs you can fulfill and whose you cannot. All customers' needs cannot be treated alike, and a company's focus must be aligned with its vision.

Define your target market. Typically begin by evaluating companies to find the right fit. Next, look closely at individuals in the company whose job titles indicate they might be in the market for your product or service. At every level, customers are trying to understand what they are responsible for and what success means to them in their role.

When you know whom you are targeting, it is easier to figure out what their needs are and how you can best address them. Once you know your target customer, dive deeper. What are they looking to achieve? What are their challenges? Only when you know your customer's needs can you develop solutions to meet their biggest challenges. Knowing their needs helps you identify what benefits they find most valuable and reduces the role of trial and error. Here are some suggestions to define the right-fit customers:

Be specific. Be as specific as possible in narrowly defining your target customer. This will help you craft the most compelling solutions to address customer needs. When your decisions are dictated by your customer's needs, it sets you up for long-term success.

Study your competition. Know your competition's market positioning and what customer needs they fulfill. What can you offer that's extra? What opportunities can you detect in your competitors' customer reviews? Depending on your competition's positioning, you can better define what exact market segment you want to go after. Are there overlooked areas of market that you can capitalize on?

Look at your business with fresh eyes. Does your business address a true need of the identified target market? How will your target market best benefit from your product or service? This will help you put the right message in front of key segments of your target market.

6. Ascertain the customer's "what": If your potential customer is already buying somewhere, you need to know who the customer's current supplier is, if the customer is happy with their supplier, and what benefit would make the customer switch to you. When you know what benefits a customer is looking for, you stand a better chance of being able to sell to them.

This is more important than ever; customers are less loyal and have more power than in the past. Also, customer diversity continues to rise, placing a premium on micro-segmentation and deep customer insight. Here are some suggestions for better understanding your customer's "what":

Imagine yourself in their place. Think beyond your business and understand your customer's full range of choices, as well as their ecology of customers, partners, and suppliers—of which you are likely a part. This will deepen your knowledge of the customer and help you better understand their needs and their motives.

Track their experience. Chart your customers' experience with your company and note where the quality of experience suffers.

Think ahead. Focus on what customers will want tomorrow, like Steve Jobs or Richard Branson did. Envision how underlying market shifts may affect your customers.

Answer the need, not the question. Even when you can understand the customer's principal need because you have seen it before, do not shut down the conversation. Conversation will help you learn why people are using your offering and what they are trying to achieve with it.

7. Know the decision maker: In selling to a business, your customer is often a combination of several individuals who may seek one or more different benefits from your product or service and must reach a consensus on what to buy. Therefore, when you are selling to other businesses, you must know which individuals are responsible for the decision to buy your product or service.

Often you will be dealing with a multi-person decision-making unit. The size of the decision-making unit will vary depending on the organization and the purchase. People with different roles have different motivations. As a salesperson it is your job to identify those roles and adjust your approach appropriately. These are the core roles involved in a purchasing decision:

Gatekeeper. This person is typically the initial point of contact between a salesperson and an organization.

Influencer. An influencer is a person who has a respected opinion but is not the decision maker. This person will likely have a sizable influence on the decision.

User. This is the end user of a product or a service. When dealing with this person, focus on demonstrating the benefits of your offering from the user's perspective.

Advocate. An advocate is a person who wants you, your organization, or your offering to win. This person is a key to handling other members of the decision-making unit effectively. Salespeople often misjudge whether someone is truly advocating for them. Sometimes this person could just be doing their job and providing the same cooperation to competitors as well.

Decision maker. This person is the ultimate decider who carries the biggest say in purchasing.

Each person involved in a purchase decision wants to choose the best solution for the organization, but will have some underlying motivation that influences them. You must have the savvy to determine each person's motivators. The most common motivators are the following:

Social. How the purchase will affect the team.

Economic. The impact of the solution on the bottom line.

Operational. Concerns about efficiency and conformity with the existing systems.

Quality. The urge to understand the technical aspects, or capabilities, of the solution, as well as warranties backing it.

Political. The personal costs or benefits of the decision, that is, how it will impact the decision maker's individual positioning within the organization.

Here are some suggestions for selling to multi-party decision-making units:

Understand the buying process. Find out how your prospect goes about purchasing the type of product or service you are offering. This will help you calibrate your offer to their matrix of cost and strategic value. Obviously, the more budget it uses and the more strategic the purchase is for the buyer, the more composite your sales cycle is going to be, involving a number of people.

Ascertain their roles. You need an idea of who is going to be involved. Try to ascertain who is involved and their respective roles and motivations.

Do your homework. Use social media and the internet. LinkedIn can help you identify specific people within an organization. Look at industry and company publications and websites. Work your network.

Identify advocates and influencers. The bigger the organization and the amount of an envisaged sale, the more corporate culture and politics come into the equation. That makes it important to find advocates and influencers within the organization to advance your cause from the inside.

Get friendly with the gatekeeper. Be friendly and understanding with gatekeepers. They do not like people who are too pushy. Acknowledge their job and help them perform it; this is a basic skill that every salesperson must learn.

8. Know your value chain: Start with your end user and track a trail back to the point at which you sell your product, noting each link in the chain where the product changes hands until it reaches them. Each link can be considered a customer. Then ask yourself how likely it is that each customer can provide relevant information to influence product sale and design.

Knowing the value chain of your offering is important; the competitive environment is demanding for organizations of all sizes in all industries. High-tech progress has empowered businesses to invent and build faster, procure through multiple channels, respond promptly to changing demands, and cut costs by outsourcing. To be able to sell, an organization must deliver more value at an equal or lower cost. Understand and study the value chain to get valuable customer feedback, find and motivate the right employees, remain relevant, incorporate technology, and engineer change.

When you know the value chain, you can identify areas and activities that will benefit from change to enhance customer value and reduce costs. It provides you with insights into elements that bring greater value to the end user and enable you to focus on enhancing the user experience. Your competitive differentiation can also focus on the perceived value to the customer. For example, rather than focusing on premium pricing, Pizza Hut outperformed the competition by offering fast delivery of a less expensive product. FedEx has made significant investments in human resources and infrastructure to improve the user experience.

Here are some suggestions to study your value chain for cost advantages:

- Understand and rate how your offering provides value to each user in the chain.
- Understand cost drivers of all the users.
- Identify connections and dependencies.
- Identify opportunities for you to reduce cost and improve value for the users in the chain.

Now a couple of suggestions to use your value chain knowledge for differentiation:

- Identify the features driven by your offering that create value for the end user.
- Identify the best opportunities for differentiation that will improve customer value.

9. Discern emotions: People buy on emotions, and identifying the underlying emotions can be helpful in determining the real need. There are only four reasons people buy something, and all of them are connected to emotions. Here they are:

- Pain in the present
- Pain in the future
- Pleasure in the present
- Pleasure in the future

No skill that you can learn in sales is more important than learning how to touch your buyer's emotions in ways that are helpful to the sale. As you work at developing the skills to arouse your prospect's emotions, keep in mind that emotions work both ways—they can trigger sales or destroy sales. Lack of control over emotional settings is bad news for a salesperson. Emotion in sales is a gun with a trigger. Each time you engender a positive emotion, you are pulling the trigger on another shot at closing the sale. Here are some emotions that can have a powerful effect on buying decisions:

Fear. Fear—of insecurity, failure, disrepute, or loss—occurs when something is not working the way it should or is not there at all, and the buyer is afraid that the status quo does not bode well for them. You can use it in a sale by enquiring what they stand to lose if things continue the way they are. Then show how your solution will solve those problems, taking away their fear. When people are afraid of change, help them realize the cost of inaction.

Frustration. Frustration occurs when something that is critical to achieving their goals is broken. It is a powerful stimulus to find a solution. You can arouse it by asking your buyer to explain their struggles and how they are causing annoyance or irritation.

Hope. Your prospect is hopeful that things will improve. They are focused on a better future. You can arouse this emotion by asking them to describe the desired future and tailoring your pitch to speak to their hopes.

Excitement. Getting the buyer excited involves imparting in them a sense of urgency and keeping them engaged. You can arouse excitement by showing the buyer an engaging demo or by letting them have a trial. Figure out what excites your buyer and then play to it.

Anger. Anger occurs when things reach a breaking point or when people feel let down. To be able to use it, first acknowledge the anger and then understand its source. Channel the buyer's emotion into something productive, like hope or resolve.

Competitive pressure. This pressure stems from the fear of missing out or losing to the competition. You can use it by providing social proof—stories of similar customers who have seen success with your solution. Also show the customer how not moving quickly will leave them behind the competition.

Desire to win. Every company needs a comparative advantage to thrive and is fueled by competitive drive. Frame benefits in terms of competitors. Tempt your prospect's competitive nature by explaining benefits in a way that helps them see how your solution will give them a competitive advantage.

Personal angle. People are always motivated to do well personally in their career; they are driven by recognition, money, promotion, perks, titles.

To use this emotion, emphasize the personal benefit to the individuals concerned—how it will make them look good to their boss or how it will enhance their performance. Help them look good internally.

Humanity factor. Most people enjoy making choices that are morally responsible and socially rewarding. Think of a greater good your offering could facilitate. Can it foster teamwork or make the buyer's customers or partners happier? Where applicable, emphasize the benefits for employees. Maybe your solution will help their morale or their work-life balance.

Pride. Pride is a powerful emotion to leverage for selling. Buyers feel it when they perceive a high identity value in an offering. To work on pride, frame outcomes in terms of images. If a customer won an award thanks to your offering, tell your prospect the story. Offer image-building exposure to the company if they buy.

Shame. Nobody likes to feel ashamed. Refer to past mistakes that can be avoided with your offering. Show the customer how your offering prevents them from letting others down.

Comfort. People value a sense of security that brings peace of mind. Find ways—case studies, awards, statistics—to reassure your customer that they can stop worrying about this one thing and focus on other important aspects of their business.

Great salespeople have high emotional intelligence that helps them distinguish a customer's emotional state and align their own emotions with it. They can establish strong emotional connections with customers and know how to fine-tune their pitches in order to pull the right emotional triggers. Here are the ten most important attributes you can work on to improve your emotional intelligence as a salesperson:

Self-awareness. You must be able to recognize and understand your own emotional state at any time.

Self-control. You must have the restraint to keep strong emotions and moods in check to obviate any unwarranted emotional reactions.

Self-motivation. You must be a self-starter who is able to generate energy, enthusiasm, and positivity even in difficult circumstances.

Curiosity. You must be a keen listener with an ability to ask the right questions and understand the responses.

Resilience. You must be able to persevere when the going gets tough.

Personal connections. You must be able to build personal connections, manage conflicts productively, and influence other people.

Networking. You must have robust social and networking skills.

Stress management. You must be able to manage stress productively.

Active listening. You must listen with full concentration and intent.

Empathy. You must have a strong ability to grasp or understand another person's point of view to be able to sell by discovering your prospect's hidden but dominant desires.

HELP

Customers want to buy solutions that will give them the outcomes to meet their needs. Once you have gained the customer's trust and identified their need, connect your offering to the need. Come around to the customer's side of the table and become a co-buyer. Not all of your customers understand and describe their need in the same way; you require more than one way to frame your offering.

HELPING CUSTOMERS

There are four starting points after customers have established their need.

1. The customer has a need but does not know how to address it: These customers know to express only the pain they feel. When you are selling to them, your indirect competitors are also in the game here. It is important for you to educate the customer to help them believe your offering is best suited to address their problem.

In practice, we are not always selling to fill an obvious need. Even if your product or service does meet a real need, does the buyer realize that they have that need? And do they know that a solution exists? A lot of salespeople face this situation, and creating brand awareness does not help. When people do not already know they need your offering, your brand is meaningless to them. You require increased need awareness followed by solution awareness. Customers often do not clearly envision the outcome they seek, and you need to figure out how you can best help them to fill their need. They need to be led to a decision, and if you do it correctly, they will show loyalty. You can address this in three stages:

Make the customer aware of the need. At this stage the customer is not aware that they have a problem that requires a solution. Show them that they do have a need. As you raise the awareness of this need, keep the focus entirely on the customer and not on you.

Show them that a solution exists. The customer is aware of the need, but they do not know what the solution is. Present the type of your offering as a good solution for their need. Once again, the focus remains solely on the customer and their need.

Position your solution as the best. The customer knows they have a problem and that your offering can provide a solution. Your job now is to show why they should buy the solution from you. At this stage you focus on your solution and its distinct advantages over the competition. Paint a clear picture of how your solution will make their life better.

2. The customer knows the need and thinks they know the type of the solution required: These customers think they know what type of product they need. The main challenge here is differentiation either by superiority (e.g., brand preference) or by greater relevance (specialization) of your offering.

Such customers are often a large segment. The customer is already looking for the product or service you offer and is not attached to any particular brand; your job is to show them that your offering best matches the solution they have in mind. They may have some inner struggles, rendering decision-making more complicated. Do not let them profit from too much of your advice without making progress in the sales process. Here are three suggestions to sell to buyers who know the need and think they know the type of the solution required:

Establish a dialogue. Get them talking, and ask questions to understand what they are looking for.

Win their trust. Once they trust you and see that you have their best interests at heart, it will be easier to sell to them.

Invoke the right emotions. Understand their emotional need and hold their hand through the decision-making process. Understand what will give them enough comfort to say yes.

3. The customer knows the need and the precise solution for it: Here your challenge is to provide a better version of what they have in mind and then show the customer how they will benefit by opting for your solution.

Often such buyers view the purchase process as an information-gathering event, are methodical, and do a lot of research before they buy. They are ready to dive into the decision-making process and can make a quick decision if they feel enthused about dealing with you and see that you understand their need. Here are three suggestions to sell to buyers who know the need and the precise solution for it:

Provide details. These are discerning buyers and they like information and details. Distinguish yourself through the fine points. Present your offer as though you know what they are thinking.

Be specific. Be as specific as possible in discussing the benefits of your product or service. Neither oversimplification nor lofty claims will cut it. Address the customer's questions directly and avoid straying off topic.

Provide proof. Back up your statements with case studies, testimonials, references, and research.

4. The customer knows the need and the precise solution, which is not you: This is a hard sell, as you are likely up against a formidable competitor the customer is satisfied with. In such a case you are not likely to win a direct one-on-one with the customer's preferred choice, so you need to find ways to gain initial traction. As you make progress, you can help the customer see the merit in migrating from their current solution to yours.

The customer is generally already informed about the solution; you need to sell them a better outcome than the competition can assure. They can be influenced by urgency and scarcity. To do it effectively, catch their attention and then prove you are a more worthwhile investment. Here are three suggestions to win over buyers who know the need and the precise solution, but believe it is not you:

Get to know more about them. Understand what makes them tick. What solution do they intend to purchase from competition? How are you different, and how can you use this difference as something that the prospect wants? Can you solve their problem faster, offer them a better ROI, or make the purchase easier for them?

Balance emotions and facts. Have a clearly constructed message that convincingly states the benefits and advantages of buying from you. Balance your message with emotional payoffs and compelling facts.

Build the case for change. Awaken the customer's desire to change and get them feeling reassured and excited to move past their reluctance.

HURRY

The final step is to move a customer to action. If a customer tries to push you around, or waffles indefinitely over their next steps, deals can drag on and may not even end in a sale. Create a sense of urgency in your prospect's mind, so they are motivated to act—and to act quickly.

HELPING A CUSTOMER TO DECIDE

Here are some suggestions for shortening the customer's path to the final decision.

1. Start by establishing the right fit: Instead of persuading your prospect to do business with you, start by determining whether a prospect is a good fit for what you are selling. If you begin every sales meeting by trying to answer this question, you will create a sense of urgency. When your prospect senses that you are trying to determine if they are a good fit instead of forcing them to buy, they will be more likely to open up and explain why they need your product or service and to say yes in the end, on their own.

Rather than seeing every prospect as a "must have," look at them as if you are looking to hire a new person. They have to be the right fit to recognize the value in your product or work. No matter who you are or what you do, you will not be the best fit for everyone. Recognize that truth the next time you take a sales meeting. Booking customers who are not the right fit is not productive in the long run, as not being the right fit prevents you from acting in their best interest. In addition to your own target market criteria, here are some points to consider for deciding whether a customer is the right fit for you:

Technical fit. The customer should have or be able to acquire the technology to get value from your offering.

Operational fit. The customer must have the functions and processes to derive benefit from the features of your offering.

Budgetary fit. The customer must have the financial resources to be able to buy your offering.

Cultural fit. To work well together in a lasting relationship, the customer should share your core values.

Expectations fit. Can you clarify expectations and provide the experience the customer is looking for?

Analytical fit. You and your customer should have a common set of metrics to gauge the performance or success of your offering.

Authority fit. The customer must have the authority to buy or you are barking up the wrong tree.

Needs fit. You must know the customer's needs to be sure that they are aligned with your offering.

Timing fit. The customer's timing requirements must conform to your ability to deliver.

2. Know the customer's decision-making process: You cannot add urgency to a sale unless you understand how the customer will make the decision. If you make it all the way through a sales process without knowing who the key decision maker is, you have likely not gotten very far. Make it your priority to find out exactly who is involved in the decision-making process. Only then can you be strategic about where to apply pressure and create urgency throughout the sale.

Every customer travels through a decision-making process before they buy a product or service. These are some of the factors that you can consider:

Internal roles. Understand who the gatekeeper, influencer, advocate, and decision maker are, and who allocates the budget.

End user. Whose problem or need does your offering target? Who will actually use it? This is the party that will most understand the better future your solution can produce. They can be much more emotionally motivated than others involved.

Information need. What information is valuable respectively to different parties involved in the decision-making? People are more motivated by social information than by what you tell them directly. Understand the sources they use for their information.

Competition. Understanding the alternatives your customer is considering in order to make the best choice will help you better position your solution against their criteria.

Social. As a salesperson you must understand the role played by the buyer's culture, subculture, social class, reference groups, and family.

Physical. Your location may weigh in the customer's decision-making process. Other aspects such as size, dimensions, area, and so on may also matter.

Personalities. Understand the personality (motivation, perception, beliefs, and attitudes) differences among the people involved in the decision. This will help you handle each person in a unique manner.

3. Understand your prospect's key goals: People execute around their priorities. As a seller you must know to connect your product or service to the buyer's priorities. For that you first need to understand those priorities. Find out which objectives they want to accomplish in the short-term. By aligning your solution with those objectives, you can generate greater urgency for even unenthusiastic prospects.

Sometimes you may need to help your customer identify the specifics of their goals. Think of both business outcomes and personal aspirations, such as increasing sales, launching new products, penetrating new markets, finding new customers, reducing costs, enhancing efficiency, training people, pleasing the boss, getting a promotion, changing the company culture, leaving a legacy, or exercising authority.

You must understand what success looks like for your buyer. Is there a gap in their strategy that you can fill? What are the barriers to achieving their goal? This will help you understand why your prospects may or may not buy your products or services.

Once you know your customer's goals, you can be more strategic in selling to them. You can align your offering with their key goals. With the right approach, you can assume the role of a trusted advisor rather than being just another vendor. The key goals of a buyer usually fall in one of the following areas:

Strategy. The buyer may be contemplating a major shift in their strategy.

Targets. These can be revenue or profit targets, as well as customer goals.

Plans. Based on what worked and what did not work in the past, the customer may be envisaging a change of plans.

Challenges. The customer's priority may be to address specific problems or pains.

Timelines. The customer may be faced with the imperatives of certain timelines.

Budget. The customer's main concern may be to meet or use a budget.

Personal. The customer's motivation may be personal, for any of the various possible reasons.

4. Sell less, listen more: The more carefully you listen, the more you will command your prospect's attention. Demonstrate your value, but make the conversation mainly about them, not about what you are selling. You can create greater urgency by helping your prospect to come to their own conclusions, instead of peppering them with sales speak.

Listening is a far more effective selling tool than some overexuberant sales pitch. When a salesperson stops talking and starts listening, it is amazing how much the customer will reveal about themselves. A great conversation is not about slick salesmanship; it is about making customers smarter. If you get a customer to talk about a need that can be filled by your offering, it can be a natural entry into positioning your offering.

5. Be a problem solver and not a salesperson: Make your time with your prospect count by communicating and sharing ideas on how to quickly address concerns that affect them. Be lucid and coherent on how you can minimize pain points and add value where they need it. Prospects respond positively to personalized attention to detail, which will allow you to have more open and purposeful discussions that eventually shorten your sales cycle.

Selling is not about convincing someone to buy something; it is about identifying a prospect's need and showing them how you can help. There is a huge difference between being a problem solver and a solution provider. Assuming a problem solver mindset can give you a significant advantage over the traditional selling mentality. This is a relational and empathetic approach. The relationships you thus build with prospects are focused on solving the problems they face rather than on the solutions you want to sell. Here are some reasons why selling is about solving problems:

Products or services are meant to solve problems. Whatever it is that you are selling has been created with a need in mind. In the absence of competition, it would be a straightforward matter to sell it based on the need it fills. However, in the face of competition, you have to show the customer why your brand solves their problem better than the other alternatives available to them. You need to be a critical thinker to deeply understand the customer's problem. Then you can show the unique ways in which your offering can better solve their specific problem.

People do not buy products, they buy outcomes. To find ways to solve problems people did not even know they had, ask the right questions and describe how your offering creates more convenience. For example, the first home-delivery or the first drive-thru service solved a problem using a product that was already in existence. Somebody thought of ridding customers of the hassle of going out of their home or workplace or of the problem of parking their vehicle and getting out. This solved a huge problem in the face of traffic jams, tight schedules, or harsh weather conditions.

Every problem holds an opportunity for a solution. People who succeed see every problem as a challenge and an opportunity. Great salespeople use their critical thinking skills to analyze and redefine the problem when necessary.

No one likes to be sold to. Most of us buy products and services believing that when the transaction is complete, our problem will be solved. When you buy a state-of-the-art modem, the problem you solve is connectivity. You may buy the latest cellphone set to solve the problem of a hankering ego. Shifting your focus to problem solving rather than selling will get people to like you better.

Benefits matter more than features. Benefits solve problems and relate to emotions. Think of a benefit that can help a customer make an emotional connection with your offering. Once you have connected to a buyer's emotions, they will likely find their own logic that conforms to their emotions.

6. Obtain real commitment: Try to elicit concrete commitment from your customers. For example, if the customer wants to buy your offering, try asking, "Mark, what is the single biggest challenge you are facing … are you committed to doing something about this right now?" Often, holding your prospect's feet to the fire at the right moment will save you much time either by consummating the sale or by stopping you from continuing to dig a dry well. Many salespeople lose sales because they never demand an actual commitment, thus diminishing any real sense of urgency.

A commitment will not automatically follow asking the right questions. You need to be skilled in getting to the stage where the prospect trusts you enough to say yes. Here are some suggestions to help you navigate to getting the commitment:

Have milestones for every stage of the sales process. Be clear what you want to achieve at every interaction. Monitor the process and do not just get pulled along by it. With each customer, know what is going to happen and when.

Recap everything the customer has said to you. Recapping builds your credibility and creates empathy. It shows that you have been listening and understand the prospect's real needs.

Paint the future with your solution. Help the customer envision the future when they start using your product or service. When they can, you are more likely to get their commitment to move to the next stage.

Address risks. Understand and minimize the risks—financial, timing, disruption, and so on—to the prospect in making the purchase.

Build urgency. Create urgency for the prospect to move forward.

Make sales a collaborative process. Instead of selling at the customer, sell with them. Get the prospect to do something; get them involved so that they feel like they are working on it with you. For example, ask for structured feedback, hand over the mouse or the marker, think of meetings as a co-production, use "we" and not "you."

Make actions time related. Stay in control of the process. Agree to deadlines and follow up on them.

7. Build a feeling of scarcity: Scarcity bias is a strong motivator of urgent behavior. You can purposely limit the supply of what you produce or deliver in order to engender a feeling of scarcity. For example, if you tell a willing buyer that you only have "four more left," it imparts a sense of urgency to the desire to secure a supply of your offering.

However, this has to be done very tactfully. Research has found that scarcity has a stronger positive effect on product or service evaluation when knowledge is of little influence on the customer, the customer's frequency of exposure to scarcity claims is low, the decision reversibility is high, and cognitive load is high.

So, customers who have a higher knowledge of persuasion or more exposure to scarcity claims are less likely to value a scarce product more. When customers interpret scarcity claims as a sales tactic, the positive effect of them on product or service evaluation is palpably diminished. Also, when customers have adequate cognitive resources available to draw inferences about the persuasion motives underlying seller's behavior, they are more likely to perceive scarcity as a sales tactic.

To sum up, if your customer sees the scarcity claim as spurious, it is going to hurt more than help.

8. Create time-sensitive offers: A good way to move your customers to act is to tie your offering to a specific timeframe or deadline. Even if you did not first intend to assign a deadline, review the situation at a later stage to determine if adding one could increase the urgency of your offer. You might be surprised by the positive effect it can have.

You often need to create some urgency in your prospect to get the deal over the line. Here are some suggestions to create a sense of urgency in selling:

Help the customer understand their needs. The prospect must appreciate that they need your product or service and recognize the consequences of not buying. Perhaps the most effective way to expedite a sale is to show them why they need it now.

Set deadlines. Do not underestimate the power of deadlines. Provide your prospect with a non-negotiable deadline for a significant incentive in the form of a discount or extra benefits. This will only work when the customer trusts you and knows that the offer is set in stone, not just a sales gimmick that they can call on after the deadline has passed. Introduce the offer early in the sales process and allude to it and the decreasing time remaining on it regularly. Adding it late into the mix will likely be viewed as just a closing technique rather than a genuine element of your offer.

Do not hound. Do not pester your prospect for their signature. Rather, instill urgency by creating a top-of-mind approach and reaching out only when what you have to say adds some value.

Seek clarity on delay. Sometimes procrastination occurs because either you have not been able to convince the prospect fully or the person you are dealing with does not have the authority or budget to buy. But mostly it happens because people are generally risk-averse and find it difficult to make decisions. In such a situation, highlight the risks of delay and show how not making a decision has its own risks.

Keep the trial period brief. For many businesses, a free trial is part of the sales mix. Cutting access to a winning solution after a brief trial period is a great way of exhibiting confidence in your offering.

9. Make it easy for customers to act: People are busy. It is your responsibility to make it as simple as possible for them to buy what you want them to buy. They must know exactly what they need to do as soon as they are done making the decision to buy.

You must be easy to do business with; do not make customers jump through hoops to do business with you. Be responsive and proactive, and collaborate with buyers throughout the sales process. Here are a few things you can do to make it easier for customers to buy from you:

Remain accessible. Make it easy for customers to reach out and have a dialogue at any time during the sales process.

Be responsive. Promptly respond to all customer questions. A fast turnaround time cuts a sales cycle and moves the customer toward a decision.

Keep it simple. Do not make things complicated for your buyer. Instead of confusing them with too many choices, tell a buyer which one is right for them or, at least, help them narrow down their options to make an informed decision.

Keep driving the process forward. Often the salesperson who does a better job of driving the sales process forward wins. You do not have to be pushy to do it; instead, ensure that each step leads logically into a next one. Make sure every interaction consummates in some commitment for the next action.

Help the buyers say yes. Ask for a decision when the time is right. When you reach the point in the sales process where the only thing left is to make a decision, do not be afraid to ask your buyers for a clear yes.

Make the payment process easier. Make it as simple as possible for your customers to pay you, quickly and easily.

10. Show the unsavory consequences of delaying: The desire to avoid losses or costs (unless they are viewed as investments) is greater than the desire to generate profits. If you can show that the buyer will lose something by not responding, then you are reinforcing that the buyer cannot afford to lose.

Help the buyer understand the cost of delay and why it matters by explaining the impact of time on outcomes. Understanding the consequences of delay helps improve their decision-making.

11. Draw on the competition: The lure of competitive gains or the fear of losing opportunities to the competition are prime motives to stimulate the urgency instinct and get people to act.

12. Use appropriate vocabulary: Use appropriate vocabulary in your interactions for your customer to feel that they do not just want what you are offering, they are convinced that they need it. Use vocabulary that elicits emotions. Prompt the customer to follow the call to action and buy. You can do this by sprinkling your delivery with certain words that capture attention and elicit an emotional response.

In order for compelling words to be effective, do not overuse them; place them well and they will serve their purpose by adding their impact to the message. Here are some of the types of words that motivate customers to buy:

Words touching sore spots. Fear is probably the most powerful emotion for attracting your prospect's attention. Use words addressing their fears and worries. Once fear comes into play, they will be fully engaged. Some words that touch upon fear are *failure, hate, afraid, danger, humiliation, alone, vulnerable, mistake, risk, devastating.*

Words underlining urgency. Using time-related words reminds the prospect to think about deadlines and to make the action they envisage taking time-bound. Some examples of such words are *now, limited time, last chance, deadline, fast, never again, do not delay, do not miss out, once in a lifetime, instant.*

Words highlighting scarcity. The fear of missing out is a powerful driver for customer commitment. Experiments have shown that we immediately place a higher value on something of which there is a lower quantity. Some words that can highlight the scarcity of your product or service are *only, one day only, final close-out, offer expires, limited offer, running out, final, hurry, now or never, rush.*

Words emphasizing an exclusivity. We are all predisposed to want what not everyone can have. People want to feel that they are members of a small elite group. The most popular clubs all have exclusive door policies. Exclusive brands charge exorbitantly more with a negligible difference in quality. Some words you can use to play on the desire for exclusivity are *members only, ask for an invitation, be one of the few, become an insider, be the first to hear about, only available to subscribers, limited, class full, login required, special.*

Words seeking to reassure. Lack of assurance can thwart an otherwise obvious closing. It is difficult for customers to be sure who among many choices is trustworthy. Some words that can inspire reassurance are *guarantee, lifetime, authentic, certified, dependable, no risk, proven, secure, safety, protected.*

13. Social proof: A powerful way to spur your customer to action is to show social proof. Social proof is a psychological phenomenon that makes people embrace the actions of people they like or trust. User-generated content such as reviews, testimonials, case studies, and social media mentions are useful. Promote positive examples of each social proof that you may have. If your customers can see their peers buy and appreciate your product or service, it will strengthen their inclination to buy.

Here are some types of social proof you can use for your business:

Popularity. Clearly perceptible signs of your product or service's popularity are a common type of social proof. They can get potential customers to feel better about buying from you and help them decide to do it.

Public approval. Customers trust what other people say about your solution more than what you say. Good reviews are helpful in conversion.

Expert endorsement. This type of social proof includes favorable opinions from industry experts and other trusted opinion makers. The halo effect is a cognitive bias in which we judge someone's opinion based on our impression of their knowledge and reliability. A stamp of approval from a credible expert is a great social proof.

Demand. This type of social proof shows that not only is your product or service popular, but people also buy from you in large numbers. People feel comforted when similar action—purchasing, subscribing, hiring, and so on—has been taken by large groups of other people. The fear of missing out can engender a compulsive concern that one might miss out on an opportunity.

Peer behavior. This is the type of social proof when you can show that similar businesses or a person's peers, friends, and relatives are buying your product or service.

This four-step process—trust, need, help, hurry—allows you to concentrate on the buyer's needs and attract, engage, and then empower them to buy.

Identifying Customer Requirements

"The purpose of a business is to create a customer."
Peter Drucker

To be good at selling you need to understand and satisfy your customers' most important requirements in relation to your products or services. You can then adapt your offering to meet their needs. Your understanding of customer needs will shape the whole of your approach to selling.

Identifying customer requirements is the process of engaging customers to discover what they need out of products and services. This is often a starting point for product or service development or sales. A good analysis of customer requirements should have these characteristics.

1. There must be a pattern to it: The ideal set of requirements will have some stability and order. If requirements are mercurial and unpredictable, then it is difficult to analyze them, except for the purpose of disaster management.

2. It must evaluate the competition: A good analysis of customer requirements will accurately assess how much better or worse various solutions (including yours) are. In addition to selling, it also provides the business with ideas for new offerings that could be developed in the future.

3. It must tell how customers measure value: A good requirement analysis communicates the norms that customers use to measure value. Only when you can measure it can you create value for customers.

4. It should be practicable: A good requirement analysis is controllable and marketable in the sale of a product or service. It outlines what function or feature a product or service should offer in order to better address the requirement.

5. It should be lucid: A good analysis is clear and accurate, to ensure that it cannot be misunderstood. Everyone in your organization should have the same idea of the customer's requirements.

6. It should identify customer preferences: A good analysis reveals the criteria that customers use to assess the value that one product or service provides over another and thus determine their preference.

7. It should identify unmet expectations: Know which of the customer's requirements or expectations are currently unmet. You can then structure your sales approach to focus on unmet needs.

8. It should be relevant to the entire organization: A good requirement analysis would help each area in your business get its job done better. While you can sell accordingly, marketing can define a more effective value proposition, strategy can identify hidden opportunities, and so on.

9. It should be uniform across the organization: Different people or areas in the same organization cannot have segmented or, worse, conflicting understandings of customer requirements. The entire organization should know and agree on a common set of customer requirements. This will make the organization completely aligned with customer needs in language, structure, understanding, and approach.

Identifying customer requirements involves five elements: need, want, affordability, timing, and buying criteria.

NEED

Creating a need in the prospect's mind creates a sense of urgency in sales. Sales dynamics have changed, because of content marketing and customer research on what they want before making contact with sales professionals. But the value of a sales professional's skills has not changed. Savvy sellers engage the customer well before the customer fully understands their own needs. They know which questions to ask in order to uncover customer needs and to guide them through a sale.

Your prospects cannot benefit from your offering unless they realize they need it. Help them see the big picture with open-ended questions that reveal where their needs are and how you can help solve them. Ask discovery questions, make the customer feel wanted, and demonstrate how your product can solve their problem. Here are some types of needs that you can analyze.

1. Business need: An example of business need would be a firm that needs to increase the efficiency of a manufacturing plant.

2. User need: This is about discovering the needs of the end users and how you can help your customer to make their experience better. The end user can be the consumer, a business within the value chain, or a department within your customer's business.

3. Problem-driven need: Identifying this kind of need requires an analysis, from the ground up, of the pain points with current situation.

4. Goals-driven need: Understand the goals of the customer, whether it is a business or a person, and the needs fueled by them.

5. Potential need: Visualize customer need in the extremes of possibilities.

6. Functions-based need: Consider the additional functions or features your offering might help a customer to add.

7. Expectations-based need: Identify the expectations that the customer assumes are always fulfilled by a product or service. Understanding such unstated assumptions can lead to more business, whereas a failure to understand them can lead to losing a customer.

8. Perception-based need: This kind of need is driven by the customer's perception of products, services, and experience. For example, when the customer perceives the ingredients of a food product as healthy, that helps.

9. Quality-based need: Understand what defines the quality of a product or a service in the eyes of the customer. That definition of quality would drive their need.

10. Inconsistent need: Different departments or individuals making a purchase together may have seemingly contradictory needs. For example, between a couple buying a house, one partner may be looking for a spacious bedroom while the other desires a large walk-in closet. An intelligent need analysis leaves such inconsistencies intact and, when it suits you, use them to advocate an option.

11. Closet need: This is a need that customers do not want to talk about but nevertheless require. For example, a secretary may want their boss to make a choice that does not result in long hours for them. Such needs also determine how people use their influence in a purchase decision.

12. Good-to-have need: These are small things that customers can get excited about such that they significantly influence the purchase decision. For example, a customer buying a house may be relatively unexcited about the colors, fittings, or ceiling height but may get very excited about living in a street that is considered posh.

WANT

Know the distinction between a customer's wants and needs. Every so often what a customer wants is completely different from what they need. Want and need represent two different motivations for the customer, and it is important for you to understand the difference. While a need solves an actual or imaginary problem, a want is simply something that is nice to have for whatever reason. What customers want is often a more influential motivation than what they need. You can ascertain the distinction by listening carefully. When customers have a strong desire to get what they want, they simply want you to show them how they can get it.

While helping them to understand that what they need is also important, as a businessperson, your job is to give customers what they want. That's often an easier sale, too. Most people prefer to buy something rather than have it sold to them; if you can make them feel they have bought it and you gave them what they wanted, they feel empowered in the relationship.

To illustrate the difference, let's take the case of Netflix. Netflix quickly became a market leader in the home entertainment space with its original model of charging a subscription to customers and sending them DVDs through the mail. But then Netflix was able to see the long-term flaw in this model. There were no barriers to entry and the dominance in this service could be threatened by the entry of a major player, which actually did happen as Blockbuster entered the market.

Had Netflix confined its analysis to its customers' needs, it may have discovered that customers needed lower subscription rates, or greater choice of movies, or faster delivery with Netflix using FedEx, and so on. But Netflix was thinking beyond the needs of its customers to what they really wanted—a quicker and more convenient way to receive more diversified content for their entertainment.

So, Netflix upgraded to address their customers' wants. A solution that most customers could not think of but that delivered what they really wanted. And that solution was on-demand streaming of entertainment content, anytime, to virtually any internet-connected device.

It was somewhat like Henry Ford's vision to transform the need of faster horses into automobiles to address the true want of customers, which was a faster and more reliable means of transportation. Steve Jobs was another visionary who was able to see what customers truly wanted and then develop products to address it.

If you can figure out what your customers really want, then you can identify opportunities to create products and services that make those customers happy. Learn not only what your customers want but also what their customers want in turn. By learning what motivates both your customers and your customers' customers, you can greatly enhance your ability to develop successful products or services before the market asks for them.

Here are a few suggestions for knowing what your customer wants.

1. Get to know your customer: Learn more about your customer. Develop a robust customer profile with relevant information.

2. Determine what type of content they like: Encourage your customer to share their thoughts and build a strong relationship with them. As you develop an effective engagement pattern, you will be able to understand the type of content they like and design accordingly.

3. Put yourself in their shoes: Look at your offering from the customer's perspective. Get your customers on the phone regularly to help you go deeper into their motivations and challenges.

4. Ascertain what drives your customers: While they may not be able to envision a solution beyond the alternatives offered by the market, think of the underlying desires that drive your customer's needs.

5. Find out where they currently buy: Discover why your customers purchase from where they currently buy.

6. Get your team to meet your customer: When all teams related to your business connect with the customer, it helps you get a better understanding of their tastes and aspirations.

7. Know trends: Keep current with the latest tendencies and technologies related to your industry. This will give you valuable information about customer behavior. It will also help you to anticipate, predict, and plan for the future.

AFFORDABILITY

Many salespeople invest too much time and effort in a sale before determining if the customer can afford to buy. There is nothing more awkward than toiling on an opportunity, developing a great solution, and presenting it to the customer and having them say, "No, we do not have the money." Sometimes customers also use this as an excuse for buying elsewhere or because they do not see enough value in your solution. More often than not, you have a chance to show the customer that they can indeed afford the solution you offer by one of these approaches:

- Showing them the difference between the price and cost, especially in relation to your competition
- Showing them additional revenues or cost savings that your solution will bring
- Showing them how your solution will generate a healthy ROI for the business
- Talking price only when you are in the lead

- Using some real examples of customers who opted for a less pricey option and ended up with a higher cost
- Closing for the technical win

In order to survive as a business, you need customers who can afford to pay for your product or service and who understand its value. There is little point in engaging with a customer unless there is a likelihood of a meaningful exchange of value. Here are some suggestions to help you identify customers that you will work best with and that will pay for you to continue to serve them well:

- Before you start selling, explore the size of the opportunity to determine if it is within the buyer's means.
- Consider what your prospect can afford to solve the problem your solution targets.
- Consider whether the customer's perception of the value of the problem's resolution lines up with your price.
- Consider what alternatives they have to choose from in the market.
- Think about the value you are creating and make sure early in the process that the prospective buyer understands that value.
- Consider if the buyer's business, their priorities, your offering, and its value are all in alignment. Get the alignment right before you push too far.
- Consider if the buyer you are targeting can be satisfied with you delivering more value rather than cutting the price.

TIMING

In almost every human endeavor—sports, politics, employment career, investment, negotiation, love—timing plays an important role. Get the timing right and you win; get it wrong and you lose. Selling is no different. The larger the stakes in a selling situation, the more central it is that you follow a reliable sales process that keeps your timing in step with the customer all the way to the final decision to buy.

Understanding your customer's timing and buying cycle is important. Customers expect different interactions with you depending on where they are in the buying cycle or how specific events prompt a buying mode. You can use this knowledge to make your selling more effective.

Imagine that you are in the process of building a new house and go into a hardware store to look at the options available for some of the items. There is no intention to buy anything particular. You are accosted by eager salespeople who feel they can get you to buy something. Their excessive attention interferes with your intent to browse in peace. Now imagine you walk into the same store a few days later and know what exactly you want to buy for your house. You want someone to help you close the purchase. However, you are left alone, perhaps because the salespeople thought you were a bit irritated by their attention the last time. You are again irritated, this time by the lack of attention. This is about understanding the timing of the customer. A more skilled salesperson would have quickly determined where you were in the buying cycle on each of the two occasions.

Similarly, you have to understand your customer's timing imperatives and then tactfully hurry them along the trajectory. Make sure that you provide all the information and assistance the customer needs to take the final step in the buying process. Also, be aware of the triggers that can rev up the customer's purchase process—for example, a new project, expansion plans, acquisition, growth, or winning a contract. Sometimes, you encounter a buyer late in the buying cycle and need to react in a hurry to address the buyer's picture of what they need, which is likely shaped by the competition.

Sales is a delicate balance of finely tuned messaging and great timing. In sales, being in the right place at the right time is less about luck than about strategic thinking and business acumen. You must build a sound foundation for the sale, through mutual agreements and mutual commitments, throughout the sales process. Closing then becomes the logical denouement of the series of agreements. Without that foundation, salespeople feel a pressure that can activate their prospect's natural resistance. Here are some suggestions to improve your sales timing.

1. Do not sell until you understand the problem: Never start selling unless you have understood your customer's problem. Ask questions to have a clear understanding of your customer's objectives and the challenges they are facing in achieving them.

2. Do not sell until you understand the value: Until you completely understand the nature and scale of your prospect's problem and what it is costing them, along with their budgets and timelines, you cannot understand the value your proposal has. Grasping the value of your solution to your customer helps you put things into perspective. Then you can evaluate the gravity of the problem and how driven they are to fix it.

3. Take your time: Before presenting a solution, take the time required to ask questions and fully understand the responses. It is important to know how your customer goes about making their decisions, what timeframes they have in mind, and whether they have the budget available for a solution to their problem. Unless you know all this, you may be presenting the solution too early.

4. Control the process: The trick to staying in control is to not point out the pain points to the customer. Instead, question them in a manner that helps the customer discover them on their own. Rather than pontificating and likely coming across as arrogant, with Socratic questioning you can command the conversation to get the right emotional reaction from your customer and inspire them to change things. To time the sale correctly, get the buying temperature up by talking about the customer's problem and the costs it is triggering.

5. Timing is about the customer, not you: Always communicate at your customer's pace. At the end of every meeting, agree on the next step or book a time for the next meeting. Try asking your customer when you can present a sales proposal. This will put the ball back in their court and make them feel in control. It will make sure that you do not end up presenting the solution either too soon or too late. Instead you present the sale when the timing is right for your customer.

BUYING CRITERIA

Buying criteria are the sum of all the factors that a customer needs to consider to make a buying decision. They can include answers to questions like these:

- What do we want to buy?

- Why do we need it?
- What are our choices?
- Why should we buy this one?
- Why should we buy it from you?
- What is the cost?
- What benefit will we get?
- What are the risks?
- What is the deal?

The answers to these questions guide the customer along the path to the purchase. Always find out why the customer chose to go with their existing solution. What features tipped the scale? When a customer opts for the competition, make it your business to ascertain why precisely you lost the sale.

As a salesperson, it is your job to understand the customer's buying criteria and help them make an educated decision. This shortens the sales cycle and reinforces the buyer's trust. The key is to provide the buyer with all the information they need and create an emotional connection. Once the customer feels that their criteria are fulfilled, they feel in control of the buying process and ready to close.

When you understand your customer's buying criteria and their relative importance, you are in a much better position to shape your message. Some buying criteria may be a given and others a distinguishing feature. For example, if you are an airline, no reasonable customer will compromise on safety and security. Hence the distinguishing buying criteria may include landside or airside service, price, comfort, type of aircraft, leg space, ease of buying, and baggage entitlement.

Here are some universal buying criteria in B2B purchases.

1. The reason: What has caused the motivation to buy? Is it a simple replacement, an opportunity to do an old job more efficiently, or a new requirement?

2. Performance: Customers want to be certain that the purchase fulfills their needs for quality, efficiency, usability, and durability. Does your offering meet or exceed the customer's expectations of performance?

3. Brand: Customers like to buy names that have a history and evoke quality, prestige, and reliability. There will always be some skepticism toward an unknown or untried brand. So ask yourself, how does the potential customer feel about your brand and how you can position it better and more appropriately?

4. Price: Customers are likely to carefully analyze the price/benefit equation and compare the cost with the budget and available alternatives. They also like to feel good about the price they pay. Hence, as you proceed along the path of a sale, keep your customer's price expectations and your product's affordability in mind. Also, be aware of the competition.

5. Look: Design and appearance are also a factor. With everything else being equal, it is a basic human tendency to prefer the choice that has greater visual appeal. Be mindful of the physical and visual aspects that your customer values. Color, finish, size, shape, and design can all be considerations.

6. Prior satisfaction: You may be faced with a customer who is already satisfied with an existing supplier. Sometimes the only way to win is to first create dissatisfaction in the potential buyer's mind and recreate the notion of what a real solution looks like. When you enter into a buying process late and the customer's buying criteria have already been influenced by a competitor, do not be restricted by the standards of a solution set by your competition. Instead, try to alter the buying criteria in your favor. There are two common ways of doing it:

Educate your customer to see the possibility of results exceeding their current expectations. Provide examples of your similar customers who have implemented your solutions with better results. It is your job to share with your potential customer the possibilities they may not yet have in sight.

Bring to their mind additional needs that your customer has not considered yet. Understand how the customer is defining their needs and point out any area they may have missed. Show how your solution addresses those needs.

However, you have to be very tactful and precise in such a situation, or the potential customer might think you are overlooking their immediate needs and offering solutions they do not need. The trick is to hike the ball without making a foul. Run the race you think you can win; otherwise, you will lose your customer's trust.

UNDERSTANDING YOUR CUSTOMER'S BUYING CRITERIA

Business purchasers usually undertake significant research, carefully examine specifications, follow a strict purchasing or procurement process, can find switching costs high, and are more concerned with functionality. Modern flows of communication, information, and interaction enable them to be well informed, and more influencers and decision makers are now involved in the buying process. Therefore, as a salesperson in business, it is important for you to understand what drives your customers' buying criteria and decisions. For that understanding, stay close to your customers. These are some of the things you can find out from them to understand their buying criteria:

- What problem are they looking to solve by using your product or service, and how?
- What are their important criteria in selecting the offering, and what makes these criteria important?
- Who is involved in the decision-making process?
- How are suppliers selected and evaluated?
- Who is involved in evaluating how well your offering meets each of the buying criteria?
- If it is a new prospect, then what do they like and dislike about their current supplier, and what would it take for them to switch to you?

More complex interaction with customers will help you discover less obvious strands of their buying criteria. These proprietary insights will help you formulate better targeted sales actions. These are some ways in which understanding a customer's buying criteria can help you:

1. Mapping criteria by influencers or decision makers: Keep track to understand how different variables—such as price, delivery times, response times, and product or service features—affect each person involved in the process. That will enable you to precisely address customer expectations and needs at each stage of the sales process.

2. Allocating resources and efforts to the activities most likely to influence decisions: Once you map buying criteria in the way described above, you can shift your efforts and resources to conform with your customer's buying criteria.

3. Aligning your organization with the customer: Sometimes, organizational structure may need to change in order to ramp up collaboration with the customer. All parts of your organization at customer touch points should be aligned with the customer experience.

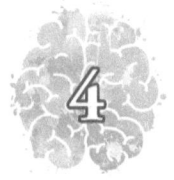

Handling Objections

"An objection is not a rejection; it is simply a request for more information."
Bo Bennett

M any sales professionals dread customer objections. They can be difficult to handle, and they usually arise after a skillful salesperson has proactively addressed all the concerns that they had anticipated during their research and preparation. While handling objections might sound like the most difficult part of the sales process, a great salesperson knows how to make it the most productive part. Besides, customer objections also give you valuable information about customer concerns, priorities, and fears.

Handling objections is an essential part of life. Since you are constantly selling in your everyday life, you no doubt also encounter objections there: your friend does not want to visit the same beach as you, your partner does not want to share the car, your parents want you home on a weekend when you have other plans. When you attempt to convince someone or sell your idea, you usually have fallback arguments in mind to get what you want while meeting the other person's needs. Life makes us skilled in handling objections.

Similarly, objections are a natural product of the sales process. Rarely will you encounter a situation where you are able to close the sale without any objections. The heart of sales is handling objections and figuring out how you can help your prospect meet their needs. It is a test of your skills as a salesperson to find the opportunity in an objection, listen to your prospect, and then respond. View objections as an invitation to continue to sell, and leverage them to build your relationship with your prospect and find the true reason for their resistance.

Customer objections can be rooted in a range of apprehensions. They can only be handled effectively if you understand the underlying reason. Often this value calculation is not scientific; it is prone to human errors, judgments, and emotions. However, an underlying motive for most buyer objections can be classified into one of these three categories: the no-benefit objection, satisfied objection, and timing objection.

NO-BENEFIT OBJECTION

The no-benefit category includes all types of objections where the customer does not see enough value in opting for the solution that you are proposing. Here are some causes of such objections:

- Price, cost, budget, ROI concerns, etc.
- Misgivings about quality of product or service
- Fears about compatibility of your offering
- Lack of trust, credibility, legitimacy, etc.
- Lack of institutional or personal relationship
- Internal pressures delaying the process

No-benefit objections can be handled by demonstrating the value of your solution and directing the buyer's focus back to the larger context in which the purchase is being made. Reframe the objection in a way that helps the customer see the bigger picture. How your solution can help the customer grow revenue, volume, or market share. How your solution can help the buyer measure their performance in the organization. Help your customer understand the economic consequences of taking action or not taking action. Or identify all key decision makers to address their respective needs. It is important to determine both professional and personal drivers, in order to align your benefits to those drivers. Talk about benefits to your customers that outweigh any drawbacks, or offer countering evidence or missing information.

SATISFIED OBJECTION

This type of objection occurs when your prospect is either already satisfied with their existing supplier or reluctant to make a change. In such cases, the best option is to create dissatisfaction with the status quo, in order to alter the customer's buying criteria in your favor. Here are a few suggestions to help you address the satisfied objection:

- Make sure you have presented sufficient value to differentiate your solution from the status quo.
- Expand your customer's vision of possibilities by showing them how your solution can help them achieve results that surpass their current expectations. Provide evidence or social proof to back your case.
- Create dissatisfaction by bringing the needs they have not yet considered to your customer's attention. Then show how your solution can satisfy those needs.
- Mitigate the risks of taking action for the customer. For example, by providing volume discounts, offering guarantees, making the transition as smooth as possible, or creatively structuring the business terms of the deal.

TIMING OBJECTION

Sometimes you are convinced that you understand the customer's goals and their problem, and that the solution you are offering is a great fit for their business. You are all set to move the process toward closing, but your prospect says something that stalls you in your tracks. For example, "Can we talk about this next quarter? It is just not a good time for us to buy right now." Not only is this a deal you had included in your pipeline, but you have also invested a lot of time working on it with your prospect. And they say that they cannot buy for now.

In many cases, this is not the true reason; it is effectively a form of satisfied objection that is used to make you either wait or walk away. A customer who wants to buy but genuinely cannot buy now will preemptively let you know their timeline and exactly what is holding them up. This objection is frequently offered when a prospect does not feel a sense of urgency, is unable to get the internal buy-in, or does not perceive enough value in your offering to buy. Your first challenge is to get to the real reason of the customer's objection. Here are some questions that you can ask to discover the motive behind the timing objection:

- "What stops you from going ahead?" Once you know their reason for vacillating, you will be able to better address it.
- "What are your key priorities?" Once you have a complete picture of their pressing concerns in the moment, you can position your offering as helpful in addressing them.
- "If money were not a constraint, would you be willing to buy with us today?" Ask this question when the customer cites lack of financial resources as the reason for not going ahead now with the purchase. If they say no, then money is not the real reason. They probably do not see the value in your product. Dig deeper to discover what is truly stopping them.
- "Is X no longer a key objective for you?" Bring up a palpable objective for their business that you had discussed during the sale process and that can be tied to your offering. That will move the focus away from the sale process and back to how your offering can play an important role in achieving their goals.
- "What is going to be different next quarter (or next year)?" This will help you surface the motives behind their effort to postpone.
- "When will be the right time to buy?" Try to understand what needs to change in order for the customer to buy.
- "What can I do to help you convince the decision maker?" When you feel your prospect is having difficulty getting internal purchase, try to help them get it through.
- "Here is the timeline for the ROI if you go ahead now." Showing them the gains related to time will underline the sense of urgency.

- "Is there anything I can do that might change your mind?" This approach ensures that you do not lose a sale that you could have salvaged.

ADDRESSING BUYER OBJECTIONS

Experienced salespeople understand the tremendous help objections can be to closing sales. As a salesperson, you must learn how to both discover and resolve customers' objections. You must respond in a way that assuages those concerns and allows the deal to move forward, helping the customer come to a different conclusion of their own accord.

View objections as a positive part of sales process that you are prepared for. Doing thorough homework helps you understand your prospect and gives you confidence that you are a genuine business partner to them. Understand what your prospect considers a risk—time, technology, changing suppliers—and address those risk factors head-on.

Knowing when to expect objections is the first step to handling them; you remove the chance of being caught by surprise or unprepared. Where possible, handle objections as they arise. Do not let them linger till the end of the sales process. The longer the customer holds an opinion, the more they become invested in it.

SOME COMMON TYPES OF OBJECTIONS

Let's look at some generic buyer objections that come up often in different guises.

1. Price: Price objections can be genuine, as well as a bargaining chip even though the buyer already intends to buy. When faced with a price objection, find ways to bring the focus back onto the value of your product or service. Often a prospect may think that a similar, cheaper product can do what they need. Make a comparison to highlight the differentiation that your prospect values; emphasize value by showing the distinction between cost and price.

2. No money: To cope with a genuine no-money objection, consider how you can help the customer save enough costs or raise money to be able to afford your offering. Share case studies of similar companies that have saved money, increased efficiency, or had a massive ROI with your offering.

3. No budget: Help the customer with justifications to obtain internal budgetary allocation, or find out when the budget will be available and make a note to reconnect at the right moment.

4. Dislike for contractual obligations: People tend to view time-based contracts with trepidation. See if shortening the contractual period or changing payment terms can work.

5. No need to change the supplier: A customer who is already working with a competitor is already educated and already has a need. Probe into the relationship to see if you can create dissatisfaction.

6. Bound by an existing contract: Try to come up with an inventive discount to balance the cost of breaking a contract early, or demonstrate ROI that will make up for the sunk cost.

7. No internal buy-in: Find out what objections your prospect anticipates and help them prepare the business case to respond. Also seek to meet with internal stakeholders and the decision maker so that you can convince them directly.

8. Not a priority: The customer may feel that the problem in question is not important for now. Find out the real reasons the need has low priority. This excuse can also indicate that your prospect understands they have a need and is trying to justify their inaction. Your challenge, then, is to create a sense of urgency.

9. Your product is complicated: Find out if the complaint is because of certain features or about the whole product. If the former, then you have a good chance of alleviating their concerns. Assure them of your complete technical explanation and implementation support. Make your prospect feel heard. Restate your impression of their situation, then align with your prospect's take and move forward on that trajectory. A lot of misunderstandings and hard feelings can be resolved simply by rephrasing your prospect's words.

HOW TO RESOLVE OBJECTIONS

Objections are not necessarily a sign of rejection. We all want to feel good about our purchases. Quite often objections are means to ensure that we are making the right decision. Sometimes, an objection is merely an opportunity for you to make the prospect feel good about what they are purchasing from you. Here are some suggestions for resolving your prospect's objections.

1. Listen carefully to the objection: First give the prospect a chance to explain the concern exactly. Listen carefully and do not interrupt.

2. Show empathy: Take a genuine interest in the customer's concern. Do not be defensive or condescending; try to understand their perspective and acknowledge it.

3. Keep the objection separate from the prospect: Be sensitive to the customer's feelings. Do not lose sight of the fact that buying is an emotional process. You can win on logic and still lose on emotions.

4. Do not argue: Arguing can lead to an impasse. As a skilled presenter, you have an advantage and are likely to win the argument. But the prospect will likely buy from somebody else to get even. Take an educational approach, instead; educate your prospect on how your product or service will add value to their business.

5. Slow down: Do not pounce on objections. Do not speak faster after hearing an objection. Do not confuse your ability to answer quickly with your capacity to respond well. Pause immediately after a customer's objection and then maintain your pace.

6. Talk less: Suppress your urge to talk more. Handling an objection is not about talking your way out of the situation. Answer precisely, with confidence and calm. This shows to the customer that you have the exact answer and are confident that you are right. If you talk too much, you will preclude your customer from engaging at a crucial point.

7. Clarify with questions: When you respond too quickly to objections, you might address the wrong issue. Instead, ask questions. Make sure you understand your prospect's objection before you respond. That way you won't sound confrontational; the objection may be a simple misunderstanding or point of clarification.

8. Repeat the objection to the prospect: When the prospect is done talking, recap the gist of what they have said. For example, "I see that you are concerned about the compatibility with your system. Is that right?" It gives the prospect the chance to either agree or further clarify. After that you can address and resolve the specific issue.

9. Discover the real reason: Sometimes the objections mask the real concern. Ask a few exploratory questions to draw the prospect out a little. It is likely that they will become more comfortable as you continue to engage them and will open up to you. If that happens, you will be able to offer the precise solution to the prospect's real concern.

10. Keep the end in mind: First, if you have not already done so, understand the customer's desired outcome. This outcome is your common ground with your prospect, the guiding light of your relationship. Resolve the objection within the realm of what is helpful in achieving their desired outcome.

11. Respond to the objection: Once you understand the objection fully, you can answer it. The most authentic answers include social proof and verifiable hard facts or numbers.

12. Lead your prospect to the answer: Present information in a way that helps the prospect make conclusions that answer their own objections. Lead them where you want them to go. Nothing is more convincing than an answer we find ourselves.

13. Use social proof: Share stories about other customers who had similar concerns during the sales process, but ultimately moved forward with your offering and saw business success as a result.

14. Confirm with the prospect: Ask to check if you answered the prospect's objection completely. Only when they confirm that you have, move on to the next step. This is important when responding to an objection: you want to make sure the customer understood your response and that you have suitably tackled their concern.

15. Refocus the discussion: Bring the focus back to the sales process and continue to move on.

16. Blunt the competition: Objections can provide you with an opportunity to talk about the competition. Bring up the competition when you see an opportunity to get ahead of them. Dealing with the elephant in the room early on will give you more influence over your prospect's perceptions of you.

17. Use the right language: We all react better to powerful words. Here is some of the vocabulary that will help you in handling objections:

Imagine. Suggesting to the customer what to imagine can be incredibly powerful. For example, "Imagine becoming the number one company in your industry."

Verbs connoting action. Explain the tasks your offering enables the prospect to perform rather than its features or how it works. Use action verbs like *mentoring, training, leading, onboarding, investigating, achieving.*

Successful. Great salespeople use the word successful quite often in their speech.

Fair: This is a powerful word. Use it often. Tag your conclusion with, "Is that fair?"

The customer's name. Use the prospect's name often, especially before making an important point.

Reassuring language. Use words that convey confidence and assurance like *definitely, certainly, we can accomplish that.*

Partner, not customer. A *customer* buys something from you; a *partner* is someone you continue to feel responsible for.

In-Person Selling

"People will forget what you said, people will forget what you did, but people will never forget how you made them feel."
Maya Angelou

I n-person selling occurs when the salesperson meets with the customer to convince them to buy a product, a service, or an idea. It requires significant personal skills and knowledge on the part of the salesperson. The strength of in-person selling is the personal touch and the flexibility it provides. Salespeople can adapt their approach and pitch to fit the needs, motives, and behavior of the customer. The personal interaction means that a salesperson can successfully respond to and overcome objections and encourage the customer to act.

PREPARING FOR IN-PERSON SELLING

Here are some ways to get ready for an in-person sale.

1. Be prepared: One area you can control is being well prepared for the meeting. Skilled salespeople do meticulous research to acquire knowledge of their customers and competitors. This makes them aware of how the people they hope to sell to will react to their products and services. Learn all that you can about the customer. Do not place yourself in the situation of asking the customer a question whose answer you could have easily found elsewhere. As you plan for the meeting, ask yourself which customer insights will demonstrate your preparation.

Also note the reason for the meeting, its agenda, who is attending, and the roles and influence of the attendees. Do some quick research on people who will be in the meeting that you do not know. Preparing for both the meeting content and the customer's situational context will influence the outcome of the meeting.

2. Plan your questions: Once you have done the research, the next step in preparation for in-person selling is to plan questions that will draw your prospect out. Smart questioning builds trust and gives you opportunities to uncover information and get the customer thinking about challenges that match your solutions.

Ask questions that converge the conversation on the customer's needs, going from the general to the specific. Think through the questions you need to ask to deepen your understanding of their needs. When you plan well and ask the right questions in the right way, you can laser-focus your presentation on just those points that will sell most effectively. Ask open-ended questions with three objectives in mind.

First, asking open-ended questions helps you establish whether the prospect is a good fit for your offering. Second it helps you discover their emotions and, therefore, the benefits that matter the most to them. You can tailor your pitch accordingly. Third, by getting them to talk in greater depth, you can slide your rapport past the prospect's "salesperson filter."

Here are some of the types of questions you can plan to ask:

Buying history. Learning about the prospect's previous buying experiences will help you understand what they value and how their mind works.

Building rapport. Ask questions that get your prospect talking about themselves and help you develop some level of rapport with them.

Gathering information. Plan questions that will gather factual information that is not available from research.

Seeking clarifications. Draw out more information, where needed.

Creating need. As a salesperson, you need to be skilled in asking questions that uncover and develop needs in areas where you can offer solutions.

Defining the impact. These are questions that explore and expand the customer's perception of the problem by investigating its impact on other areas of their business.

Related to purchase. These questions relate to the specific sale you are targeting. They will help you understand what is important to the prospect, their timeline, their budget, and their decision-making process.

Underlining differentiation. Plan questions that you can ask, instead of you doing the talking, to lead the customer to differentiate your offering from the competition.

Quantifying the benefit. Learn to ask customers intelligent questions that help them quantify the potential benefits of buying your solution.

Drawing out objections. It helps to get the prospect to voice the objections that you sense are on their mind so that you can address them.

3. Identify "the" problem: While the prospect may enumerate a litany of problems, there is always one specific problem that is responsible for the issue you are pitching to resolve. Therein lies your opportunity. Therapists know they cannot solve any patient's problem until they understand the story hidden behind the problem. Similarly, the real problem is lurking somewhere behind the various issues that a customer cites. People do not care how much you know until they see how much you care about their business. Forget about what you are selling and focus on what the customer is selling. Your customer wants someone who understands their pains, problems, opportunities, goals, and challenges. Stop selling and show them how you can help them with the problem they are facing.

It is difficult to convince businesses to buy unless they have a major problem on their hands that is creating frustration and inefficiency. The problem can lie in any area of their activity—finance, operations, technology, sales, and so on. Whatever it may be, this is what motivates a business to purchase or to change. You need to be good at probing and identifying the problem.

So, how do you identify the problem? The first thing you can do is to shun the "tell and sell" approach, delivering canned pitches without truly engaging the customer in a dialogue. The best sales meeting is neither a speech nor an interview; it is a discussion. Keep it pleasant and friendly. Make the customer feel that you are on their side and trying to learn more about how their business could benefit from some new ideas.

To get the customer to talk about their organization, ask open-ended questions. Open-ended questions elicit detailed and individualized responses; they help you conduct effective qualitative research. Your customer's problems are mostly subjective. Even when two customers have identical pain points, the underlying cause (the problem) can be very different from one customer to the other.

Here are some questions that can assist you in teasing out the problem:

What is your biggest obstacle to growth? This question can drive to the core of the matter. Every business strives for growth, and the problems it faces must in some way be hindering growth. Getting prospects to talk about their present business situations not only increases your understanding of their business, but it also builds your credibility with them by demonstrating your expertise without having to flaunt it. Once you are on the trail, get down to the customer need analysis. Ask them about their plans to tackle it, about their timing, and if they have a supplier in mind. The discussion will then become more open, helping you learn a lot about the customer's problem and how best you can solve it.

What keeps you awake at night? This question is more personal and is likely to kindle your customer's emotions and get to their fundamental need. Getting your customer to talk about what they are most aggravated by will get them enthused about a potential solution.

What is your company's most important performance goal? Talking about the most important goals will surface the issues that need to be addressed for optimal performance. What do senior managers talk about incessantly? Helping your prospect look good within their organization makes them likelier to champion the purchase within the organization.

What are the drags on your time? This question will lead to a discussion where you can explain the value that your solution could bring to your prospect on a personal level. It could be a problem whose resolution will impact their team and help the prospect save time spent in solving their issues.

What makes you unhappy? It may seem a trivial matter, but responses to this question can offer a lot of insight. A problem may look small, but a skilled salesperson can ask further questions that unveil a larger issue.

Once you identify the problem, continue to make progress on the sales process. Here are some suggestions to proceed further:

Use your customer's terminology about the problem. Using their language to describe and discuss the problem will build trust.

Discover who has the buying authority. Identify the decision maker. Determine whose budget will be used to support the purchase.

Find out who else needs to be involved in the decision. Ask what teams need to be involved in a decision to purchase, and identify key stakeholders. As early as you can, you need to know the people and the teams involved and their priorities—which may be quite divergent.

HANDLING THE MEETING

How you handle customer meetings plays an instrumental role in closing a deal. Here are some suggestions for better handling a meeting.

1. Make a good first impression: Start by thanking the customer for their time. Do so even if the meeting was requested by the customer.

2. Outline the agenda: Define the agenda of the meeting at the outset. This shows that you have done your preparation and that you respect their time.

3. Use the agenda to reveal requirements: The agenda forms the spine of your meeting. Keep coming back to the agenda to ensure that the meeting is moving forward and that you are making good use of your time with the customer.

4. Balance talking and listening: Do not overwhelm the customer with information. Listen with empathy; this also allows you to better understand the customer's emotions and attitude.

5. Keep everyone involved: Do not just speak to the senior manager. Others in the room are likely to have some input in the decision-making, and you need to convince them to do business with you and your company.

Speak to all of them and make eye contact with each person around the table.

6. Discover their timing: It is not productive to focus too much on prospects who are not going to make the purchase decision anytime soon. A good way to ask this is, "If I provide you with a solution exactly as per your requirements, what timeframe are you looking at to make the decision to buy?"

7. Anticipate and address objections: Some objections are inevitable; some others you can sense coming up. Preempt such objections by handling them before the customer brings them up.

8. Do not be unfair to a competitor: If a competitor's name comes up, do not be unfair to them in their absence. Praise them for what they do well, but then show the customer why it would be a better business decision to work with you.

9. Be flexible: Most meetings do not exactly go as planned. There is always some need for flexibility in how the meeting is to be run and accommodating what the customer finds important. Spend time within the context of your agenda to work through what the customer deems is important. Be flexible at the same time as maintaining control on what is to be discussed.

10. Be authentic, add a personal element: During most customer meetings, conversation takes place at two levels. One is a person-to-person conversation and the other is the business conversation. Do not underestimate the power of personal impact on a customer meeting; you can add a lot of value to the meeting through meaningful personal interaction. People relationships also play a role in shaping buying decisions. Be yourself and use that to your advantage.

11. Convince the customer: Make a demo, answer all questions, handle objections, and lead the customer to the decision.

12. Close the business or agree on the next step: If it is time to push for closing, do so. Otherwise, do not end the meeting before moving the sale process to the next step. Agree on a tangible action point.

METHODS FOR IN-PERSON SELLING

Here are some methods that can be used for in-person selling.

1. Sales presentation: In-person or virtual presentation to apprise prospective customers of a product, service, idea, or organization.

2. Conversation: Relationship-building discussion with prospective buyers with the intent of persuading or making sales.

3. Validation: Demonstrating how a product or service works, the benefits it offers, and how it resolves the problem the customer is faced with.

4. Addressing objections: Responding to the concerns of prospective customers to remove any perceived or stated obstacles to making a purchase.

5. Bold calling: Sales calls by a sales representative to connect with target customers in person or via phone.

6. Outlet selling: In-store assistance from a salesperson to help customers find, select, and purchase products or services that meet their needs.

7. Door knocking: Offering products or services for sale by going from door to door.

8. Counseling: Consultation with a prospective customer, where a salesperson learns about the problem the customer wants to solve and proposes solutions.

9. Referrals: Seeking satisfied customers to share their positive experiences with other target customers.

Influencing

"The ability to influence people without irritating them is the most profitable skill you can learn."
Napoleon Hill

D o not think that once a prospect has been bombarded with a product's features, advantages, and benefits, the sale is guaranteed. Selling is not something you do to someone, but rather something you do with someone, gaining trust and rapport and then influencing the buying decision. Salespeople rely on their capacity to forge human relationships and influence those relationships to guide their customers along the path. Influence is described by Oxford dictionary as "the capacity to have an effect on the character, development, or behavior of someone or something, or the effect itself." The ability to influence others in the area of sales can transform your business and your career. It enables you to get people to make a commitment to you. There is real power in influence. It is effective during sales interactions or in contracts and other in-person negotiations. In essence, influencing is the heart of the sales process.

Through hundreds of controlled tests, psychologists who explore the principles of influence and persuasion have sought to understand what influences people to say yes to requests of all kinds. And they have demonstrated that you can produce a yes response to almost any request if the request is presented in the right way. The principles discovered by these researchers are basic to our human nature, deep-seated, and powerful. They work because our brain is built to help us simplify life by identifying patterns moment-by-moment, and automatically setting in motion habitual sequences of standard, well-rehearsed behavior. Yes, as you might argue, human triggers and response patterns are more varied and complex, and certainly less predictable. And people are more aware than ever of the manipulative nature of selling and advertising. However, if you can discover the most powerful human behavior sequences and find the thing that triggers them, you can lead people to say yes to your requests more often.

Psychologist Robert B. Cialdini (in his 1984 book, *Influence: The Psychology of Persuasion*) identified six principles for influencing a buyer and sales success: authority, reciprocity, scarcity, consistency, liking, and social proof.

AUTHORITY

People are instantly deferential to those in positions of power. It is not just police officers and people in uniforms who command our obedience, though, it is anyone with authority, special knowledge, impressive credentials, or even an air of confidence. People are more willing to follow the suggestions of those who appear credible and authoritative. Establish yourself as the authority or the expert. Your questions and third-party stories are indicative of your expertise and offer social proof. People appear hardwired to respond to authority. When your product conjures something familiar, such as a celebrity, industry expert, or even a memory, people will feel that your brand possesses similar qualities to that familiar entity. They have recognized expertise in the space, and you can reap the benefits by associating your brand with authoritative figures, thus establishing your own sense of authority. A stamp of approval from an expert in your industry could provide just the authority you need to instill customer confidence and persuade browsers to buy.

We respond to authority figures because we grow up surrounded by those bigger, smarter, and more experienced than ourselves. As we grow up, we all learn to take shortcuts to help us make decisions based on very limited information. Since our reaction to authority is so powerful and immediate, those "in the know" can use this principle to get a yes response more often. Psychologists call the rule of authority a "decision heuristic," which is a highfalutin way of saying a shortcut for making decisions. Acquire knowledge and then change the look and tone of your messages to project more confidence and authority.

ELEMENTS OF CREDIBILITY

One form of authority that is important for a salesperson is credibility. According to a mountain of psychological research, there are four basic elements of credibility: expertise, trustworthiness, similarity, and physical attractiveness. The first two are most important, but they all play a part.

1. Expertise: Having relevant knowledge is the key to expertise. What special education do you have? What kind of experience? Have you demonstrated unusual competence in a relevant area? What are your big successes? What about awards or public recognition? People look for clues about what you know and what you have done. However, these clues must be relevant to the subject at hand.

Here are some suggestions to sell like an expert:

Sell within your area of expertise. Sell only when you have identified the customer's deeper-level problem and you know that you are good at resolving that problem. Do not think it is your job to convince the customer that they need whatever it is that you are selling. Make sure that the customer has the problem that you are good at solving and you have the resources to address their problem.

Educate, do not cajole. Be passionate, but do not be more passionate than the customer to solve their problem. Do not cajole your prospect into buying your solution; instead, educate them to make the decision that is right for them. Remember what the famous author Dale Carnegie said: "The only way on earth to influence the other fellow is to talk about what he wants and show him how to get it."

Ask more questions than give answers. Ask questions to discover and understand your prospect's problems. Ask questions to sustain the discovery process till the customer can decide for themselves. Your desire to get to the truth earns you credibility.

Listen. You do not need to out-talk your prospect to show your expertise. Instead, first get the best information by listening and then demonstrate your expertise in the matter.

Do your homework. Great salespeople practice and rehearse before they sell. They spend hours researching and finding the best answers to anticipated questions and likely objections. Do not turn up for a meeting without doing your homework.

2. Trustworthiness: Perhaps even more important than expertise is trustworthiness. When considering credibility in a sales environment, trustworthiness may be vital because of suspicions about salespeople and their motivation for selling.

Trustworthiness is built of a blend of personal integrity, truthfulness, and your reputation. Nothing else you do will work if you are not able to get people to trust you. Customers can tell when they are only getting a sales pitch and not an honest opinion. They can also sense when you are not being yourself. You cannot rush it. Establishing a bond of trust with a customer will take as long as it takes; it may happen in an instant or it may take a long time, but it cannot be pushed.

Do people feel they can trust you? The answer is based on what people perceive your intentions to be. People want to know why you take the position you do. Among the reasons for people rating you low on the trustworthiness scale are a "knowledge bias" or "reporting bias." If your prospect thinks your background or particular experience prevents you from being objective, there is a "knowledge bias." If your prospect thinks you are just saying what they want to hear, there is a "reporting bias." So, you'll be more persuasive when you come across as saying what you really believe. That often means admitting that there are two sides to an issue or acknowledging flaws before presenting your position.

Buyers rely greatly on their capacity to judge another person based on their perceptions of the person's characteristics. That will affect whether they consider a salesperson worthy of trust. It is vital, then, to make a favorable first impression in order to attain trustworthiness. Expertise also enhances trustworthiness. Buyers are likelier to trust salespeople they deem competent. Another factor that can affect trustworthiness is likability. Salespeople who are liked are more effective in selling.

3. Similarity: Similarity can also figure into credibility. We tend to pay more attention to those who are like us. Deep down in our minds, we ask: Do you think like me? Are your ideals like mine? Are you from the same social class as I am? Do you look like me? And the more similarities we come up with, the more likely we are to like that person and grant their requests. Of course, similarity depends on relevance.

Research suggests that business buyers may judge their degree of similarity with a salesperson in terms of visible characteristics (physical characteristics and conduct) and inner characteristics (insights, feelings, attitudes, and values). Most often, visible similarity has little effect on a buyer's perception of a salesperson's effectiveness. In contrast, there is substantial evidence that inner similarity can augment a business buyer's willingness to trust a salesperson and follow their guidance. It is more significant for buyers and sellers to think alike than to look alike. As a salesperson, you must have the flexibility to identify potential areas of inner similarity with your buyers and build upon those aspects to cultivate positive perceptions.

Besides inner similarities, incidental similarities also help build connection and credibility with buyers. Incidental similarities usually refer to trivial aspects of our lives that we share with another person—like a common name, birthday, or birthplace. Research indicates that these types of similarities enhance a customer's favorable attitude and likelihood to buy. Being aware of this phenomenon can help you make connections with the buyer. Experiential studies show that the existence of incidental similarities bends toward such positive outcomes as increased liking, persuasion, and cooperation between individuals. Thus, incidental similarities have both an immediate and a long-term benefit. As a salesperson, consider how you might connect with buyers with whom you may share some common ground. A buyer may be more inclined to work with you if they know that you share a similarity.

4. Physical attractiveness: The final key to credibility is one most of us will not want to admit to: physical attractiveness. There's no way around it; we are more likely to pay attention to attractive people. This is for a variety of reasons. Attractiveness produces the "halo effect"—the pleasant feeling we get from an attractive person is associated with the message that person delivers. And according to various studies, attractive people are seen as better communicators and more fluent. In addition, liking and identification play a part, since people like and identify with attractive people, thinking "I can be like that person if I believe what they believe, say what they say, or do what they do."

There is enough research that investigates the dimensions of physical attractiveness in sales settings. A 1986 study by Shelly Chaiken confirmed a strong relationship between physical attractiveness and social influence. The impact that physical attractiveness has on a salesperson's credibility varies according to the situation. A 2008 study led by Michael Cunningham conveyed that attractive people have an advantage in selling products that relate to physical appearance. Therefore, an attractive salesperson would likely have direct persuasive credibility with products that pertain to sports, fashion, cosmetics, or hair products.

Attractiveness does not always give a credibility or persuasion advantage in a business situation. In most business selling, factors other than attractiveness are far too influential for attractiveness to be of any real consequence. However, research suggests that physical attractiveness can play a role in perceived credibility when two salespeople are equal in expertise, competence, trustworthiness, and similarity.

GAINING AUTHORITY

We are all wired to respond to authority. The power of authority can get people to do things that would normally conflict with their deeply held values. As a salesperson, you can use authority to build confidence in your prospects. Establishing your authority also helps you stay in control of the sales process. Here are ten suggestions for what you can do to gain authority.

1. Establish your expertise: Prepare with plenty of information. Back up your confidence with capability. Display your know-how and experience. Show your credentials before presenting your argument. Better still, allow people to discover your expertise indirectly, so it seems more natural and not part of a sales pitch. And make sure all the symbols of authority are in place.

Here are some suggestions to demonstrate expertise to sales prospects:

Earn professional qualifications. One way to easily demonstrate expertise is to get some widely recognized professional accreditations under your belt. You can use these designations or certifications in your introductions.

Use testimonials. If you have received customer endorsements or recommendations, add them to your social media presence, especially on LinkedIn. You can also include links on your social media profiles to other sites that contain content showing your expertise.

Share your expertise outside of your target market. Seeing that your expertise is valued outside of your sales focus enhances your authority in your prospects' minds. Volunteer to speak at public events. Publish articles in newspapers and industry publications. Join local trade associations.

Build your own stories. The most effective stories you can tell are your own customer case studies. Prospects will always find it easy to relate to a case study that tells the story of another customer's experiences and how you solved their issues. Show that you have a track record of successful experiences.

Become an author. If you do not have enough time to write, then remember that most sales books are co-authored. Or use professional organizations and writer groups to find a project where you can contribute without having to write an entire book on your own.

Write a blog. Make a website of your own that can demonstrate your expertise and share your knowledge with the world.

Expertise is not just information. Bombarding people with information and data alone does not build your expertise. Expertise is more than knowledge; it is an amalgam of knowledge, performance, credentials, skills, flair, and credibility.

Specialize. Do not be a jack-of-all-trades and master of none. Specialize in something so that people will regard you as an authority in solving their specific challenges and needs.

Use the right channels. Do not waste time establishing your expertise in places where your target market does not spend time. Consider what the best channels are to communicate with your prospects and share your expertise. If you use social media, do your prospects spend time on Facebook, YouTube, Instagram, LinkedIn, Snapchat, or somewhere else? Also consider how your prospects consume content—articles, videos, graphics, eBooks, podcasts, or another form of content? Knowing this will not only enable you to create content that gets more engagement but will also help you select the social media platforms where your audience abounds.

Offer value. Do not just create content for the sake of it; it has to be valued by your audience. We are so flooded with content that every bit of it has to compete for attention. Ask yourself not what you want to share but "What is in it for them?" Look at content from your audience's perspective; if they see no clear benefit, they will most likely not invest time in it.

Persevere. Expertise cannot be established overnight. It takes time because it requires building a reputation. Be regular in creating and sharing content or in networking.

Connect with your audience. Be open and engaging with your audience; respond to their comments and answer their questions. Ask what is important to them and share expertise accordingly.

2. Create trustworthiness: Inspire trust by avoiding any appearance of bias. Take a position that people do not expect you to take. Say what you truly believe and say it with conviction.

The trust of your customers and colleagues is imperative for success. If you get others to trust you, it is easier to grow and nurture your authority. Here are some suggestions for you to become trustworthy in a business environment through communication, commitment, and competence:

Show compassion. Pay attention to and care about a prospect's problem. Be genuine; never fake compassion. Be willing to lend a hand to people and help them solve their problems.

Show humility. When success is hailed as identifying champions and winners, business culture often induces us to double down on pride, leading to arrogance. Humility, however, is what breeds trust. Humility gives you the capacity to position yourself as an authority without being afraid to be corrected.

Show confidence. Make sure that you both know what you are doing and also appear to. Competence backed by confidence in your ability to help attracts trust. When you are confident and humble, you are comfortable in presenting divergent ideas but also open to feedback.

Be reliable. Follow through on every little commitment you make. Be prompt and punctual. Every small detail counts, especially at the beginning of your relationship with a buyer, when they have little information to gauge your trustworthiness. Be careful not to oversell; promise only what you can deliver without fail. When you cannot fulfill your promise for some reason, go back and explain the situation to the customer in advance.

Show trust in others. Trust begets trust. Be generous and forgiving with others. Show trust and give other people the benefit of the doubt until proved otherwise.

Build win-win relationships. A customer should clearly understand the value of your product or service to them. Show them that you care about their problems and their goals.

Address complaints fast. Every interaction with a customer is an opportunity to build trust. Resolving problems and conflicts quickly goes a long way.

Be truthful. Not lying is not enough; be willing to tell the truth when it is needed. Be as honest with people as you expect them to be with you. Think about what is realistic and live up to your word.

Be flexible. Be willing to meet the person in the middle. Consider uncommon alternatives for problems that cannot be resolved by the usual methods.

Respect your customer's time. Raise your awareness of other people's time and schedules. Promptly return phone calls and reply to emails. Be on time for meetings, and finish them on time too.

Exceed customer expectations. To pleasantly surprise customers is a good way to deliver trust. Deliver more—in service, product, time, convenience, or sensitivity—than the customer bargained for. Exceeding customer expectations adds real value and trust.

3. Mention weaknesses or drawbacks: Be willing to acknowledge weaknesses in what you are saying or selling. This will appear to be contrary to your own interests, but it is not, and you will appear more trustworthy. If you do mention weaknesses, bring them up before you list strengths—this generates greater belief in your position and lowers resistance to your arguments.

Confidence is an important skill for salespeople. It helps you to have conviction in what you are selling and inspires the buyer to trust your authority and capability. However, everyone feels vulnerable at times. It is acceptable to show weakness.

Do not worry about looking good to hide what you do not know or hide your weaknesses. Be accepting of your mistakes and shortfalls. Being able to admit and share times of weakness is a way for sellers to earn trust from those they want to sell to. Take time to identify your vulnerabilities. As a salesperson, you need to know all you can about your product or service, company, and industry. But there will be times when you will not know the answer to a question or problem. Admit it; do not be afraid to show it to your buyer.

4. Try the "convert effect": Someone who has converted to another lifestyle—to something opposite—is always more credible. The "convert effect" plays on the feelings of similarity between the convert and the prospect. The convert seems to have overcome a "knowledge bias." The convert has made a voluntary decision to do something different and has not been forced into the decision by circumstances.

5. Show similarities: Find and discuss similarities between you and your prospect, customer, or donor. Show that your thoughts, ideals, social class, or appearance are alike. Demonstrate similarities that are relevant to the selling situation.

6. Show purpose in your meetings: Make the best of your meetings by following an agenda and asking questions. Be flexible and willing to adapt according to what your prospect wants. By being adaptable, you are demonstrating that you are an expert seller—all while making your prospect feel as comfortable as possible. Intelligent questions show that you are in control.

The purpose of the sales meeting is to create the need for your offering. For that you need to connect, to establish credibility, and to drive action. Here are some suggestions to help you conduct a purposeful sales meeting:

Connect with the prospect. Make eye contact and break the ice with some small talk to start connecting. Do what you can to build rapport early in the conversation.

Reiterate the objective of the meeting. If you set the meeting, set forth its specific premise. If the customer called the meeting, listen to them and then confirm the agreed reason for the meeting.

Outline the agenda. Spell out the agenda for the meeting. Ask your prospect if there is something else they want covered in the meeting. If the buyer has already set the agenda for the meeting and there is something more you want to discuss, ask them to add it. The tact of suggestion works to guide the conversation without appearing to dictate the agenda.

Ask questions. The conversation should not be one-sided; engage your buyer. Also, if the buyer is the only one asking questions and you just keep answering, the buyer is in control of the discussion. Ask your own questions and where necessary act to keep the conversation on track.

Tell stories. Use the power of story. Stories are more convincing than preaching. Use stories to educate the buyer, to inspire them to think differently, and to influence them to take action.

Balance inquiry and advocacy. Employ a blend of inquiry and advocacy to turn the opportunity you have created into a sale. Frame questions in a manner that includes both. For example, "Why wouldn't this work here? What could get in the way?"

7. Be yourself: Be professional, but be yourself. Like trust, authority is easier to gain if your prospect believes you are genuine. Being yourself also enables you to build personal rapport with the customer.

In the long run, being yourself consists in being honest with your strengths and weaknesses. Getting to know yourself and then being yourself are outcomes of a personal process. You do not have to be a consummate speaker and you do not need to know all the answers. But you must stay true to yourself and show your personality in your sales message.

Be authentic: not someone you think you should be, but genuinely and authentically who you are. As a salesperson, what you are selling is first and foremost you, and then your product or service. You, as the salesperson, are often part of the perceived value difference between your offering and the competition.

8. Dress appropriately: Dress to look attractive but professional. Dressing inappropriately can prevent you from being taken seriously.

Dress well to make the first impression count. Your influence starts when you walk through the door. What you wear plays a role in the impression you create and the authority you gain. Dressing appropriately affects how seriously some people will take you. If you wish to be taken seriously, you had better look the part. Here are some suggestions for dressing appropriately as a salesperson:

When in doubt, be overdressed rather than underdressed. Be careful not to overdress, but if you are not sure, err on the side of too formal. You can always dress down by removing a tie or jacket, but you cannot dress up if you turn up underdressed.

Dress like your buyer. As a professional, it is always best to dress the part. Dress equal to or slightly above what your customer is wearing.

Enquire about the dress code. When you are invited to an event by a customer, it is wise to ask what the dress code will be.

Think locally. Keep your dress in tune with the part of the world you are in. When you travel, pack clothing to match the attire to the place you will be in.

Look neat. Whatever you wear, stay neat and tidy. Check your appearance just before the meeting. There is little point in wearing expensive clothes that are wrinkled or fashionable shoes that are unpolished.

Beware of offensive odors. Be mindful of the odors you carry into the meeting—alcohol, garlic, perfume, bad breath, cigar, body odor, and so on.

Dress to feel comfortable. Wear something in which you feel easy and comfortable. Clothes that are oversized or too tight will make you feel uncomfortable. To be at your best, you have to be comfortable in your body and relaxed in your mind.

Dress according to the weather. Wear attire that is in accordance with the weather conditions.

9. Give guarantees: Guaranteeing in some way the performance of what you sell is a great way to gain authority, because it reduces the customer's risk. Different customers may buy your product or service for different purposes, but they are aligned in their goal to avoid regret. Your guarantee exercises authority in getting them to take a leap of faith. Make sure that your guarantee is attractive to the buyer but tight enough not to invite abuse. Here are some suggestions for types of guarantees you can offer:

Money-back guarantee. This is the most popular type of guarantee. Almost every major retail establishment, such as Walmart, Best Buy, chain book stores, Amazon, and Apple (online), offer a guarantee of this nature. If you offer it, do not hide it in the fine print. That is a poor idea. You will have a higher success rate if you make the benefit clear.

Risk-free guarantee. Giving your customer a chance to try your product or service before they commit to buy, a risk-free guarantee is a variant of the money-back guarantee that works well with high-cost products. It helps your customers move across the line from considering to trying your product or service.

Free trial. In today's world, a free trial has become a customer expectation. Most online services—Dropbox, LinkedIn, CloudApp, Evernote—offer a free service and a premium service, often with a free trial, hoping to attract some of their free users into becoming paid users.

Price guarantee. For example, amazon.com guarantees that you will be charged the lowest price the item has been sold for, rather than the price at the time of purchase. Many retailers guarantee a low price for 30 days after purchase, meaning that if the item you bought goes on sale, you will get a refund of the difference in price.

Satisfaction guarantee. A satisfaction guarantee not only ensures that the customer will be happy, but also makes sure that you will get another chance to save the sale by offering an exchange or remedy.

Forever guarantee. This guarantee is offered for high-quality durable items. It tells your customers that while they may spend more to buy your product, they are in effect saving by never having to buy again.

A guarantee is a powerful tool—both for achieving a high-quality offering and for marketing it. Apart from adding to your authority, here are some further advantages of backing your offering with a guarantee:

It lifts sales. This is the main motive for a business to offer guarantees. Offering guarantees increases sales by minimizing purchase risk.

It hastens decision-making. Once a customer is satisfied with your offering, a guarantee can quickly move them to buy it, thus shortening the sales cycle.

It reassures buyers. A guarantee encourages customers to purchase by reducing the risk of the purchase decision. For a buyer with more than one choice, a guarantee can make the difference between buying from you or from someone else.

It imparts competitive advantage. A guarantee is an opportunity to build competitive advantage. When other things are equal, a better guarantee compared to the competition adds competitive advantage. Organizations that work out how to offer and deliver a guaranteed high-quality product or service discover an authoritative source of competitive advantage.

It helps you command a better price. A robust guarantee somewhat releases the pressure on price negotiation. Buyers are willing to pay a higher price when they feel less at risk.

It buttresses the quality of your offering. When you are bound by a guarantee, it becomes imperative for you to deliver quality offerings and measurable results. You cannot afford to relax or lessen your focus. Hence, it drives the entire company to focus on customers' definition of good product or service—not on managers' suppositions.

It enhances performance standards. A guarantee sets clear delivery standards, which lift the business's all-round execution and performance. It informs everyone in the company what the company stands for. For example, FedEx stands for "absolutely, positively by 10:30 a.m."; Walmart is committed to providing "low prices every day, on everything." Salespeople, therefore, know exactly what their company can deliver and will represent that correctly.

It generates useful feedback. Payouts or performance under a guarantee generate valuable data to improve the areas of concern. A guarantee helps you know when you go wrong on something you must do to fulfill your customer's expectations.

It creates customer focus. Taking all of these factors together, guaranteeing a product or service forces you to focus on customers. Completely understanding what the customer wants is a prerequisite in offering a product or service guarantee. You must identify your prospect's expectations about the elements of your offering and the importance they ascribe to each.

A guarantee will be productive only if you begin with a commitment to the customer. It will not work in the long run to design a guarantee to maximize your selling punch without pulling up your socks. When you develop a guarantee program, make sure it is worth the effort and the cost and is not prone to misuse. Here are some suggestions for an effective guarantee program:

Only promise what you can deliver. Your guarantee is your commitment; only make a commitment that you can fulfill.

Use impact words. Use words that inspire trust, such as *guaranteed, warranted, 100%, authentic, certified, zero-risk.*

Make sure your customer also has a stake in it. Depending on what you are selling, you may require the customer to hold up their end of the bargain before they can call on your guarantee.

Fulfill your commitment. Make sure you fulfill the commitment that your guarantee entails.

Differentiate. Find creative ways to distinguish your guarantee from the competition.

10. Present testimonials: Use experiences of satisfied customers who are similar to your target audience. Testimonials are effective in helping you gain authority and converting skeptical prospects into buyers. Testimonials are a persuasive way to show that people who trust you get the results they are promised. They humanize your business; they make it easier to relate to what you sell and help your prospects imagine themselves enjoying its benefits. Here are some of the ways you can use testimonials:

Embed them in your promotional videos. Happy customers sharing positive experiences make for the most effective type of video content.

Share them on your website. Your website is the first place you might post your testimonials. It is an effective way to gain authority with visitors to your website. A posted testimonial must support your value proposition. Apart from the homepage, you can also create a dedicated testimonial page or place testimonials on your sales and landing pages.

Include testimonials in your promotional campaigns. Use testimonial videos in your email campaigns. Video content increases email click-through rates.

Include them in your follow-up or thank-you messages. Include testimonials in your messages when you send out thank-you notes or respond to questions and objections you receive from customers or prospects. Use compelling content to move your prospects further along in the buyer's journey.

Use them in trade shows. With a large number of interested, interconnected customers in the audience in one place, trade shows are a great place for video testimonials.

Use visuals. Hearing from another customer is effective, but seeing a real person is far more reassuring. Where videos cannot be used, use photos. Research shows that photos make facts and statements more credible. Human faces are an attention-grabbing element in all forms of promotional materials, from billboards to flyers to web pages.

Use stories. Comments from customers do not have quite the same effect as real stories that potential buyers can relate to. Stories have always enchanted us; great communicators know to use the power of story to convey their message. When told effectively, stories absorb us in their details and persuade us without our realizing it is happening. A good story connects a pain with a desirable outcome and manifests how your offering was able to bridge the gap between before and after.

Emphasize benefits. A good testimonial is focused on what your offering can actually do for the customer. For example, "This product made the pain in my neck vanish completely—and fast!" is far more effective than "This is the most effective painkiller I have used!"

Use data. It has never been easier to gather and compile data across a wide range of situations. When you use data, convey results precisely. Precise numbers enhance credibility—"77%," for instance, looks more authoritative than "around 80%."

Show comparison. Make your testimonials comparative, using them to set you apart from your competition. Your testimonial informs your audience what your product or service can do that others cannot.

Emphasize similarity. Buyers are more receptive to hearing from customers who bear a resemblance to them.

Use them as proof. Rather than just singing your praises, a good testimonial provides proof that you will solve the problem. Use case studies as evidence, showing in detail that the problem was solved.

Focus on outcomes. Showcase results achieved in real-life situations. Get customers to provide quantifiable results in their own words.

Make them real. Make the testimonials you use as real as possible by including the identity and details of the person or company that provided it.

RECIPROCITY

A second principle of influence is based on the law of reciprocity. Social psychology defines reciprocity as responding to a positive action with another positive action. In other words, in response to acts of kindness, people are often nicer and more helpful than usual. Our need to reciprocate a kind or generous deed can influence our behavior without our being aware of it.

Returning a kind gesture or favor is a basic human instinct. People are more likely to treat others in the same way that they have been treated. That is why it is so valuable in the realm of sales. Even a small gift goes a long way in helping a customer remember you when the need arises.

Reciprocity works when a good deed is done without any expectation of return. The sincerity of the deed is what gives it power. The need to return a favor is strongest when the initial favor is perceived as sincere and with no expectation of a payback. Cultural anthropologists Lionel Tiger and Robin Fox go so far as to claim that we live in a "web of indebtedness." This web, they say, is central to the human experience, responsible for the division of labor, all forms of commerce, and the organization of society into interdependent units.

The method for employing the rule of reciprocity to your advantage is simple: Give something away—a gift, a service, valuable information, assistance—to produce in the other person a sense of obligation. By appreciating the principle, you can exploit its full power more effectively. Here are some suggestions to help you influence customers and others in your network to reciprocate your positivity and perceive your interest in them as genuine.

1. Think service rather than sale: As a salesperson, focus on what is best for your customer rather than being preoccupied with selling your product or service. Help your customer find the right peg for their hole instead of shoving a square peg into a round hole. When you advise a customer to buy a less expensive option because it suits their needs better, even if the customer was prepared to spend more money on a pricier option, it produces an ecology for reciprocity to flourish.

Such a culture at a business drives every employee to focus on delivering a superior customer experience. No matter what insights you have to determine what to deliver and when, and how personalized and persuasive your message is, you will not reap the full benefit of your interaction if the experience is not focused on being of service to the customer. Here are some suggestions for cultivating a value-based approach to sales:

Think of building a business and not selling. As a good salesperson, you are building a business and not just trying to make a sale at all costs. Think of the business and the relationships that have to last beyond one sale.

Leverage your customers. Do not forget about a customer after making a sale. Nurture your customer relationships and use them to discover new relationships and customers.

Set yourself up to do well regardless of the market's ups and downs. As a salesperson, rely more on your actions than on macroeconomic indicators. A good salesperson does well in any economy; they create their own economy and can always make something happen.

See problems as opportunities. Problems are a part of sales and business. When a problem occurs, view it is an opportunity.

2. Make your customers feel special: Even when you are selling a generic solution, the customer should feel it is meant especially for them. Give the customer your complete attention, emphasize any unique benefits that the customer may derive from your product or service, and offer a gift or benefit that the customer is likely to value. Even a minor personalized gesture, such as a handwritten note, can make a generic offering to a customer feel special. Here are some more suggestions for making your customers feel special:

Give them personal attention. Make your customers feel that they are always in the top drawer of your mind. Keep track of their birthdays and send them a note on the day. When you meet them, always give them your undivided attention, greet and address them by name, and make them feel like they are your top priority.

Remember, they are people too. You may be doing business with large corporations, but the buyers you transact business with are people like you. They like to be acknowledged, even in small ways. Treat them like real people and not like a legal entity on the other end of a bargain.

Value their feedback. Show customers that you place a premium on their feedback. Show them that, when warranted, you can make necessary adjustments to your offering or your business based on their feedback.

Give them your business or make referrals. Reciprocate by giving customers your business, where appropriate, or by making suitable referrals.

Manage their expectations. Manage customer expectations from the beginning. Find out what they expect. Ask open-ended questions to understand their perceptions. Tactfully weed out unrealistic expectations. Make only promises you can keep and surpass. Communicate with them and keep them informed, especially of any unforeseen situations.

Be authentic in your interactions. You can never make an intelligent person feel special by feigning attention or adulation. Buyers are particularly sensitive to affectation and pick up the signs quickly. Be authentic, communicate honestly, and help them understand you.

Show gratitude. Manifest genuine gratitude by thanking your customers at every opportunity. Do not fake it; always be genuine and appropriate to the occasion. Send them small gifts to show your appreciation.

Be the best of yourself. When people inquire about something and you respond promptly, it makes them feel good. When you turn up smartly dressed and well-turned-out to meet them, people feel respected. Always be presentable as a business by making sure that you, your workspace, and your employees are clean, neat, and professional.

Celebrate their success. Celebrate your customers as being successful professionals and businesses. Keep an eye on the news for their triumphs and be quick to congratulate them. If you stay abreast of their successes, it makes people feel that you value your relationship with them.

Be proactive. When you apprise a customer of an upcoming circumstance that will benefit them, warn them to take a precaution, or give them information that will help them look better in their job, they will feel special as individuals.

Do something unexpected. Receiving a kind deed as a surprise always makes people feel special. Send a customer a gift when they do not expect it. Add a little surprise to their purchase. Forward some useful information or share a tip to make them feel that you are thinking about them. If they sense that you are looking out for them, it makes people feel valued.

3. Be the first to give something: Psychologists have established that giving gifts is a complex and important part of human interaction, helping to improve relationships and reinforce bonds. The person who gives first is in control, and that is the situation you want to create and maintain. Give something, without the perceived expectation of return.

What can you give? Anything. You can offer exclusive information, a concession, samples, a free trial, bonus points, discounts, a free booklet, planning kit, gift, survey, catalog, special report, or virtually anything else that is related to your product or service, or something exclusive to the customer that is not offered to the general public. Give away a sample of your "what" and "why." Give away inspirational content. Give away content that shows people what is possible. Give away case studies. Give away stories. Give away market intelligence. Give away your best thoughts on a subject. To keep the circle of goodwill going, offer another incentive when the sale is made.

People generally love freebies. At first glance, giveaways appear to be obvious money losers. But experience shows that, when handled wisely, giveaways are likely to reinforce reciprocity. Their power goes deep. Here are a few of the surprising ways giveaways affect people:

They feel obligated to buy more. Marketing research has shown that promotional events offering freebies are huge moneymakers. In a well-known 2005 study, Randy Garner, a professor of behavioral science at Sam Houston State University, showed that people feel obligated to reciprocate a favor even when they "may never have requested the favor in the first place."

When given something for free, people are likely to pay more for it later. Studies show that when an item is thrown in as a giveaway with a more expensive good, customers deem the freebie a higher-quality product and are willing to pay for it.

People perceive getting more as superior to a discount. In a marketing study, people were given a choice between getting 33% more coffee or a 33% discount on the regular price of coffee. More people chose 33% more coffee, even though getting a 33% discount was a better deal in terms of the price of coffee per ounce.

4. Offer customers a selection: Offer customers alternatives for selection instead of making the final choice for them. Give advice on the ultimate choice only when you are asked. Feeling the power of choice motivates recipients of goodwill to return the favor. According to psychology, the power of choice makes us feel more in control. The more options customers have, the more empowered they feel with their buying choices. Today's customer lives in a world where they not only have choices of products and services, but they also keep in constant touch with trends and happenings in the business world. Smart businesses, therefore, focus on providing their customers with multi-channel support, top-quality service, and a range of products and services—all different forms of choice for customers. Giving customers choices is part of delivering a high level of customer service and it also reinforces reciprocity.

Customers like usable and practical choices. The more pertinent choices a customer has, the more important and engaging a product or service becomes for them. However, the idea is not to overwhelm and confuse the customer; it is to build their trust through a thoughtful variety of quality offerings and top-class customer service. By offering the customer diverse yet simple choices, you can become a preferred partner for them.

In order to offer the most suitable and seemingly customized selections, you must gather as much data about your customer as possible. By using all the information about a customer, your business can put together a more inclusive strategy and be better positioned to create choices that the customer is likely to love and be able to use instantly.

One way of offering customers selection is to present a range of options that can be mixed and matched to put together a solution that perfectly fulfills customer needs. By offering customers choices, you are empowered to compete in a wider target market. Here are some suggestions for offering the customer the power of selection in a productive manner:

Keep it simple. If you want to help customers make better decisions, offer a handful of strong, clear, and simple choices and variables.

Make it specific. First understand the customer and their needs, and then offer specific and targeted solutions.

Do not put the cart before the horse. First fully understand, clarify, and agree with the customer on the problem they are looking to solve. Then give two or three options to solve that problem and explain how they will help. That helps guide customers in the right direction in the sales process.

Spot lack of decisiveness. When you perceive a customer is not able to make a choice, take more control of the process to funnel them to the decision-making stage. In such instances, you might make it simpler by advocating for a default choice.

5. Give something that is clearly and wholly for the benefit of the recipient: Do not allow your gift giving to come across as an apparent ploy. Your gift should be solely for the recipient's benefit and must not be selfish or qualified in any way. It must help the recipient, whether or not you get anything out of it. Give them a gift of value that profits their lives outside their relationship with your business or the use of your product or service.

It is not just about giving; it is about giving in the right way. As a business, you must be able to measure what works and what does not work, and then act accordingly to give back to others. Apart from the customer's reactions, here are some other ways in which giving back reciprocates to gain for your business:

Connection with the community. We are not wrapped in a bubble; it is important for any business to gain traction in the community. By giving away, you can forge a stronger connection with the community. This also allows you to understand and serve your customers better.

Stakeholder engagement. When you sacrifice your time and align your business with a good cause, you are able to align your employees, customers, and suppliers alike for the purpose. This is an excellent way to distinguish your organization from the competition.

Positive perception. When you give away your money or your time in a meaningful way, it generates positive publicity.

6. Give something that has tangible value to the recipient. The more valuable, substantial, and truly helpful your offer is, the more grateful your prospect will feel. Chest-thumping corporate brochures do not generate indebtedness, because they are all about you. What you give should be all about the person you are giving it to.

It makes sense for a business to be generous in offering gifts. The act of giving is itself part of the gift, but giving thoughtlessly is not enough. The value of a gift stems from the calculation that goes into its choice: What will it actually mean to the recipient? Giving such a gift requires a mental leap from your mind to the recipient's mind.

It requires a lot of empathy in order to attempt convergence with the mind of another person, but it is worth your while. Even if you fail to do it as precisely as you desired, the effort will be noted and appreciated by the recipient. It signifies generosity of time and attention, not just of money, and generosity of time and thought reciprocates in more ways than we think—an investment that is worth making.

A study led by Jeff Galak (Carnegie Mellon University Tepper School of Business) indicates that gift givers tend to focus on the moment of exchange when selecting a gift—the "wow" factor—whereas gift recipients are more focused on the gift's long-term utility or practical attributes.

Galak and his co-authors make recommendations for those hoping to choose better gifts, advising them to better empathize with recipients when thinking about gifts that would be both appreciated and useful. "We exchange gifts with the people we care about, in part, in an effort to make them happy and strengthen our relationships with them," Galak wrote. "By considering how valuable gifts might be over the course of the recipient's ownership of them, rather than how much of a smile it might put on recipients' faces when they are opened, we can meet these goals and provide useful, well-received gifts."

7. Make it personal: Whenever possible, make it clear that what you are giving comes from a particular person. It is easier to feel indebted to a real person than to a faceless corporate entity. Knowing what business gifts to give and how much to spend can support business growth—or hurt growth, if you get it wrong. A gift can impact the recipient's opinion of a business partner positively or negatively, so you have to be careful. Make it appropriate for the recipient's personal use. For example, gifts that bear company logos in a prominent manner are the least desired; they make the recipient feel less than appreciated and result in lower levels of satisfaction. Such items are often seen as marketing collateral and not as gifts.

Companies often feel compelled to put their logo on gifts so that recipients will remember them. However, research shows that practice to be counterproductive. A good gift is one that communicates "How much I think about you" and not "Think about me and my company." This is why a gift card is also not a good gift; it fails to be personal and memorable. A memorable gift is more likely to strengthen personal connections.

In order to be memorable, a gift must be selected just for the recipient and should include a personal message. Personalizing it with one's name or initials can add further value. It is also important to consider practicality. Focus on how the recipient might use a gift, and not just on its desirability.

Prefer to give handmade or homemade gifts over mass-produced items. Such items convey more love to the recipient.

Privilege experiential gifts over objects. Research shows that people who receive gifts such as concert passes or tickets to a sports game find the gift more memorable than people who received material items.

8. Keep on giving: Reciprocity is more than a technique to get one order, one lead, or one donation. The key is to create a feeling of gratitude and to maintain that feeling of gratitude. So, offer something extra that your customer or prospect didn't ask for. When you make a sale, deliver more than expected. And continue to give before, during, and after every transaction. Keep the circle of goodwill going.

Gifts are but one way of continuing to give. Sensible and thoughtful gift giving benefits your business in several ways. Promotional gifts have been used in business for generations. They are a means to continually remind customers and stakeholders of your company. Giving employees gifts is also a way of telling them that you value their commitment and hard work. Prefer practical items and keep your business gifts appropriate to the relationship. If possible, give a gift that reflects the recipient's personality.

Another way to give continually is through corporate social responsibility (CSR), which includes initiatives by a business for the betterment of society. These initiatives can be effective in garnering wider goodwill in the community. In order to participate in CSR, pick a cause that your customers or employees are passionate about. This will elicit greater reciprocity, and you will have a constant supply of ideas and volunteers.

One more way of continuing to give is to offer help or knowledge. Figure out what you have to give and how it will help your recipients. It can usually be your expertise, your knowledge, or your time. You can offer a tip, provide a little help, or impart a colossal idea that enables a paradigm shift or a quantum leap. Be clear whom you can and want to help or educate. Dedicate your wisdom or efforts to your target market. For that you need to measure. It is a bit more complex than other metrics, because what you need to measure is relations and not transactions.

I have observed that leaders who give the most of themselves to their teams receive the most from team members in terms of performance and effort. It fosters mutual giving within the team and reinforces engagement and learning. When we live as givers, we receive an enduring affirmation of our value to others. What we do fashions who we become.

Studies show that givers are the most effective salespeople, showing higher results across industries. A giver's basic instinct is to help customers solve their problems. When you continue to give, you build more supportive networks, you inspire higher creativity from your colleagues, and you are more likely to achieve successful negotiations.

9. Help customers reciprocate: Make it easy for your customers to thank you and help your business grow. Offer them opportunities to provide referrals, do some volunteer activity, provide testimonials, and so on. Give happy customers a voice by providing forums where they can describe and rate their experience with you.

If you can get your customers to reciprocate, it reinforces their loyalty. Once you inspire reciprocal loyalty, it will take your business to the next level. Customers will support your business through reviews, advocacy, referrals, purchase behavior, and community participation. There are myriad platforms available to get your customers to tell the world that they love you or your company and why.

Aim to nurture the emotional response that is most likely to drive loyal behavior—gratitude. Reciprocity is more about emotion than behavior. Repeat purchase behavior is a manifestation of reciprocity that is powered by emotion. The emotional connections that a business makes with its customers go the deepest and last the longest. When you empower customers to reciprocate you are, in effect, cultivating emotions.

One way to foster reciprocation is to find and advance a shared purpose with your customers, and to help them to share that purpose with others. Shared purpose is not something you do for your customer, but rather with your customer. When you transform your product or service into a social currency—like Apple did, for instance—sharing the experience with the world can become a shared purpose between you and your customers.

There is nothing better than turning your customers into your ambassadors. The perceptions you or your business have in the marketplace start and end with customer interactions. Customer enthusiasm reinforces a sequence of support and investment in one another that helps your business flourish over the long-term. Actively encourage your customers to reciprocate your dedication to them, and make it easy for them to do so.

10. Get to know the customer and begin to relate to the person: Try to build genuine relationships with your customers. The better you know a person, the more you can relate to their way of thinking and their preferences. Building relationships requires effort and time, and attention to detail and customer needs.

Connect with your customers and understand what they need. In this age of technology, it is very easy to keep customers engaged—on both organizational and personal levels. Use online tools and social media. Here are some suggestions for establishing relationships with customers:

Develop and nurture communication. Great communication is the foundation of any good relationship. We all have a need to be recognized and understood. Follow up with customers in an opportune manner, and answer their questions and complaints.

Foster feedback from customers. Encourage your customers to share their feedback to show them that you are keen to listen.

Understand what they value. Listen and ask to understand what your customers value and adjust your approach to match their expectations.

Exceed their expectations. Understand the experience customers are looking for in purchasing from you, and find ways to make it better than they expect. Exceeding expectations requires more of a mindset than an investment in additional resources. For example, delivering earlier than expected is a simple way of exceeding expectations. Delight your customers with the unexpected.

Show that you care. Show that you genuinely care about what customers want and value. Be friendly, be authentic, and show empathy. Enquire about their personal wellbeing and their families. Find out what you have in common with customers and engage on that subject.

Do not compromise on customer support. Commit enough resources and skills to customer support. For a good support experience, use a software that allows customer support to keep track of conversations that occur across different channels with the same customer. As customers, we hate to repeat ourselves every time we speak to a new person in the company. Also, if your support people have the relevant customer data when assisting customers, they will be able to take a more personalized approach.

Reward loyalty. Every good business must acknowledge and reward customer loyalty. Loyalty programs continue to grow in popularity. Rewarding loyalty is not only an effective marketing tool that companies use to retain their customers, but it can also be very helpful in building relationships that last.

Show flexibility. Be attentive to a customer's needs and complaints and quick to respond. Follow company policies, but do not be overly rigid or unbending.

11. Understand what it feels to be in the customer's shoes: Put yourself in the shoes of your customer so that you understand their pains and problems better. Putting yourself in your customer's shoes means that, organizationally, you need to understand their business, markets, industry, key success factors, key challenges, and organizational dynamics. At an individual level, know their motivations, fears, and personal goals, how their performance is appraised, their routines, and so on.

The more you gain insights about your customers, the better you will be in identifying how you can package solutions that help them achieve their goals. This process never ends. Great salespeople continuously learn about their customers. Here are some suggestions that can help you walk in a customer's shoes:

Know your customer. Learn their goals, strategies, priorities, performance, and financials. Know about their key performance indicators, organization, structure, and decision-making process. Find out how their customers and competitors perceive them. Think about their problems, the tiniest gap in their desires, and how you might fill and fulfill them.

Understand their "why." Go beyond knowing your customer's business, wants, and needs. Understand the "why" that propels their decisions. Identify their wants—physical, intellectual, and emotional. Focus on their experience. Consider how they actually feel in the situation where you want to create difference for them.

Understand their industry. Know as much as possible about the industry your customer is in. Find out what publications they read or what thought leaders they follow. Attend some of their trade shows. Learn the dynamics of the industry, its key players, issues, and threats. Learn the industry jargon so that you can speak their language.

Talk to their customers. Learn how your customer's customers view them and why they buy their products. Find out what makes them choose your customer over the competition and how your customer creates value for them.

Hang out where your customers hang out. Spend time where your customers are, both online and offline. Go to the places your customers frequent. Go there to meet them and to listen, learn, and build relationships. In online venues, follow the discussions; learn and ask questions.

Think local. If you work for a global company, it is imperative to respect the local culture, tastes, and ways of doing business. How your brand operates in one country or region may not work exactly the same way in another.

12. Listen carefully to what they say and how say it: Mutuality is the foundation of reciprocity. It is surprising how we often miss the most shared and influential form of reciprocity—listening. Nothing builds rapport like listening with attention and empathy. Listen to what your customers have to say as well as to what they leave unsaid. Ask them why they want something done.

People want to be heard, and listening carefully builds reciprocity. Listen, and only then offer advice. Reciprocity means, if you listen to me, I will listen to you. Listening is more than just nodding your head and waiting for your turn to speak. How much do you really hear of what your customers say? People are attracted to good listeners, and remember, they will buy from people they like.

Listening attentively to a customer allows you to develop a conversation, an exchange of ideas about how they feel. It enables you to see the world from their perspective and to understand their needs, characteristics, tastes, wants, and fears. It also projects respect, which, when reciprocated, is instrumental in building a long-term relationship.

Listen to learn and understand what your customer is saying: openly, keenly, and without judging. When a customer is talking to you, just listen. Pay attention to their tone of voice and body language. Empathetic reciprocity requires an ability to understand people's emotions and respond the way they expect you to respond.

13. Offer a solution to their business needs without asking for anything in return: Make helping the customer, rather than selling, your primary reflex. For an act of kindness or help to have the most import, it needs to be presented in a way that is perceived as sincere, with no anticipation of return. In business, there generally is an expectation of return, but the principle of reciprocity works best when you offer customers incentives, gifts, services, and complaint resolution in a manner that inspires trust.

Nobody cares about what you sell; they want their problem solved. Until a prospect or customer feels that you understand the problems they are trying to solve, you cannot make a real connection with them. Research shows that delighting customers is less important for building reciprocity than reducing their effort in getting their problem solved, without asking for anything in return. Customer satisfaction is merely a par; today there is little relationship between satisfaction and reciprocity.

Instead, businesses breed reciprocity by helping customers solve their problems quickly and easily. Make it easy for customers. Remove obstacles. Customers dislike having to contact a business repeatedly, to repeat information after being switched from one department to the other, or to grapple with an inefficient website in order to resolve a problem. Here are some suggestions for reducing customer effort in solving their problems, without asking for anything in return:

Be proactive. Customer problems are often downstream issues related to the problem that prompted the original interaction, even if that problem itself was sufficiently resolved the first time around. Most companies are well equipped to anticipate and tackle such issues in advance, but they rarely do so.

For example, Bell Canada studied its customer interaction data to understand interrelated customer issues. Based on what it learned, the company identified "event clusters" and started training its reps not only to resolve the customer's primary issue but also to foresee related downstream issues. This sort of forward resolution has enabled Bell to reduce its call time by 16%.

Pay attention to customer's emotions. Learn to detect when a customer is not satisfied, does not like an answer, shows signs of mistrust, or feels that you are hiding behind the company policy. Listen for clues to understand the customer's personality type, and adapt your approach accordingly.

Use customer feedback to reduce customer effort. Do not just resolve customer issues; also collect useful feedback. Learn from the data you thus gather from the customers. Some companies monitor online behavior in order to identify customers who are stressed. To foster reciprocity, salespeople must focus on reducing customer effort.

14. Leverage giveaways: Free giveaways represent the most basic way to build reciprocity. Those who are offered something for free will feel good about it.

It is important to keep your business at the top of your prospect's mind when you are looking for growth. Getting people to talk about your brand is a great starting point. Giveaways are not just about the person you give them to; they also affect the people in their networks. Give items to your prospects and customers that resonate with your business and encourage them to talk about you, thus telling others about your products or services.

When you think about the law of reciprocity, the benefits of giveaways become obvious. Giving products or services away is a powerful method that can create and strengthen customer reciprocity by providing someone with something useful at no cost to them. The recipient, in return, will begin to build trust with your company and will be more amenable to doing future business with you.

Choose giveaway items that represent the guiding message of your business and that the recipient will use each day. That will stop them from forgetting about you. In order for your giveaway items to beget reciprocity, they have to be useful, attractive, and relevant. For example, if you turn up at a sports event in the realm of your target market and hand participants an attractive water flask with your logo, you will make an impression in their mind. Similarly, consider what you can offer free of charge that your prospects would consider valuable and that you can obtain economically.

Giveaways, when used intelligently, trigger the law of reciprocity. For instance, the Disabled American Veterans organization relates that its plain direct mail request for donations found a response rate of 18%. But after they began giving away personalized mailing labels to potential donors, their success rate nearly doubled to 35%. It worked like a talisman.

Information is also a great example of a free giveaway that that generates a high perceived value at a low product cost. This is why it is clever for businesses to distribute special reports carrying the latest information and useful insights to their target market.

15. Use the power of service: Quality customer service often inspires customers to reciprocate. Those who receive better service than expected feel the urge to reciprocate. The goodwill you generate through excellent service extends to your product and company.

No doubt there are a lot of subtle elements that nurture reciprocity in any business relationship, but do not underestimate how effective providing above-par service can be. They will at least pay attention when you ask for something. If you set a certain service expectation, then exceed it in unexpected ways. Do this often enough and customers will start to evangelize.

When you really overdeliver, you will see your customers reciprocating without even being asked. Commit to excellent and error-free service; this commitment is a constant tool for self-improvement. It is an advantage to performance, and the reciprocity it generates can be a locomotive to market dominance.

To create a sustainable impact that goes beyond quarterly statements, businesses need to embrace a purpose beyond themselves. They should be able to create, serve, build, and improve in the service of a broader, more long-term goal. When combined, purpose and service are the fuel for transformation. However, many businesses overlook this imperative to focus on more practical, short-term objectives, serving only their more immediate agenda. For a business to unleash its potential, it must help its customers experience the power of service.

Unleashing the power of service, first and foremost, is about putting aside internal concerns to prioritize customer needs. It requires aligning organizational strategy to customer service, demonstrating customer service behaviors at the top of the leadership, making customer service a value that shows up in performance measurement, connecting customer service to teamwork, and using the service platform to develop further business. The law of reciprocity is best served by the desire to help your customers accomplish their goals. It is not about you; it is about what you can accomplish together with your customers.

SCARCITY

In general, the fear of loss is more powerful than the hope of gain. By influencing the instinctive tendency to avoid losing what one already possesses—or avoid losing the chance to possess something desirable—you can trigger a favorable response.

Something that has limited availability often piques people's interest. Businesses use scarcity to encourage purchasing behaviors, as people value things that are scarce. A designer may only have few suits left in your size. A special sale offering may be for one day only. A builder may have only one house with the features you want. Collectible items fetch a lot of money in special auctions.

People also tend to assign value based upon availability, the law of supply and demand. If something is in shorter supply, people want it more. Scarcity forces action. The limited offer is a proven selling technique, especially when done honestly with justification. The limitation can be a time-based deadline, a limited quantity, or exclusivity. Show genuine scarcity in the most tangible way you can. Point out what will be lost by not responding. People fear loss, so generate a feeling of potential loss. Make sure your scarcity offers are consistent with your product and the expectations you have set.

Here are some of the reasons why scarcity works so well on us.

1. Decision-making: We use the attribute of limited availability to help us in our decision-making processes. If something is scarce, it makes decision-making simpler. We often see scarcity as a shortcut to the best choice amid plenty of alternatives.

2. Value-perception: We view things that are difficult to possess as better than those that are easy to possess. Even buying simple things like cookies, chocolates, or pastries from the same outlet, we often prefer items that seem to be more in demand, as evidenced by a low supply on the shelf.

3. Restriction to freedom: If something is scarce, is likely to be unavailable in the future, or can be possessed by only a few, that is seen by many as a threat to freedom of choice. We feel in control when we possess exclusive things or rights, for example, membership in a club with limited membership and a demanding selection.

4. Loss aversion: Scarcity triggers a subconscious impulse to avoid regretting having not taken a decision to act by acting now. When we view something as scarce, it leads us to want it.

5. Status: Scarcity is also fed by our anticipation of social effects. When we see others with the item that we wish we had, we start seeing that item as a status symbol and think that the person who has the item enjoys a higher status than those who do not.

CONSISTENCY

Consistency is a valued adaptive behavior. Communally and personally, it is an applied survival skill in a complex world. Doing things the same way or maintaining the same ideas about things offers us helpful shortcuts. People are motivated to be consistent in all domains of life—in their words, actions, choices, beliefs, values, habits, and relationships. Once a person makes a decision, takes a stance, or performs an action, they endeavor to make their future behavior consistent with their past behavior. People will go to great lengths to appear consistent in their words and actions, even to the extent of doing things that are basically irrational. As a salesperson, if you can understand the psychology of buying and get customers to make a small commitment to you—like signing up for your email newsletter— they are more likely to eventually purchase from you. Consistency will make a huge difference in any long-term relationship you want to develop with a potential customer. Sales is about building trust and following through. Being consistent will help you do both.

Similarly, customers also have a desire to appear consistent. You can skillfully use that desire in the sales process. Consistency is another example of a "decision heuristic"—a shortcut for making decisions. In addition to simplifying our thinking, consistency helps us avoid unpleasant emotions. It helps us stick to what we know and avoid the chance of disappointment, embarrassment, failure, and loss.

Moreover, people are not only motivated to be consistent but are also motivated to appear to be consistent. That is because, socially, consistency is a looked-for personal trait. It is perceived as balanced, dependable, logical, and focused. Inconsistency, in contrast, is generally frowned upon. It is viewed as unsound, dishonest, illogical, and vacillating.

Commitment is the key to activating the rule of consistency. If you can get someone to make a commitment, even an apparently unimportant one, you inevitably activate the rule of consistency, which can then help elicit the yes response for later, and more important, requests.

USING CONSISTENCY TO SELL

Here are some suggestions for using consistency in selling.

1. Start small and build: The foot-in-the-door technique is effective. Start by asking your prospect to accede to a modest request or a small transaction. By getting them to decide, take a position, or undertake an action, you have found a new psychological "commitment." This changes your prospect's self-image just enough to trigger the rule of consistency. You can build on this new self-image and make requests of increasing import.

2. Build on existing commitments: In addition to creating new commitments, you can also work on commitments your prospects have already made. Get people to take a position on what they already agree with. Align your offering with your prospect's current sense of consistency. You can also drop a hint about how refusing your offer would be inconsistent. For example, "No one who admires Monet can afford not to have this print in their collection."

Engaging your prospect in a series of small commitments is a thoughtful process. By asking them to make small commitments, you create a journey of their own making, a story that requires them to remain consistent. Here are some suggestions to forge your process to extract and knit together little commitments:

Create engagement. It starts with getting them engaged in the process. Build rapport and provoke your prospect's interest. Take it to the point where they trust your input. Engage all the stakeholders, as you proceed.

Educate. Understand and agree on the customer's problem. Provide information, make a demo, and ask provocative questions. We all crave information that is tailored to our situation or need. Allowing the customer to personalize information they receive from you is a powerful tool to build trust. Take it to the point where they know they can count on you for the solution they require.

Guide them along in decision-making. Once you get your prospect to trust that they are now getting the best possible information to resolve their problem, you can build on a succession of tiny commitments, leading them to the point where their next commitment involves their wallet.

3. Get prospects and customers to participate and keep them involved: People judge others and themselves more by their actions than by their words. Therefore, the more active a commitment, the better. Where possible, rather than getting your prospect to think something, have them spell it out loud; rather than saying it, get them to write it;

and rather than writing it, have them do it. What you ask should not be difficult, just active, necessitating some involvement. Involvement generates inward pressure to regulate the self-image to match the action, which is how others see us.

Strengthening your bond with the customer fosters consistency. Businesses have much to gain from actively pursuing and pushing customer participation. Amid the deluge of promotions all around them, today's customer values interactive involvement with a purpose. Here are some suggestions to get your customer participating and then keep them involved:

Build engagement. Let your customers know that you expect them to engage. For example, post interactive content on social media that elicits participation in asking you questions, answering your questions, and partaking in competitions. Be active on social media platforms, such as Pinterest, that generate a higher participation rate. Know where your customers are found in order to engage them.

Foster emotional connections. It pays to build emotional connections with your customers. An effective way to build emotional connections is to cultivate personal interactions. Think how Steve Jobs did it as Apple's brand ambassador.

Create a community. Create an in-person or online community of your target market. An online community enables you to directly engage your customers by answering their questions, supporting relevant discussions, keeping them abreast of developments, and sharing information that they value. Use this community to methodically encourage customers to recommend your company to others.

Involve them in product development. Foster customer input. Encourage your customers to volunteer constructive ideas and suggestions to improve your product and service offerings. Research corroborates the value of involving the customers in new product or service development. Not only does it reinforce customer engagement, but customer interaction in new product development also has a positive effect on new product success.

Organize a contest. Give your customers a chance to win free stuff. You will gain their attention and you can also reward their participation.

Hold an event. An in-person or online meetup is a great way to engage your customers. They will learn from their peers or feel like a part of an exclusive community. Participate in industry trade shows that allow you to mingle with your customers. Host webinars.

Build excitement. Businesses often engage their target market by getting them curious or excited about something. For example, share teasers about a new product to keep people wondering or announce an event first on social media to build anticipation.

Ask for feedback. Encourage customers to share their views about your company and its products or services. Do not hesitate to ask for feedback and reviews. See if customers are willing to share it publicly or even be featured. If you encourage satisfied customers to provide feedback and suggestions, it helps bind them to the business. Transform their satisfaction into active involvement as your ambassador.

Keep it simple for them. Customer participation should not be complicated. The easier it is for customers to get involved and the less time it takes, the more likely it is that they will engage.

Make them feel in control. Be creative and sensitive in pulling customers into the process. Make it feel voluntary and unforced. Customers want their participation to benefit themselves, other customers, and the company. As you ask them to invest time, let them feel that their involvement can make a difference.

Form path breaker partnerships. Look for opportunities to partner with your business-to-business customers on initiation of ideas. Help your customers promote their ideas and breakthroughs. Highlight the problems you have solved together. Join hands for the causes you both support. This strengthens the involvement of a valued partner and boosts your opinion shaping credibility.

Keep participants informed. Inform participating customers about how you are using their input and how their involvement is shaping your business. Show evidence that prior customer involvement has contributed to the community, improved the experience of other customers, or boosted efficiency.

4. Sometimes, you may need to make them work a little: There can be a benefit to demanding some effort. Effort increases the power of commitment. The more work someone does to get something, the more committed they are to it and the more likely the rule of consistency will come into play. For example, writing takes effort, and it is more likely to influence behavior than speaking or thinking. The rule of consistency pulls one to adjust one's actions and thoughts to what one has written. Evidence shows, for example, that customers who fill out their own order forms are less likely to cancel.

Every business knows that one way to make customers work for you is to ask for referrals from them. Not only do you advance customer involvement, but instead of spending money on advertising, you can pass on the savings to customers.

5. When suitable, make commitments public: The more public a commitment, the greater the pressure for consistency. That is because people are not only wired to be consistent, but also to appear to be consistent. Find ways to make engagement public when it is appropriate. For example, getting satisfied customers to write testimonials makes them even more committed.

The more public a commitment people make, the stronger the influence that action has on future actions. When we do something that others see, we feel a greater need to be consistent. If someone has made any commitment at all to your company, product, or service, you can reinforce that commitment by asking for a more public show of support.

For example, a customer survey is mainly a way for you to get information and feedback about your products and services, but it can also be a way to get customers to publicly commit. You can even engage people who are not yet customers by asking them about their perception of your organization, products, or services. If they provide positive responses, that is a form of mild commitment and they will be more open to dealing with you in the future.

The more public the commitment, the more it will stick and the more it will impact your customer's behavior. For example, completing an identified survey invokes a stronger commitment than an anonymous one. But eliciting a testimonial or recommendation or getting customers to write a review that is posted publicly will arouse a much greater commitment than participating in any survey. That is because testimonials or reviews are not merely a measure of social validation, they also act as a form of commitment. They make the giver more likely to take action to be consistent.

However, never pay people to get a commitment. When a public commitment is given for a reward, then the giver is not likely to be deeply committed. Instead, if we act voluntarily out of our beliefs, we feel an inner responsibility for action.

6. Try to interest customers with offers directly connected with your product or service: If prospects feel they tried your product or service because of the lure of a gift, they will feel no commitment or need to be consistent. But when they respond to offers that are directly related to your product or service, prospects will take ownership of their behavior, thinking, "I responded because this offer looked interesting to me. This is the kind of product someone like me would use."

This approach makes your total offer much more than your product or service. For example, you can add value by providing expert advice that will enable smooth installation or use of your product and services. In order to deliver real value, offer a level of advice that is better and more valuable and state-of-the-art than the competition.

If you as a business possess ability as knowledge, skills, and experience, you can offer extra value to your customers by enabling them to learn how to do something. Take your cue from Home Depot, for instance, and start teaching your customers how to do things they want to be able to do. This will reinforce consistency in your customer experience and enhance the value they perceive as related to your product or service.

Another way to add value to your product is to increase the speed of delivery to your customers. There is a direct positive connection between speed and the perceived value of your offering. You do not need significant investments to increase your delivery speed, but if you can put in place efficient logistics systems and processes to deliver as quickly as possible, you will create consistent positive experiences and a palpable competitive advantage.

7. Exercise commitment management: The desire for commitment is a general human drive. From the perspective of behavioral science, customer commitment is seen as a psychic construct of an individual's or a business's obligation to and solidarity with another individual or business relationship. From the positive or negative evaluation of the relationship emanates the corresponding inclination to behave in a certain manner. Customer commitments deliver the continuity of the behavior in the business relationship.

Commitment is a reciprocal relationship; investing in your customers will strengthen their desire to remain consistent in their behavior to use your product or service. On the other hand, consistency on your part can reinforce and consolidate customer satisfaction as the basis of long-term commitment.

For every sale, consider the current state of your prospect's commitments. Ask yourself: Is there a commitment I must produce to sell this? Is there an existing commitment I can use? What is the right pace to build commitment? One critical factor in any business relationship is to consistently respect promises related to deadlines or time.

The likelihood of customer commitment rises with the anticipation of sufficient gratification with regard to interactions. Communication within business relationships also enhances commitment if it adds to the customer's satisfaction and thereby stabilizes the business relationship.

Business relationships can be influenced positively with strategies of customer commitment, and you can use various tools to manage and strengthen commitment. For example, you can get more feedback on the ease of use of your products or the services that support them. Or you can engage customers in focus groups. Showing customers the alternatives available, and highlighting why you are better, can improve commitment. Here are some types of customer commitments that you can identify, build, and manage:

Unique commitment. This happens when the customer believes that no other offer or company could better address their needs. The solution you offer them meets all their needs, and they are extremely satisfied.

Relationship commitment. This is when a customer becomes highly attached to you, your colleagues, or your company and an emotional link is forged. When customers are pleased to say "my realtor," "my jeweler," or "my banker," they feel a sense of personal identification with that individual or team. This commitment takes shape when a customer believes that an organization or its people are better than competitors in ways that matter.

Belief commitment. This type of commitment happens when the customer feels their core beliefs are aligned with those of the company. Customers can have varied core beliefs, for example, environmental protection, honesty, water conservation, child protection, education, family orientation, and so on. These beliefs are often a blend of cultural norms and personal values. A similarity in these values is likely to elicit superior customer commitment. Businesses everywhere benefit from belief commitment. For example, Body Shop inspires customer commitment because of its refusal to source products tested on animals and its support for community trade, human rights, and the environment. Hence, personal value orientation does have an impact on professional business relationships and commitment.

Habitual commitment. This commitment is rooted in repetitive and automatic behaviors. For example, a customer continues to purchase from a company because that is what they have always done, and not necessarily because of superior quality or a better bargain.

Coherence commitment. This is the commitment between business partners that arises when their technology, process, policy, or potential are mutually compatible. This aspect of commitment is often manifest in longer-term business relationships in the business-to-business sector.

Identity commitment. This is the "we" feeling of mutual solidarity with a business partner that arises when customers see a business as consistent with their lifestyle and personality. This feeling addresses the emotions, motivations, and attitudes that influence the customer's psychic commitment.

LIKING

We tend to be influenced by people and things that we are attracted to. No matter how reasonable we may think ourselves to be, we will be more likely to say yes to those we know and like. We readily comply with requests from those who are similar to us and for whom we have good feelings. That is why people are more likely to buy if they like the salesperson.

Sympathy for a friend is one of Cialdini's most famous principles of influence. If you want to influence someone, try to please them. The quickest way to create sympathy is to find what you have in common.

The role of the right moment cannot be underestimated. Timing is everything. Another well-described principle, "priming," is also associated with wise timing. It involves introducing a variety of incentives that change the behavior of people immediately. As a rule, people are completely unaware that their actions were influenced.

Stressing similarities is a powerful tactic for building sympathy. If someone tells you that you went to the same school, support the same football team, or have a common hobby, then you are more likely to succumb to their conviction.

Cialdini lists the following factors that cause the liking rule to take effect.

1. Physical attractiveness: "Research has shown that we automatically assign to good-looking individuals such favorable traits as talent, kindness, honesty, and intelligence."

2. Similarity: "We like people who are similar to us. This fact seems to hold true whether the similarity is in the area of opinions, personality traits, background, or life-style."

3. Compliments: "We tend, as a rule, to believe praise and to like those who provide it, oftentimes when it is clearly false."

4. Contact and cooperation: "Becoming familiar with something through repeated contact does not necessarily cause greater liking.... we must be working for the same goals ... we must 'pull together' for mutual benefit."

5. Conditioning and association: "Compliance professionals are incessantly trying to connect themselves or their products with the things we like. Did you ever wonder what all those good-looking models are doing standing around in those automobile ads?"

SOCIAL PROOF

Cialdini's social proof theory argues that when we do not know what the appropriate behavior in a situation is, we will look to other people to seek guidance for our actions and to imitate what they are doing. This theory accentuates the significance of social influence on our own behavior.

Like other influencing techniques we have discussed here, social proof is a shortcut for making decisions. It is a sound and logical adaptive behavior. When you understand the rule, you can trigger it to generate a positive response to your offers and requests.

Social proof is connected to the principle of liking. Because we are social creatures, we tend to be biased toward things that other people already like, whether we know them or not. We all look to others to help us decide how to act and choose. The more people are doing something, the more correct it seems. We do it all the time, at the office, on the highway, at parties, and in the neighborhood. We are driven in so many ways to conform. As a salesperson, you can use this tendency to your advantage. Smart retailers or pub owners design in a way to keep people waiting in long lines outside. Fund collectors announce the names of those who pledge. Why? Because of the rule of social proof. It works.

MOTIVES OF SOCIAL PROOF

Social proof works best under two conditions: uncertainty and similarity.

1. Uncertainty: When faced with an unaccustomed situation, an uncertain individual feels the need to refer to other people for guidance. Social proof will help when your prospect is uncertain about your offer or some aspect of your message, or when your prospect is unfamiliar with your product, your company, and so on.

2. Similarity: When we are still undecided, we are prone to adopt the behavior and outlooks of people whom we perceive to be similar to us. The perception of similarity may be based on facets such as age, gender, school, community, physical appearance, beliefs, income levels, education levels, vocation, and common experiences. Social proof helps when your prospect sees similar others using your product or service. They then feel, "Yes, those people are like me and they are using it. So, I am the type of person who would use it, too."

CATEGORIES OF SOCIAL PROOF

Broadly, social proof can belong in six categories.

1. Customers: Testimonials, case studies, or other means of endorsement from your existing customers.

2. Experts: Endorsement from credible and respected experts and thought leaders in the industry.

3. Celebrities: Advocacy from celebrities, stars, and personalities who have bought your product or service or have visited your premises.

4. Crowds: Large numbers that evidence the popularity of your offering, like the number of customers, subscribers, hits, likes, and so on.

5. Friends and family: People who are members of your prospect's circles.

6. Certifications: Accreditations, qualifications, and official recognitions that vouch for your quality and reliability.

USING SOCIAL PROOF TO SELL

When you use social proof effectively, you communicate to potential customers that buying your product or service is the safe thing to do. This is vital for the success of the sale because people are risk-averse. Here are some ways of putting social proof to work for you as a salesperson:

- Demonstrate your social credentials: awards, best-selling products and services, independent surveys, customer reviews, and so on.
- Quote information on your market leadership in any aspect—qualitative or quantitative.
- Show important or well-known and well-liked people using your product or service. (It appeals to the good feeling the buyer may have toward a celebrity.)
- Show an approval or endorsement by a rating organization, a trade association, or an industry body.
- Display industry certifications or accreditations.
- Show people like your prospect using your product or service. The more similar, the more effective.

- Show testimonials of satisfied customers.
- Use customer logos to evidence positive adoption.
- Show testimonials by those who have been "converted" from another product or service. Converts are always more credible than typical customers.
- Show pictures or videos of people using your product or service. Seeing is believing. You can also use real-time stats. Showing how many people are currently viewing the page or how many customers are currently purchasing a product is not only a form of social proof but also adds a sense of urgency.
- Show case histories of some of your best customers. Studies show that tangible case histories can be more effective than impressive statistics. More formal in nature, case studies provide high-authority social proof.
- Show the excitement of others on discovering your product or service. Acceptance and enthusiasm create a supreme emotional stroke.
- Mention how long your company has been around.
- Show the number of products sold.
- Show the number of customers you serve. Show the number of subscribers or users.
- Create a sense of short supply triggered by demand. This deploys popularity plus scarcity.
- Create a sense of urgency due to demand.
- Cite media coverage. Newsworthy products and services, such as magazine features, unsolicited reviews, TV segments, and podcast interviews, inspire trust. A simple strategy is to integrate the logos of media outlets you have been featured in.
- Cite available compatibilities as a social proof that puts your product in the company of credible, familiar brands. For instance, if your product or service offers platform integration with other companies' services, you can mention that or add a logo of your integration partners.

- Social share counts are most often used to provide social proof on blog posts or any website page.
- Like Amazon, you can show prospects similar products that your customers bought along with the product they are currently viewing.

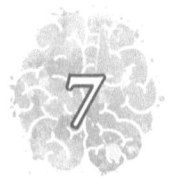

Negotiating

"In all negotiations of difficulty, a man may not look to sow and reap at once; but must prepare business, and so ripen it by degrees."
Francis Bacon

S elling is not a black and white proposition that dies if the buyer does not say yes. Good salespeople view negotiation as an important part of selling. More sales fail because of lack of agreement on terms than because the solution is not good enough. Prior to a sale, make a list of all the points that might come up or that you can use for negotiation. You may need to change gears during the process from salesperson to consultant to negotiator in order to conclude an agreement that is a win-win for the parties involved.

THE ART OF NEGOTIATION

These are some of the negotiation skills that you will find useful in sales.

1. Prepare well: Prepare thoroughly for every round of negotiation. Set aside time to do your research. Studies show that underprepared negotiators make needless concessions, fail to see sources of value, and walk away from beneficial agreements. Being prepared before entering negotiations leads to negotiation success. The better prepared you are, the more likely the negotiation outcome will be positive. Prepare for detailed negotiations and plan strategies for every encounter. Be adequately knowledgeable in all areas of the sale you are conducting. In this case knowledge is power; it will make you a more skillful negotiator.

The best salespeople know that they must plan carefully. Build powerful negotiation skills to become a better dealmaker. Like other skills, negotiation skills require regular practice to keep them sharp for when they are required. Simulate and practice important conversations in your mind beforehand. Practice both your delivery and your body language. Here are some suggestions for you to put in practice:

Be clear about your goals. A successful negotiation is one that delivers both your goals and your customer's. Your goals are the measure you set to gauge the success of a negotiation. Determine them in advance. Once you are clear about your goals, they will guide your negotiation. Take time before the negotiation to think through what you want to get, what you need to get, and what would be nice to get out of the interaction.

Know your customer's goals. During your preparation, consider what your customer seeks and what they want to avoid. Knowing your customer's goals and positions will allow you to position the negotiation.

Look for symbiosis. You know your own goals and have taken an educated guess at those of your customer. Now consider how to best shape a solution to connect them. This solution is often the missing link between your and your customer's objectives. Try to find it. Good salespeople start preparing for the negotiation at the start of the sales cycle and never stop.

Know the threshold. If you are clear about the point where a deal becomes unattractive for you and you are better off walking away, you will not hurt yourself in trying to elicit an agreement. Identify the point at which you will stop negotiating and move on to other opportunities. Setting a bottom at the start of your negotiation makes it easier to resist the temptation of agreeing to an unprofitable deal.

Do your research. Read about your customer's industry. Develop a clear understanding of the value of your product or service to your customer. Find out who your likely competitors are.

Train. Do not just read or listen to tips. Consider how these points apply to your practice. Simulate real-life situations and make note of what you learn and what concepts or moves apply to your own negotiations.

Be open to learn. Participate in role-play exercises with your colleagues or at home. Seek feedback and be open to correcting flaws in your thinking or style. All of us are susceptible to judgment biases that color our negotiation approach. Feedback on elements of your behavior is useful for improving your negotiation skills.

Use everyday situations to learn. Treat ordinary interactions like negotiations. Practice your skills. Simple discussions with your friends and family can help you practice active listening, empathy, or taking cues from body language. The more you practice negotiation skills in everyday interactions, the more you begin to see negotiation as a process toward an agreement, making you feel more comfortable in high-stakes situations.

Be mindful. Maintain a sense of vigilance to apply what you have learned to your negotiations. You can only embed what you have learned by continually using it in real-life situations.

2. Ask the right questions: Start by investigating the key issues from the customer's perspective. Be curious about their position, intent, goals, motivation, limits, and areas in which they can be flexible. Listen carefully to their responses, and at various points during the negotiation, recap the other side's point of view out loud so there are no misunderstandings. Being alert to the buyer's verbal and nonverbal communication will also help you uncover any hidden agenda and recognize when your negotiating partner is ready to close.

You will be amazed how asking the right questions can help you find a way through impossible situations. During the course of negotiation, you can often ask questions to do the following:

Solicit information. Do not assume anything, ask. You are not supposed to have all the information; ask questions to fill any gaps.

Check knowledge and commitment. Ask a question to make sure that your prospect fully understands the information you are providing and has the knowledge necessary to make an educated decision. Also determine how committed they are to the outcome of the negotiation.

You do not want to overinvest where you are unable to create the required level of interest.

Determine the personal style. Orison Swett Marden, who founded *Success* magazine in 1897, wrote, "The golden rule for every businessman is this: 'Put yourself in your customer's place.'" Ask questions that provide you with some insight into the behavioral and decision-making style of your counterpart so that you can adapt your approach to their personality.

Encourage participation. Good salespeople know to ask questions to get the customer to talk and participate in the discussion.

Provide information. You can also ask questions with the intent of providing information. For example, you could ask, "Do you know why Mrs. Brown's house sold well over the asking price?"

Seek an opinion. When you ask questions seeking someone's opinion, you are not only seeking information but also conveying that you are interested in what that person has to say.

Bring attention back to the topic. You can ask a question to refocus attention on important issues. For example, "Can we get back to the resistance you anticipate from your board?"

Establish agreement. Ask questions to ensure that you and your counterpart have the same understanding on a topic. You do not want to be surprised when you try to draw on that understanding later and discover that your prospect had a different interpretation.

Circumvent roadblocks. If negotiations start to get stuck or become tense, it can be helpful to ask smart questions. If you understand concerns or sources of stress before further aggravation, it can help you restructure the negotiation. For example, "Every time I talk about training your concerned staff at our plant, you object. Can you help me understand why you are opposed to this idea?"

Show empathy. Showing empathy makes your customer feel better. Suppose your prospect looks unusually off-color during your meeting; you might ask, "All good? Are you having a tough day?" Author Tiffani Bova rightly states, "How you sell matters. What your process is matters. But how your customers feel when they engage with you matters more."

Close the sale. You can ask skillful questions to move the sale process to closing. For example, "Have I answered all your questions?" or "Are you in a position to proceed now?"

3. Balance inquiry and advocacy strategically: You can gain leverage in negotiations by paying attention to advocacy and inquiry. High advocacy / high inquiry fosters two-way communication and learning—I state my views and I inquire into yours; I invite you to state your views and inquire into mine. A balance of advocacy and inquiry is necessary, but their quality is also critical. High-quality advocacy involves providing data and explaining how they support your view of the situation. High-quality inquiry involves seeking the buyer's views, discovering their needs, probing their biggest challenge, and encouraging them to find out more about your solution or service. A balance of high-quality advocacy and high-quality inquiry leads to highly productive negotiations.

Negotiation may or may not involve agreement or disagreement, compromise or dispute, and approval or argument, but it invariably involves communication. Poor communication thwarts the progress of negotiation. Many salespeople chatter away when they should be listening. On the other hand, some salespeople talk too little. Some are good listeners but do not know to ask questions. Some ask question after question, tendering no advice, setting no agenda, and adding no information.

Each party engaged in a negotiation gains by maintaining clear two-way communication. A balance of advocacy and inquiry ensures the flow of two-way communication. As you communicate during the process of negotiation, the act involves both informing and questioning. Effective negotiation means more than just selling what you want. It means arriving at a solution that satisfies all parties and creates future opportunities.

Most people are hardwired to lean toward either advocacy or inquiry. Fine-tune your communication style and cultivate self-awareness to maintain the right balance between advocacy and inquiry.

4. Maximize your negotiation leverage: Many salespeople think that the customer has all the power and will only care about price. If that is the case, then you had better be the cheapest option or you will lose. Think of levers other than price. For example, work hard to develop a stronger value proposition than the competition and confidently assure your customer that you have a unique offering that solves their problem in ways that no other solution can. Here are some examples of the circumstances that will give you more leverage:

Best solution or unique features. Begin with the customer's goal and focus on the specific benefit that best addresses their concern. For example, "We manufacture ourselves and are in the same location as you, so you will no longer lose money because of delays. Plus, you will be able to cater to unforeseen spikes in demand by getting supplies from us at short notice." If the unique value you have is a customer priority, you have significant leverage to use in your negotiation.

Ability to meet deadlines. Timeliness is important for any business. When you consistently deliver on time, you establish a reputation for being a reliable and dependable business. Show the prospect your demonstrated dependability, plus any advantage you have in this respect because of your location or processes. Explain to the buyer how your continuously meeting deadlines will ensure that they stay on budget, a financial benefit that can add up over time.

Delivery capabilities. Amazon's example shows delivery capability can build a business. Your ability to deliver rapidly and consistently can bring an advantage to your negotiation. Show the buyer how your standard procedures are able to achieve a faster response to their demand, how you can ensure a fast turnaround time for their special needs, and how your unified information system makes data on customer needs quickly available for delivery planning.

Issues with the competition. A big challenge for a business, while negotiating with a prospect, is to demonstrate a sustainable competitive advantage over its competition. In all of your sales interactions, keep in mind the imperative of creating a competitive advantage. When you can identify legitimate issues with your competition, that gives you strong leverage. A competitor may be vulnerable in one or more areas, such as these:

- Quality issues (features, benefits, durability, reliability)
- Price issues
- Cost issues
- Low levels of productivity
- Low capacity utilization
- Incompatible systems
- Production methods

- Ineffective distribution
- Poor ability to execute

You are selling so that you can tip the playing field in your direction. You want an unqualified advantage over your competitors.

Ability to tailor or customize the solution. When you are able to provide a bespoke product or service to a customer, it empowers you in negotiations. Research shows that when users have a say in designing and personalizing the product or services they need, they are far more likely to buy them. The 21st century is witnessing a growing clamor for choice, away from the mass production of the previous century. Today's mass production must be accompanied with many options to suit different preferences. Therefore, companies that strive to be a leading force in the market have to be innovative to satisfy this growing demand for choice.

Customer relationship. To build and leverage a good relationship in negotiation, ask questions, listen carefully, work collaboratively, and build agreements that benefit both sides. A relationship in negotiation is a perceived connection that can be personal, economic, or political. You can use a good relationship to inspire trust in your commitment to the buyer's interests. It will be difficult for your customers to reproduce a strong customer relationship.

Industry knowledge or expertise. Knowledge is growing in importance as access to it broadens and deepens. Those able to cultivate and use it well will learn that knowledge is becoming a big differentiator in selling negotiations. A salesperson with good industry knowledge knows what is going on in their industry and who their competition is. Industry knowledge not only helps you explain the value you offer to your customer, but also helps you understand the vulnerabilities of your competition's products, procedures, and systems.

Power of an existing relationship. Soviet leader Mikhail Gorbachev surprised President Ronald Reagan in September 1986 by requesting him to meet face-to-face in Iceland. Reportedly Gorbachev was exasperated with the Soviet and American bureaucracies that had been conducting arms control negotiations. Reagan, a believer in personal diplomacy, was intrigued and accepted the opportunity. The dynamics of negotiations that

Gorbachev identified as crucial for progress in arms control are exactly the dynamics that many salespeople overlook.

Quite often salespeople give too much attention to short-term economic rationality aimed at maximizing the benefit of a transaction, and not enough to what relationships exist and how they affect negotiations. Existing relationships have an impact on expectations. A skilled negotiator knows the relationship history, and can use a negotiation strategy that is consistent with expectations.

5. Sell first, negotiate second: Selling first gives you the ability to understand the customer's key needs. It also allows you to gain a benchmark as to where the customer stands, and ensures you know what it is you are negotiating about—should it come to that. Also, it helps in ensuring that you negotiate with the decision maker. As Eleanor Roosevelt nicely stated, "Never allow a person to tell you no who doesn't have the power to say yes."

Too many salespeople negotiate when they should be selling. If you begin negotiating too early to get the deal, you risk giving up on the value and margins. Spend time building up the value side before you start negotiating. Selling first allows you to build a compelling value. Once you have invested sufficient time selling, then, when negotiation begins, the customer's perception of value is likely to be high.

Negotiating is not really productive unless the two parties have agreed on what they are negotiating over. Make sure you accurately identify the customer's problem and understand its implications for them. Understand what is at stake in terms of financial cost, business and personal reputation, business strategy, legal implications, and so on. Communicate the value of what you have to offer to address the problem. The more convinced the prospect is of the benefits of your product or service, the less likely they are to negotiate. You may even sell without any negotiation taking place.

6. Be clear about the concessions you can afford to offer: It is important to establish your limits so that you can kill the expectations of a discount or an allowance that you cannot afford before you look obliged to accept them. Clearly understand the limits on price discounts, freebies, or other add-ons before you meet with your prospect. Then you can control the negotiations accordingly and, in the heat of the moment, you will not end up accepting a concession you can ill afford.

When you are clear about the concessions you can afford to offer, you will be able to time them better during negotiations. Some salespeople make concessions early in the sales process before formal negotiations begin and end up offering concessions they could trade later. Also, making concessions too early detracts from your original offer. The buyer might interpret it as a sales ploy and might not view your moving from the original offer as concessionary behavior. Your concessions carry more power when first your buyer is convinced that your initial proposition is firm, reasonable, and serious. So, first establish your initial offer as an anchor.

Skilled salespeople know exactly what they can trade in return for the things they want and how much they can afford to concede on any given issue. Smart customers, on the other hand, try to extract concessions during the sales process before proper negotiations start. This gives the seller the impression that they have to agree to these demands in order to continue the sales process. Defer the temptation to make piecemeal concessions until you are ready to negotiate. Otherwise, even though you make excellent progress, the deal may still fall apart because, when it comes to the crunch, you have nothing left to trade.

Make sure any concessions you commit to are related to getting the things that really matter to you. Skilled salespeople make their concessions conditional, linking tradable issues. For example, "If you could give me X, I might be able to move Y." Trigger an obligation to reciprocate. Remember nobody knows what you value better than you. If you do not articulate it, you will get what is most convenient for the buyer to give or, in the best case, what your buyer thinks you value.

Do not assume that your actions will speak for themselves; emphasize the concessions you make and their importance to the other party. Explain how what you have given up is costly to you. Underline the benefits of your concession to the buyer. People tend to reciprocate in accordance with their perception of their own benefits, regardless of what the other person is sacrificing.

Where possible, break the concessions you can afford to offer into installments. House sales data show that sellers who make concessions in smaller installments are more effective than those who hastily drop to their bottom price to close quickly. Most negotiators expect to swap offers back and forth a few times before the deal is done. When you concede a little at a time, you might be able to close the deal before using up your entire capacity to offer concessions. Moreover, offering multiple, small concessions gives the buyer the impression that you are flexible and willing to listen to their needs.

7. Let the buyer start the negotiation: Never rush to discount in eagerness to get the sale. Once you have made the quote, let the buyer respond with their price or terms. Do not offer a discount or an adjustment before the buyer even opens their mouth. It pays to listen first and then speak.

Getting off to a good start in business negotiations is likely to influence the final agreement. Keep focused on finding the buyer's needs and selling the solution for them, and let the buyer start the negotiation. This allows you to gather and exchange information without making early concessions.

When your buyer opens negotiations, their offer is also reflective of competition dynamics. It gives you a better idea of your next move to remain in contention and, if necessary, to take charge of the discussion through questions. Also, when you wait for the buyer to open the negotiation, you can be sure that most other factors that the buyer can use to negotiate are already taken care of.

8. Pay attention to body language: Body language will always divulge the truth even when the words being spoken convey something else. It may be easy to say anything, but it is not easy to back a lie up with body language. Pay close attention to the other person's body language, in particular, their eyes.

Skilled salespeople read their customers' body language. They know when a customer is convinced to move ahead, is still undecided, or is desperate to escape. They also know when someone is purposely trying to maintain a poker face. We are hardwired to give off signals of how we are feeling. Reading and interpreting these signals is an important part of a salesperson's skill set.

When it comes to reading body language, the most important thing is to notice subtle changes in behavior. For example, when a person stiffens their posture and crosses their arms mid-conversation, it is quite different from having their arms crossed throughout as their typical posture. A few examples of behavior changes are crossing arms, men touching their face or neck, or women touching their hair.

When people are relaxed and comfortable, they make frequent eye contact, they face you directly, and their motions are calm. There are four major areas of body language that you need to focus on reading and deciphering:

Eyes and brows. Notice eye contact and brow movements. When people have direct eye contact with you and relaxed brows, they like you and are interested in what you are saying. When they avoid eye contact, they are either lying or are uninterested. Tension in the brows shows stress or fear. When someone starts glancing away often, they are probably not understanding you. People most often avoid eye contact when they cannot tell you their honest feelings. Squinting the eyes is the most common signal when someone hears or thinks of something they do not like. Excessive eye blinking suggests irritation. Raised eyebrows betray surprise.

Mouth. The most important of facial gestures are by the mouth. Upward turns in the corner of the mouth are usually positive signs; downward turns are negative. Observe the lips, whether they are relaxed or tightly pressed together. When someone keeps moving their tongue inside the lips, it indicates discomfort.

Arms and upper body. Crossed arms usually indicate resistance or close-mindedness. Open and relaxed arms mean comfort and cooperation. Shoulders hunched forward indicate a lack of interest, whereas someone comfortably leaning forward is likely interested. A rigid body posture denotes anxiety. Fidgeting with hands or objects shows the person is bored. Tapping fingers show anxiety. When interlocked fingers are placed behind the head with elbows and armpits open, the person is very comfortable and open to ideas. When someone starts mirroring you, they like you. Being still with regular eye contact means that the person is paying undivided attention to you. A two-shouldered shrug means "I do not know." People who hide their hands are perceived as dishonest.

Legs. Fidgety leg movements are a negative behavior, usually indicating anxiety. Crossing one foot over the other while standing is a sign of feeling comfortable.

In addition to being able to read your customer's body language, also give them signals they can understand. Make sure your body language is open and confident, and be expressive to build trust. Use your hands often and expressively. When you observe different areas of body language separately, you can read a person much better. For example, crossed arms alone can mean that the person is feeling cold but if you see a person has their arms crossed, their torso is slumped, and they are bouncing their legs, then it is most probably anxiety. Your success in sales depends a lot on being able to read the body language of your prospects and effectively modify your behavior to adapt to the situation.

9. Do not give a range for price reduction: Once you give a range for discount, the highest number becomes the threshold. Even if you are able to pull off the sale with a lower discount, the buyer will never see it as a win-win bargain.

10. Do not confirm in writing until the conversation is over: Negotiations can go back and forth and around. A salesperson would be wise not to revise the contract until the meeting has ended, and all parties have verbally agreed to the terms.

Moreover, what you thought were pre-contractual negotiations could amount to a binding contract regardless of your intentions, even where some of the terms have not been finally negotiated and no formal contract has been signed. Email exchanges are often involved when the negotiating parties try to reach agreement in an informal way. If you use email, clearly and consistently articulate the intention not to be bound until a formal offer is sent out and an agreement is entered into.

If certain offers or concessions are tentative or conditional, communicate your intention through your words and conduct. Make it clear that the arrangements offered are not binding until they are part of a duly executed written offer. Do not sign agreements without seeking appropriate legal advice. Watch out for any communications from the prospect that do not reflect the agreement that you think you have reached. Write back to set the record straight.

11. Negotiate with the right people: Try to get to the decision maker before making concessions. Many salespeople make the mistake of negotiating with the wrong person. Then, when talks begin with the true decision maker, they have to start at the already discounted price.

The purpose of a negotiation is to reach a deal with the customer. Therefore, no matter what negotiation style or techniques you employ, you will not get anywhere unless you are negotiating with someone in the position to take the action you desire. One of the most important things to find out is if the key decision makers are even in the room.

Sometimes the people sent for preliminary negotiations are there to navigate the negotiation zone and identify a common agreement so that the decision makers can save their time and execute the agreement reached. However, that happens more often in politics and statecraft than in business. In business, you are better off not yielding too much ground unless you are sure that you are talking to the right people. Or you may waste your productivity and show your cards too early in the process. By the time you face the right people, they will have a stronger hand and you may end up conceding ground in order to reignite the traction.

If you invest too much of yourself in negotiating with people who cannot ultimately make a decision, you may look inexperienced. When there are many people in the room on the other side and you continue to focus on the most vocal or most attentive ones without determining who the real decision maker is, you may inadvertently alienate that person by giving the impression that you do not care enough to deal with them directly. Gain an idea from their tone of voice, their body language, or verbal cues.

If the decision makers are not present, then who is? Are you dealing with people who will simply convey information about the negotiations back to their managers? When you discover that you are negotiating with someone who do not have the authority to make a purchase happen, do not give up. Instead, use them as influencers. Use your time to gain new insights that will assist when you do deal with the decision maker. Provide them with the information that they need to relay to their management.

Sell to them; convince them of your value. Be sure not to make the mistake of negotiating with them. If you do so, you may need to do another round, thus yielding further ground when you negotiate with the right people. Simply put, you will wind up having to negotiate twice.

To make sure that you are negotiating with the right people, identify each person on the other side and fully understand their roles, responsibilities, and motivations. When a number of people are involved in a negotiation, keep track of who is who. Update your information if your perceptions of their roles alter as the negotiations unfold. Often things are not as they seem, and the most important person in the room may be sitting off to the side quietly observing. Thus, the real decision maker may be hidden in the corners.

To determine if someone is the right person, ask yourself if they can deliver. Know your prospect's organizational structure. Find out how the customer has handled other buying decisions similar to what you are offering. Two things help determine who the right person to negotiate with is.

The first is contextual competence. That is the person who has the most suitable expertise and skills to reach the decision. You can ascertain this by determining who knows the ins and outs of all the issues and is looked up to by others in the party for expert opinions. If the desired contextual competence is political and not technical, then do they have the organizational know-how to get things moving or are they merely talk and bluster?

The second is a simple question of power. Who has the authority to sign off and the budget to cover the offering?

12. Look for a quid pro quo: Salespeople need not accept every demand of a buyer without making some requests of their own. By keeping the negotiation a win-win for both sides, the salesperson and customer remain on equal footing. Since you gave a little on price, ask for something in return. Although the possibilities are unlimited and vary according to what you are selling, here are some of the things that you might ask in return:

- Shorter/immediate payment terms

- A larger order (up-sell)
- Additional products/services (cross-sell)
- Opportunities for recurring revenue
- Higher or broader access within the company
- Another meeting
- Additional information
- Use of the customer as a case study
- Recommendations, reviews
- Longer delivery schedule
- Referrals
- Access to industry events

As a salesperson, be mindful that effective negotiation is not about winning or losing; it is about finding a solution for the customer. To underscore the value of your solution, seek quid pro quos for your concessions. Making concessions without getting some value in return communicates to your buyer that what you conceded to them has little or no value and you are still getting the better deal. Thus, you do not get due appreciation for what you have given away.

The idea of quid pro quo is the very spirit of a win-win outcome; it is only fair that as a salesperson you have the right to seek equal benefit from the deal. In a win-win negotiation, both parties need to give and take along the way. The right balance in that give and take makes the negotiation and the relationship healthier.

Find a way to create equality from the start of the negotiation, instead of expecting one very large thing in the end as you get your signed contract. Whenever a buyer asks you something, tactfully negotiate on what you can get in return before you give the concession or information.

Prior to any sales negotiation, prioritize the buyer's needs and your objectives, including the benefits you envisage for the buyer. This will help you better align your goals and your buyer's. You will also be able to better articulate the context when negotiations start and the buyer begins to make demands. Finally, remember that effective negotiation is not just about the deal—it is about your long-term relationship with the buyer and about your reputation.

13. Stretch the negotiation beyond price: As price is tied to value, which in turn depends on a customer's perception of and satisfaction with a solution, consider offering other add-ons or freebies in lieu of a lower price.

In a time when buyers have instant access to volumes of information at their fingertips, soft factors can matter a lot. People like to buy from someone whom they see as the best fit, they trust, and they feel gets their business and their culture. To stretch negotiations beyond price, use a consultative selling approach to help differentiate yourself and your solution from your competitors.

Do not just present yourself as someone who can supply good solutions; show that you are fully vested in your customer's success and are not just trying to sell. Understand what matters most to the decision makers and then demonstrate how your solution aligns with their priorities. Lean on real value, not generic value but value to the customer. Get your prospect to want that product or service of yours. The more they want it, the easier the negotiation on price becomes. The desire to acquire something makes its cost a secondary consideration, providing the buyer can afford it and cannot get it for a lower cost elsewhere.

When you are in negotiations, wield the full weight of the strengths of your company and your offering. Communicate what makes your company stand out and provide real-world evidence to prove it. Often salespeople do not understand all the ways their company or their offering brings value. When you highlight the value of your offering, do not vacillate on price. Avoid wording that suggests pricing flexibility, for example, "normally, we charge" or "your price." Mention the price without getting defensive.

14. Drop your price slowly: When negotiating a discount, every time you have to lower your price, do it slowly. The faster you reduce your price, the less valued your product is understood to be. So, do not lower your price rather than negotiating. If you are not prepared to defend your price, your customer will lose respect for you. It is your job to convince your buyer what your product or service is worth.

When you do reduce the price, do it hesitatingly and ask for something in return. Establish the value of your product or service and present your price with confidence. Do not be defensive about it. When you drop the price slowly, you preserve the integrity of your pricing structure. Each time you lower your price, be sure you made your buyer earn the concession.

When you appear too willing to negotiate your price downward, the buyer either perceives you as desperate or, worse, sees your offering as having less worth. One recurring price negotiation in my career has been with customers who have received a proposal from the competition that undercuts the price just to break into the account. To handle such situations, you have to be confident of your long-term value rather than keep reducing the price.

The most common impediment that obstructs salespeople from getting the price they want is the fear of losing the sale. The easiest way to overcome that risk is to lower your price. However, a better way is to overcome your fear by perfecting self-assured negotiation skills. When you do it right instead of rushing to drop your price, not only will you command a better price, but both you and your customer will feel a greater sense of satisfaction. The concessions for which customers have to toil hard also feel more gratifying for them.

15. Maintain bonhomie: Do not get worked up or pulled down; keep the conversation professional, light, and jovial. Learn to deflect the other party's attempts to grab power without impairing your relationship with them. Do not become defensive, ever. When you become defensive it is difficult to argue for your interests and concerns.

There is an underlying relationship that develops whenever people negotiate. When we are negotiating price or performance, we are also negotiating our relationship. Remember, if both parties did not have divergent need, there would be no need for negotiation. In most business negotiations, both parties are clawing their way to a deal, each trying to make it better for themselves. The better you are able to identify your customer's negotiation moves, the better you can keep your cool and, therefore, the greater your chances of a successful negotiation. Many of these moves are legitimate negotiation tactics and not an intent to manipulate. For example, your customer may use one of these tactics:

- They may challenge the value you offer. "You price is way above what you deliver."

- They may attack your ideas. "You cannot be serious about this proposal."
- They may question your behavior. "You seem upset."
- They may threaten to walk out. "If you do not reduce your price, there will be no deal."
- They may appeal to your nobler motives. "Times are tight, please help with the price."

All of these are legitimate tactics to gain control of the negotiations. Once you understand the move, you will neither get upset nor become defensive. Either deflect the move through, for instance, pattern interrupt—an unexpected response that interrupts the flow—or reframe it in such a manner that the customer understands that you do not accept their position.

Do not take things personally. Smile often to experience and cause positive emotions. You can release tension and improve your mood by the simple act of smiling. Do not get caught up in the frenzy of one moment; step back and take a broad view. Try to rise above the stress of the moment and take stock of what is at stake. For example, you may have a relationship to preserve over winning a point.

16. Do not cease selling: "Don't stop selling, until your customer is done buying," says serial entrepreneur Vicki Fitch. When negotiating, if you have gotten the customer to the point of saying "Yes, I want what you sell," never stop reminding them of the reasons they gave for wanting to buy your offering. Continue to sell till you close the deal. A skilled negotiator sells in a consultative manner. However, you still need the customer to come through on their commitments, so be sure to repeat them in a polite manner. Keep an eye out for buying signals. Some are obvious, like the customer repeatedly nodding their head in agreement. Others are not that straightforward to identify and may even be couched in objections.

Remember not to get carried away by the fact that you have almost secured an order. Do not to stop selling. If you do, you are prone to start again and appear to be getting desperate to close. Be prepared to resolve further issues if the customer still has objections. One effective form of selling is to continually reassure the customer that they will be in safe hands once they sign up.

If you cannot close on the day, make sure you have the date and time for the next meeting confirmed. Have the necessary paperwork ready to obtain the customer's commitment. Once the negotiations are successful and the order has been signed, consolidate by taking the customer through the next steps. Follow up with a call at key moments to keep them informed about the progress. When the delivery has been made, call up to check that they have received exactly what was agreed and on time. Be available to answer questions when the customer starts using your product or service.

Once you have fulfilled an order to the customer's satisfaction, it is still not the end of the sales process. Establish how you can build or deepen the relationship. Stay in touch. Aim to create a relationship where the customer looks up to you for advice. Ask for referrals or testimonials, as appropriate.

17. Manage the pace: Know when to hurry the customer and when to slow down. Experienced salespeople say that one of the easiest ways to prevent a sales negotiation from getting out of hand, and to remain firmly in control, is to slow down the process. Do not arrive too early at the price-tag discussion. Instead make sure that by the time you are discussing price, a whole lot of other issues have been addressed.

In order to get the deal that you want, learn to control the negotiations. Take control of their pace so that you can determine how the negotiation proceeds. More often than not, the one who controls the pace also controls the negotiation.

As negotiations gather momentum, things seem to pick up speed. The discussions move quickly, with rapid back-and-forth. As a seller, be concerned about making too many concessions in haste. Seize control, sometimes by slowing things down. For example, ask for clarifications and examples. "Can you tell me more about when this happened the last time, so I get a clearer idea of the issue?"

You might realize that the customer is trying to take control of the negotiations by slowing things down themselves. In such a case, do not hand control of the negotiations over. When you notice that they are trying to alter the pace, move quickly to subtly let them know that you are pleased with how the negotiations have been going. Sometimes, there may be a good reason for the customer to slow down, as they may have a valid concern or objection. Get to the bottom of what is going on so that you can address that concern adequately to take back control of the negotiations.

18. Think long-term: Do not just focus on closing the transaction at all costs. Instead, nurture relationships to develop more loyalty and referrals. To develop long-term relationships, aim at win-win scenarios, instead of striving to get as much as possible in the moment.

Good salespeople prioritize their connection with the customer over other aspects of the sale, thus resisting the temptation to close at any cost. Your customer needs to feel they can depend on you and that if something goes wrong you will be there. Here are some suggestions for a long-term approach:

Bring value. Find ways to add value to your prospect's life. You may be able to help them with useful suggestions during the negotiation, provide them with links to helpful content, promise to make an introduction, or offer something else that benefits them.

Get to know the customer well. As you discuss, dig into their business challenges and their personal and professional goals. This information will also help you make sure that your offering is a win-win solution.

Make sure what you sell is the right fit. Do not sell to anyone who is not the right fit. It will be counterproductive in the long run.

Appear specific and not generic. Prescribe a strategy or a solution that seems highly specific to the customer. Provide tailored advice. Give examples of customers who have been in similar situations and were helped by you.

Show empathy. Understand the customer's situation. Resolve objections with care instead of steamrolling them to rush to the sale. Be patient and answer honestly. Act like a win for your prospect is a win for you.

Build trust. Nothing underpins a favorable long-term outlook better than trust. Do not fake anything for the sake of a sale. If you are honest from the start about everything from pricing, solution fit, no hidden contract surprises, and so on, your relationship will be off to a better start. Always keep your word.

Follow up. Do not vanish after making the sale; keep adding value. Look for reasons to reach out to the customer from time to time. Think long-term and stay on their radar. Interact with them on social media, send them value-added emails, and ask them about their kids, pastimes, and goals.

19. Be prepared to walk away: Do not accept any curveball a prospect throws at you; walk away from unreasonable demands. Even if you bow to their demands to make the sale, unreasonable customers are likely to cause problems down the road. Do not put yourself in a position where you accept a less-than-satisfactory outcome just to close the deal. If you are too anxious to close a sale, you may not be able to say no to unreasonable buyer demands later. Instead, do not be afraid to let the buyer know that they have pushed you as far you would go.

Often your willingness to walk away may force the buyer to act with reason. Skillful negotiators are always testing to see how committed you are to your position, and when you are willing to walk away it demonstrates your commitment to your position. When the buyer sees that, they may learn to be more reasonable in the negotiation. Sometimes, the buyer you are negotiating with may have to justify their position to someone higher up in the chain of command. Once they know that your position is final, they will be more committed to selling your position to their bosses.

This is easier said than done. Walking away from a deal can be difficult for a salesperson who has worked hard on it and has already invested a lot of time and energy. But sometimes knowing when to quit can save you a lot of time. It may also foster a healthier relationship with the customer in the long run.

When you are negotiating, you must know your absolute deal breakers. A clear perception of what is acceptable and what is not acceptable to you can save you a lot of time. It can often save a relationship. Even though there is no perfect science to this, here are some red flags that may warn you to not to invest yourself further in a negotiation:

You continue to coach instead of selling. Thought leadership is effective in selling. But if the customer continues to use you as a source of free knowledge without looking to make the deal, then you are better off letting them understand that they must now make up their mind. This can happen when the prospect either lacks authority or does not have the budget to make the purchase. The sale is, therefore, not going to happen unless the prospect engineers a change in their circumstance to remove the hurdle.

Unbeatable competition. It is important to recognize when you cannot beat the competition. Sometimes, it may be a wise thing to step out of an arena where you are either disadvantaged or not a good fit.

Buyers lacks financial resources. Once you know the buyer cannot afford you, there is little point in continuing the negotiation.

Not a good fit. When you have determined that your product or service is not a good fit for the customer's problem, you are obliged to walk away. In such cases, the intelligent thing to do is to tell the customer that your solution is not the right fit for their problem.

Customer has unreasonable demands. When your product is the right fit, but your prospect has needs or conditions that you cannot afford to meet, the deal may not be right. Unreasonable demands and customizations are not only hard and costly to deliver but, despite your best efforts, may still wind up in a difficult and unhappy customer.

Leaving the table tactfully is a huge part of salesmanship. When you need to walk away, do it in the right way. Walk away in a highly professional, civil, and courteous manner—in a way that displays confidence, courage, and integrity and not arrogance, defeatism, or frustration. Remember to thank the other party profusely for their time. Preserve the relationship. Never burn any bridges; you may need to cross them at some time later. Remember, sales is a long game and the world is small.

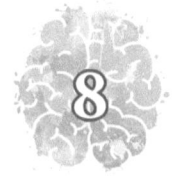

Assertiveness

*"If you doubt yourself, then indeed
you stand on shaky ground."*
Henrik Ibsen

Assertiveness is being confident and direct in dealing with others. Assertive people know what they want and are not afraid to ask for it. They also respect the feelings and needs of others and are prepared to negotiate solutions that are acceptable to both sides. Assertiveness in sales is critical. If you are not assertive, you will not be able to change buyer thinking and influence agendas. It is also one of the most misunderstood sales attributes. It requires finesse, confidence, bravery, and a good dose of aplomb. Great salespeople are assertive, but also have a deep fount of emotional intelligence. They push back when they think the buyer is wrong. They question the status quo. They are change agents. They put themselves into situations where they can help buyers. They are bold, but not arrogant.

Develop an assertive sales demeanor by showing genuine interest in your customer. Ask questions and sharpen your listening skills. Before visiting a potential customer, prepare and polish your sales presentation. Practice your sales pitch at every opportunity. As you gain experience, your presentations will become better, giving you more confidence to be assertive. Know the fine line between being assertive and aggressive. Aggressive behavior can irritate and intimidate your customer. Assertiveness, instead, is the act of recognizing your customer's needs and communicating with confidence the benefits of your product or service.

When meeting your prospective customer, try to reflect your customer's body language. If they are sitting, sit; if they are standing, stand in front of them. Mirror their body language and tone of voice back to them.

USING ASSERTIVENESS

Skilled salespeople can use assertiveness in three ways.

1. Pattern interrupt: We are all subject to getting locked into stereotyped views on what is possible. Pattern interrupt is a way to get your prospect to think differently. Skilled salespeople know when they need to interrupt the flow of thinking or a pattern of action a buyer is considering. When a buyer is set in their thinking or pattern, they are on autopilot. The salesperson's challenge is to get the buyer to question their direction and strategies, to get the buyer thinking and opening their mind.

A pattern can be interrupted by any unexpected or sudden movement or response. For example, when you spoil someone's story by asking a question and they cannot recall where they were. Or when you start to do something and after being interrupted forget to resume what you were doing. Similarly, you can make a sudden movement or drop something to break the buyer's pattern. Or you can turn the conversation in another direction by asking a different question. These interruptions break the buyer's thought pattern on one subject and get them focused on answering another question.

2. Reframe: A buyer often misses opportunities because of their mental models. When a salesperson reframes issues to introduce the buyer to new models, they open up new possibilities for strategy and action. Reframing an experience can influence how people perceive, construe, and react to that experience. Reframing also enables you to answer common questions and concerns before the prospect can ask, and thus decrease resistance.

Politicians are masters at reframing. No matter what happens, they can put a positive spin on it for themselves or a negative spin for their opponents. In the 1984 campaign, there was significant apprehension about Ronald Reagan's age. Speaking during the presidential debate with Walter

Mondale, Reagan said, "I will not make age an issue of this campaign. I am not going to exploit, for political purposes, my opponent's youth and inexperience." Reagan's age was not an issue for the rest of the campaign.

A father brought his strong-willed daughter to see Milton Erickson—the famous hypnotherapist. He said to Erickson, "My daughter doesn't listen to me or her mother. She is always expressing her own opinion." After the father finished describing his daughter's problem, Erickson replied, "Now isn't it good that she will be able to stand on her own two feet when she is ready to leave home?" The father sat in brooding silence. That was the end of the therapy—the father now saw his daughter's behavior in a new light.

3. Direct: Direct buyers to ways they can solve problems and reach goals with your help. You can often do so by offering the conclusion and then the explanation. When you put forward a question, do not explain why first. Just ask. The briefer and simpler your questions, the smaller the speed bumps you will encounter. Offer an explanation behind your question only when your prospect asks for it.

LEARNING ASSERTIVENESS

Here are some guidelines that can help you learn to be assertive.

1. Mind your optics: Pay attention to how you appear and to your body language. Dress suitably and make eye contact. Try to look and sound confident. Sales is a funny business; you will be judged not only on your knowledge of the product or service, but also on the impression you create. The initial impression you create is often burned into your prospect's memory.

It is not just about looking attractive. If your appearance is attractive but not businesslike, you can make the wrong impression. The idea is to gain your prospect's trust so that they take your word as good advice.

Your body language also matters a lot. Sit up straight, make regular eye contact, and shake hands firmly. You want to convey an impression of confidence and competence without coming across as aggressive.

If your customer is meeting you in your office, then prepare your space to convey a clean and professional image. Look organized and keep unnecessary stacks of paperwork and other clutter discreetly out of sight. Provide a chair for visitors at a comfortable conversational distance from your own and ensure a supply of basic items such as paper and business cards.

Your appearance and conduct not only form your own brand but also reflect on your company and offerings. It is easier for you to be assertive when you feel good about yourself and when people take you more seriously.

2. Speak with conviction: You do not need to be loud, but do speak in a clear voice and a confident manner. We are all drawn to people who speak with conviction and confidence. Customers like to align themselves with someone who is assured and knowledgeable, who can direct, advise, and lead them to the best solution or action. The more conviction you show, the more confidence you inspire.

Make sure you have a high level of conviction about your industry, your company, and the products or services you offer. Your conviction about what you offer to customers directly affects your confidence and assertiveness. If you make a claim, but are unsure of its validity, your body will give you away. For most of us, the body refuses to lie. You must be consistent in what you say, what you mean, and what you do. Confidence in the salesperson is what augurs the result the prospect wants and motivates them to make a buying decision.

3. Keep the end in mind: People like it when you know what you want from them. That makes it much easier for them to deal with you with clarity. The imperative in getting your product or service in front of your customer is to deliver the results they are seeking. Learn about your customer's problems, then follow up with how you can solve them. The more information you have on each prospect, the more you will start to see patterns and commonalities.

4. Be realistic in your expectations: Have a clear objective for what you can get. Do not be afraid to ask, but pick the right battles. When you are realistic in your own expectations, you can also manage the customer's expectations better. Defining clear expectations is an important step to getting on the same page and working toward the same outcome.

Only when clear goals are established can you make progress toward them without distraction. Be transparent about what you can and cannot accomplish and any limitations. Under-promise to give yourself some cushion for the unforeseen, and then overdeliver. Unrealistic expectations only harm relationships and undermine trust in the long run.

5. Do not get frustrated: View the buyer as a potential ally and not as an aggressor. Be patient, where necessary, and make your point respectfully. Learn to reduce your sales frustrations and make your selling easier by focusing on the sales process and accepting that you cannot control what other people do. Your job is to help buyers make a choice and not to make them do what they choose not to do. Pay attention to what is working as you follow your sales process. Notice what is not working, and look to improve the process.

It is wishful thinking to expect every prospect to be sales-ready. Have a basic understanding of what a customer needs before engaging with them. Take a consultative approach. First use their time to help them uncover inefficiencies and issues in their business; position yourself as a valuable resource.

When you sense frustration, focus on solutions and options and not on helplessness. Sharing your frustration with the customer is like expressing any other emotion. Share in a constructive manner only to help the situation. A customer does not need to hear all your opinions and emotions. Salespeople achieve the best results when they contain their communication to facts and how they feel about them—not their sentiments and perceptions.

6. Practice: Imagine and rehearse important discussions in your mind in advance, both your delivery and your body language. Learn to be assertive in your everyday interactions. Discover suitable ways to assert yourself in each specific situation. Over time, you can learn to be more assertive by identifying your needs and wants, expressing them in a positive way, and learning to say no when you need to. Here are some suggestions for training yourself in assertiveness:

Use the right language. When you describe a troublesome situation as you see it, be specific. Be precise about time and actions, for instance. Do not generalize. To show that you take responsibility for your feelings, use "I" when describing how you feel. Make eye contact, be firm, and do not get emotional. Focus on positive feelings and not on resentment. Be specific about your expectations and the actions you would like to see. Try using verbs that are definite and emphatic when you communicate. Use "will" instead of "could," "want" instead of "need," or "choose to" instead of "have to."

Simulate assertive responses. Role-play potential situations with a colleague or friend. If your partner plays the role realistically, you will realize that no matter how calm and tactful you are, you can still sometimes sound aggressive to the other person and provoke a strong reaction.

Practice assertiveness in daily life. Look for ways to hone your assertiveness skills. Ask for favors, stand up for your rights, give compliments to friends and strangers, praise others when they have done well, narrate your experiences to friends and family, and so on.

Do not feel ashamed. Learn not to feel guilty or ashamed for expressing a need or want or for articulating dissatisfaction. Politely and reasonably ask for what you want and wait to see how the other person responds. View an unreasonable response as a further opportunity to practice assertiveness instead of losing your cool.

Practice self-assured body language and tone. Do not mumble; speak up with conviction. Always make a request or state a preference with confidence. Stand or sit up straight, lean in a bit, smile or keep a straight face, and look the person in the eye.

Stop offering unnecessary explanations. When you express a choice or state an opinion, do not automatically follow up with an explanation. Providing unnecessary justification gives people an opportunity to counter your reason and show why you should go along with what they want.

Learn to persist. When you do not get what you want, do not become resigned or aggressive. Assertiveness requires you to be persistent while remaining cool, calm, and collected.

Learn when not to engage. Sometimes, when the other party wants you to lose your cool, deciding not to engage is the right assertive behavior.

7. Be courteous: Being assertive does not mean being rude. Be polite and respectful. Assertiveness is the art of acting in a way that is self-assured, outspoken, and confident without being overbearing or aggressive. It is acceptable for you to be a little pushy in business, as long as you are courteous and considerate at the same time.

One of the key points in assertive communication is the courtesy to listen to others' needs and opinions and fully consider them before confidently presenting your own. Allow the customer to speak before you, and be an active listener to make them feel that you truly value what they have to say. Invite input from others and let them speak without interruption. Pay attention to customers' emotions carefully to ensure that you are not making anyone else feel uncomfortable.

Try to say something that shows your understanding of the other person's feelings. Give your undivided attention to the person you are interacting with in the moment. Be punctual; respect the customer's time. Smile and make eye contact.

8. Ask questions: Clarify where needed. Ask questions to explore potential solutions and to navigate toward what you want. Be truthful in saying what you think, but in a polite manner. Salespeople often feel they should steer clear of asking tough questions to keep prospects content. However, you cannot help buyers resolve their challenges unless you touch upon them. Assertive questioning will only help you earn respect from prospects, as tackling challenges head-on will help customers see the bigger picture. Ask assertive questions to highlight your buyer's problems.

Pay attention to the buyer to raise the proper issues at the proper time. This will not only guide their thoughts in the right direction but will also help you form a good rapport. Thoughtful questions can open your customer's mind to a new possibility, compel them to action, discover relevant information, or obtain buy-in for the next step.

Keep your questions simple and short. Generally, longer questions feel more aggressive than assertive, because the other person feels that you are leading them on with context to respond in a certain manner. When you get right to the point, the customer feels like they can answer as they want. Cut out any unnecessary preface and focus on the core ask.

9. Be comfortable to say no: If you give reasons for everything you cannot do, the other person can use those reasons as negotiation points. If you are short and to the point, your decision comes across as more firm. Offer an explanation only when you owe one. Here are some suggestions for saying no without being rude or aggressive:

Listen to the customer attentively. Use empathetic language to make the customer feel heard and understood.

Appear logical and not arbitrary. Convey clearly why you cannot deliver their ask. Offer informed insight to help them better understand your decision.

Be confident. Assertiveness, delivered politely, will give your customer a much better understanding of your refusal and a base to move forward from.

Offer an alternative. Where possible, tell the customer what you can do as an alternative or ask them questions to uncover another solution. Getting to the bottom of what the customer is trying to accomplish can help you solve their problem in a way they may not have considered.

Reframe. It is possible to convey an unambiguous no without actually using the word. Done well, positive, honest language keeps the goodwill flowing.

10. Do not lose your temper: Anger never helps make a sale or solve a problem. Keep a sense of perspective as well as a sense of humor. You must manage your emotions well to be assertive. There often is a fine line between assertive and rude; be ever mindful not to cross it.

Assertiveness is the best antidote for anger. Know your triggers for anger and learn to replace anger with assertion. Often anger is a result of poor communication. When you are not able to express yourself clearly and assertively, you end up getting angry.

When you are assertive, you have high self-esteem and know the importance of making yourself heard without getting angry. You are able to handle unreasonable or menacing behavior with grace. To make buyers feel at ease with you, work through the sales process in a fair and emotionally stable way and use a calm tone and open body stance. With assertive behavior, you are not focused on convincing or winning arguments; assertiveness is about fairness and empathy.

11. Focus on the big picture: Do not lose the forest for trees. Keep the big picture in mind. To be able to relate to the big picture, you have to understand the overall strategy of the business you are selling to. Determine exactly what is important to your customer. It is not a product or a service that you are selling; it is the benefits that the customer will enjoy by using your solution. Also think of what is important to your company in the long run. Deeply analyze the competition and eliminate any elements that reduce your competitive edge. Study buyer personas. Keep your finger on the pulse of external factors that impact your industry and your company.

Look beyond short-term and medium-term goals. Each sale has its own peculiarities and must be carefully worked as you navigate until the closing is achieved. As you do so, you might realize that there are some longer-term goals that extend beyond that sale only and thus force you to step back and look at big picture.

A focus on the big picture enables you to be more assertive about closing the sale. You understand your customer's environment and goals better and truly believe that the solution you propose will help them. Here are some fundamental reasons to look at the bigger picture:

To build lasting personal relationships. Good salespeople look to build long-term relationships within their target market. These relationships arch beyond one sale and form the foundation for future sales. As the people you build relationships with move on to other companies, they can be a source of business for you where they land next.

To carve a long-term place with the prospect company. Look to build a relationship with your target by making yourself valuable to them. Great salespeople are expert consultants in their own right. Create a partnership that pays off steadily over time, rather than once.

To ensure a happy, satisfied customer. You do not just have to close the sale; your sale has to result in a customer who is entirely satisfied with their interaction with you as well as with what they bought from you and its delivery. Make sure you keep every promise you make to the customer.

To develop an outstanding reputation for yourself. You want the customer to have a great memory of you, your company, their buying experience, and the service. Go the extra mile and give them a little more than they expect.

To create your ambassadors. You want reviews, recommendations, and testimonials from your customers. You want them to be a reliable source of future business and a source of referrals.

12. Argue calmly: Speak to someone the way you would like to be spoken to. Handle arguments with assertive behavior, presenting your arguments with conviction without being condescending or ignoring the opinions and needs of others. Calm, assertive salespeople can make reasoning look effortless.

Speak calmly and clearly without raising your voice, and use relaxed and open body language. Be specific, be respectful, and use polite phrasing. At the same time, do not get defensive; get the customer to analyze the situation together and figure out what the best solution is. Remember that finding the solution your customer is looking for is more important than winning an argument.

Do not say anything that you are not sure of. When you are sure of the argument you want to present, boil your thought down to its most understandable form. Stay on message and say exactly what you mean. Some people are more difficult than others. Do not hesitate to repeat yourself calmly and succinctly until the customer gets the message.

13. Be friendly: Make yourself likable through correct and charming mannerisms. Being assertive in a nice, friendly way is the essence of good salesmanship. Seek first to understand, then to be understood. Always begin with a disarming statement. Compliment the prospect in a sincere manner.

Being An Agent of Change

"Without change there is no innovation, creativity, or incentive for improvement. Those who initiate change will have a better opportunity to manage the change that is inevitable."
William Pollard

Whatever you are selling, it promises to change something in the buyer's business. Your job is to build and sell a compelling case for change. Great salespeople make a case for change and then they deliver that change.

A successful change requires commitment from all those involved—for a business, that can include a complex collection of people with varying needs, goals, and passions. That makes building a consensus important. You have to demonstrate that the change you are promising will move the individuals and the organization to a state that is better than the current one. And then sell that bright, shiny future.

As a probable distraction to business, change always involves some risk. That is why a proposal that entails change is often met with resistance by some in the customer's organization. In order to convince them to accept change, you have to make them dissatisfied with the status quo and help them envision a better future. They need to see that the outcome your offering promises is worth it for them to fight resistance and overcome internal politics. For that you have to win over the skeptics instead of overlooking them or trying to bypass them. Identify the zones of struggle within the customer organization, and equip those who support your proposed change with commanding arguments to convert the doubters.

The more complex the solution you offer, the more likely it is that several stakeholders in the customer organization will be impacted. You must know to manage the intricate web of relationships in any organization that you sell to. Undertake a stakeholder analysis as a part of your sale process, knowing the profile, role, and priorities of everyone likely to influence the decision-making. Ask your contact to get an idea of the people who will be impacted by your solution. Identify people with influence whom you can convince to support your solution. The better you understand the goals and concerns of different stakeholders, the better equipped you are to enlist their support with a solution that addresses their needs.

To help you drive and sell the idea of change and then execute it, develop alliances with decision makers, decision influencers, decision implementers, and stakeholders. Ask yourself relevant questions. Who stands to benefit from your solution? Who controls the budget? Who has the greatest leverage in the decision chain? Who can be impassioned to champion your solution within the organization?

Identify the obstacles to change. The status quo often has many defenders, as it is easier to make a case against change than for it. Show how the status quo is riskier than change. Figure out the motivations of those who oppose the change. Do they have a close relationship with a competitor? Are they eager to claim credit? Is their power threatened by the proposed change? Or are they against change simply because it pulls them out of their comfort zone? Once you understand their motives, you will be better able to assuage their concerns.

Be aware of conflicting interests within the customer organization. While your solution may make life easier in one area of the organization, it may create difficulty for someone else. These can be turf issues or technical hassles. Before you present your solution, try to understand all the technical challenges and conflicting interests and develop a plan to address them. Your initial proposal should leave as few unresolved concerns as possible. Seek to meet the conflicted stakeholders so that you can understand their objections, and address or mitigate their anxieties as well as you can.

Making A Presentation

"The mind is not a vessel to be filled, but a fire to be kindled."
Plutarch

A sales presentation or sales pitch is a convincing narrative or demonstration of your product or service to your potential customer. This is a critical phase of the sales process that usually follows when you and the prospective customer have qualified each other. If successful, it leads to the phase of negotiation. The quality of your sales presentation will often determine whether a prospect buys from you or from one of your competitors. Hence, your presentation must be compelling enough to motivate a buying decision.

BEFORE THE PRESENTATION

Here is some groundwork you must complete before the presentation to make your presentation a success.

1. Know what you are selling: Good salespeople know their product or service inside and out. They keep abreast with the latest developments and research impacting their offering. The more you know about what you are selling, the better able you will be to impart this information to your prospect.

People are not interested in buying your product or service; they are interested in the benefit that comes from buying it. Someone who buys a weight-loss product is actually investing in a leaner self. That is why you must ask yourself what you are really selling. Figure out what the customer really wants and present that to them.

Apple is one example of such an approach. Rather than concentrating on how cutting-edge the technology is, they stop to ask what people really want. They sell you a cooler self-image with products that also function as fashion accessory. Disney is another example. While it may seem that people visit their parks for the rides, that is not the case. They visit for the family experience and the memories. Disney knows this, and their advertisements do not boast of their exhilarating rides; instead, they show how families visiting Disney share a memorable experience.

2. Be aware of your competition: Gain as much knowledge as possible about the competition. Not only will this help in answering questions and objections from the buyer, but knowing what you are up against will also lend direction to your presentation. You cannot effectively communicate your uniqueness and value unless you have a complete understanding of your competition and how they sell. Not only do you have to fully know their product or pricing, but you also have to be comprehensively aware of their messaging.

Identify your key competitors on the deal you are presenting for. Look for articles or ads in the media and industry publications. Read their marketing literature. If it is a public company, read a copy of their annual report. Go to exhibitions and trade fairs. Check their website. Ask one of your staff or friends to get their brochure and price list. Talk to your suppliers to get an idea what their other customers or prospects are doing.

Evaluate the information you gather to see if there are any gaps you can exploit. Do a comparison to see what your strengths are and where you can learn from the competition. Highlight your strengths and be ready for questions in areas where you think they are ahead of you or you are just the same.

3. Make sure you know your customer's business: When you are making a pitch or a presentation, a customer expects you to know their business, customers, and competition almost as well as you know your own product or service. Know your customer's industry, its opportunities, and its challenges. Find out your customer's position in the industry and their key competitors. If you study the market that your prospect is selling into, you can better determine how you can help them realize their goals. This will be an important selling point for you.

You can leverage the information you acquire by implementing the right processes and focusing on key data points. Be sure of any information you use and use up-to-date data; do not make assumptions. In the questions you consider about customers, also focus on "why," along with "what" and "how," to get a clear picture of how you can position your solution to provide a superior customer experience.

4. Write down what you intend to present: Do not go presenting on the fly; assemble and note all your points. Think about the major selling points of your offering. Anticipate objections and be ready to handle them. Develop leading questions that will steer the discussion toward the sale.

Make sure your presentation has a clear and compelling agenda. Begin with persuasive reasons to consider your proposal and culminate with a specific request for the business. Your presentation can start by illustrating the opportunity or challenge that your customer is overlooking or experiencing. If you make this argument compelling enough, you will have your customer's attention for the rest of the presentation. Talk about the benefits that your customer will derive from your solution, and prepare a couple of case studies to present. End with a solid request for business.

5. Anticipate how to handle objections: When you review your presentation and get to a point where you think there might be an objection, write it down. Continue doing this until you think you have found all of the possible objections. Answer them, and include them as part of your presentation in the form of positive statements.

Find out from your colleagues what objections they encounter. Prepare a comprehensive list of objections and their answers. Preparation will make it easier to handle objections. Anticipating and tackling the toughest objections will make it easier for you to handle the smaller ones. Remember, people want to do business with someone they can trust.

6. Present according to the person you are talking to: Are you presenting to the decision maker or an influencer or a gatekeeper? Do not spend all your capital before reaching the person who decides on the sale. Find out who will make the buying decision. Making a great presentation to the wrong person is of no use.

Before you start crafting your presentation, find out who your audience will be and get into each of their heads. What are their roles in the organization and in the buying process? Get to know about their personal style, if possible. What do they already know about your solution? What misconceptions or resistance will they likely have?

DURING THE PRESENTATION

Remember, it is not always what you say to the prospect, but how you say it that creates an impression. Here are some of the elements of a successful sales presentation.

1. Build rapport: Creating a connection with your prospect starts from your very first interaction. Try to build some rapport before you delve into business discussions. Do some research to find out if you have common ground to talk about with the customer. Has the prospect's company been in the news lately? Are they interested in sports? Get some insight on the subject you want to use to create rapport. During your presentation, too, there will be times when you must communicate assurance, empathy, and support for the prospect and their needs. If you can do this well, you can often establish a strong bond.

Use what you know to establish a connection. Start your conversation with a clear idea about the people in audience, particularly when it comes to work. If you have a good sense of humor, tell a joke. However, if you are unsure, stick with sincere, simple compliments, like complimenting their office or their website. The key is sincerity; people can sense when you fake it. Keep it honest.

2. Use the power of story: It makes sense to open with a brief story to get your audience fully engaged with your sales presentation. If slides are involved, use them with minimal text to keep the focus on what you are saying. Just a concise and simple message for each slide will suffice. Your objective is to get the customer to spend most of their time engaging with you.

Storytelling is the most powerful form of communication. It will never get outmoded, because our brains have an embedded need for narratives, cognitive maps, and scripts. A story is not just about an anecdote; it is also about the storyteller. When you tell a story, you reveal a part of yourself. Stories we tell give a glimpse of who we are. Telling a story is a great way to establish a connection with your listener. Be attentive to how they respond, and engage with them. Your story is a talking point. Use it to get your prospect to open up and to steer the discussion in the direction you want it to take. As a salesperson, you must have a set of stories ready to go in different situations.

If your presentation does not have stories, then you are likely providing rote information without connecting. Presentations without stories can make prospects feel that you are talking at them and not with them. Use stories to personalize the information you are delivering; a good presentation blends information and stories.

When you want to establish credibility, tell stories that feature previous successes in similar circumstances. This will show that you understand what your customer's needs are and that you have successfully dealt with such needs before. In order to handle an objection, acknowledge how the customer feels and narrate a story where a previous customer felt the same way and you produced results to dispel all their misgivings. Recount personal anecdotes to create common ground.

Every story you tell has to belong within the context of your presentation and tie in with your content. Disjointed stories sound forced and have the opposite effect. Stories you tell must have a point to them that your audience can identify with. Make your stories clear to support the information in your presentation, and keep them short by removing unnecessary details.

When you consider a story to accompany an idea in your presentation, think of it like painting an image of your idea. Make it easy to visualize as something that happens in a specific time and place, including characters that your audience can connect with. If the context allows, tell a personal story. Personal stories appeal to emotions and connect you to your audience.

However, do not overdo the storytelling. When you are in doubt about a story's pertinence, err on the side of caution and do not tell it.

3. Deliver steadily: Always speak in a self-assured tone of voice, at a good pace, and very purposefully. If unease builds up during any part of the presentation, breathe deeply, focus on friendly faces in the audience, and keep going.

Ask for silence, if necessary. Appear confident at all times and make sure your physical behavior is in line with your presentation's intent. Different postures convey different moods: your posture can be formal and still, or relaxed and active. Make eye contact with your audience. Use your hands for gestures like welcoming your audience or emphasizing a point.

Always remember to breathe steadily and deeply. Use language that involves your audience. For example, use "we" or "you" instead of "I" or "they." Speak loudly enough to be heard clearly by everyone in the room. Vary the pitch of your voice with the message. Keep the pace of your delivery easy to follow; speak neither too quickly nor too slowly. Use pauses to your advantage.

4. Keep the prospect engaged: Be enthusiastic. Make sure that the audience is following what you are saying. If you feel they are losing you, ask them if they have any questions.

If you do not work to maintain your prospect's engagement throughout your presentation, it will lapse from time to time. It is critical to the success of your presentation to keep your prospect's engagement while you build a persuasive case. To maintain their engagement over a longer duration, let's say 60 or 90 minutes, you must build in places to renew their attention every once in a while. Here are some means for renewing engagement that can be used during a sales presentation:

Change of topic. The simplest and most usual point to reengage your prospect is when you move from one agenda item to the next.

Change of tack. When you sense the attention in the subject you have been talking about waning, break the presentation up with something new but connected. For example, tell an anecdote, cite a case study, write something on the flipchart or whiteboard, or show a video.

Check in. Ask if they have well understood and if anyone has any questions on what you have covered.

Ask a question. Ask a question about what you just said. Elicit feedback.

Use names. Check in with one or more people by name. Nothing gets people's attention like their own name or the anticipation of it being called out next.

Do a quick survey. If the context lends itself to it, do a quick poll or ask for general opinions on a subject. Being asked to make a choice reengages people's attention.

5. Ask questions: Do not sound like you are delivering a prerecorded spiel. Ask your prospect questions to probe and see where they lead you. Carefully structure your questions to draw out the customer needs that your product or service matches.

Asking questions is an extremely powerful tool. It affords the customer an opportunity to get involved in the presentation. Here are some reasons why asking questions is so effective:

It is a source of information for you. Questions can help you discover information needed to steer the presentation in the right direction. You may end up correcting misconceptions you had.

It prompts introspection. Intelligent questions can help the prospect make useful discoveries on their own. For example, when the customer says, "I do not think this will work for us," instead of harping on why it will work, the skilled salesperson asks, "Why?" The customer is now forced to think. By posing a line of self-revealing questions, you can get them to dismiss their own apprehensions or misinformation.

It bears out your interest in the customer. When you ask a question and actively listen to the response, it demonstrates a genuine interest in the customer. It gets you connected with your prospect.

It makes the presentation interactive. Asking questions turns your prospects into active participants in the presentation.

It puts you in control. In a two-way communication, you can gauge the tension and level of bonding much better than you can by merely talking on your own. Dialogue also helps you control the timing of different aspects of the presentation.

6. Keep your questions open-ended: Ask questions that necessitate more than a yes or no, and that involve more than just costs, price, procedures, and the technical facets of the prospect's business. Most important, ask questions that will divulge the prospect's main reason to purchase, their problems and needs. Also find out about the prospect's decision-making processes. Ask your customer why they feel a certain way. That is how you will get to understand them.

Each sales presentation requires its unique insight. The knack of asking open-ended questions helps you shape the dialogue from the start. They are not just a source of insight but they also enhance engagement by driving the prospect to talk for an extended period of time. Here are some of the aspects in which open-ended questions can be helpful:

- Getting the respondent to ponder and reply with creativity
- Building rapport
- Building credibility and trust
- Exploring and understanding customer needs
- Getting to the heart of customer objections
- Understanding, calibrating, and mitigating risks
- Driving the sales process forward and shaping opportunities
- Upselling and cross-selling
- Nudging for a closing

It takes practice to employ open-ended questions successfully. Too many questions can be unproductive. Questions that are too broad can derail the discussion instead of leading to the purpose. The idea is for control of the discussion to alternate between the salesperson and prospect. If control of the conversation remains solely with the salesperson, then the questions start to resemble an interrogation.

7. Provide social proof: A presentation can be engaging, but if it does not build credibility, it will not go far. A good way to build credibility is to provide social proof, for example, through a case study. Case studies should include the problems another similar customer was confronted with, what you did to resolve those challenges, and the outcome you helped the customer achieve. Case studies peppered through your presentation convey a picture of what your solution will look like. This is using the power of storytelling to its fullest.

Social proof in your presentation can range from informal commentary to testimonials to past experiences. In professions that require a formal qualification, evidence of top-quality formal qualifications is also an effective social proof. The value of testimonials lies in their being attributed and not nameless. The most effective testimonials come from people your prospect can readily identify with and respect.

Besides building your credibility, social proof also resonates with the prospect's desire for transparency. Reviews, testimonials, or qualifications come from independent parties. They are not provided by you or your company and there are no marketing filters involved.

8. Be specific: Do not let your presentation look or sound generic; make it look precise with a laser focus on the prospect. Adapt the discussion of your product or service to each prospect, and amend it to include specific points that are unique to that prospect. If you use PowerPoint, place the prospect's logo on your slides and make it appear that the key slides exclusively relate to their situation.

Make it the customer's story, with your product or service playing a key role. Know the persona of the people you are talking to, their role within the organization, and their technical background. Apart from researching business information on the company, also consider the company's technological preferences and dependencies and its purchase behaviors. Where possible, use examples specific to your prospect's organization.

9. Take notes: As a salesperson you need to develop the skill of taking notes. Note taking helps you remember what the customer said, shows that you care about what they have to say, and puts the customer at ease that their message is being registered accurately.

Do not rely on your memory; note down important points. Write down everything you think you will need to refer to later during the sale process. Noting points made by your prospect shows that you are paying attention. Write down any objections so that you can specifically handle them.

Here are some suggestions to take good notes while showing the customer that you are fully engaged in the conversation:

Ask for permission. It makes sense to get the customer's permission to take notes.

Note key words. Do not note full sentences. Write down key words and numbers that capture important points for you to recall later. Acronyms also help.

Review the notes later. Review your notes quickly after the meeting before you begin to forget. Enhance them to a level good enough for you to remember the discussion accurately.

Do not break eye contact. Do not completely lose eye contact when the customer is talking and is looking at you. Note key words quickly and maintain as much eye contact as possible.

Put the pen down, when needed. If the customer starts talking about something confidential or sensitive, stop taking notes and put the pen down to make the customer comfortable.

Note the customer's vocabulary. Write down words the customer frequently uses. Make them a part of your vocabulary with this person. Make sure you know exact meanings of the terms before you start using them.

10. Be a good listener: Salespeople who dominate the conversation are generally not the most successful ones. The best salespeople spend about 70% of their time listening. Be aware of the temptation to interrupt your customer. Listen carefully to ask questions, like a skilled interviewer. To improve your focus on listening, pay attention to the customer's body language as you listen instead of rehearsing in your mind what you will say next.

As a salesperson, you must master listening and the ability to identify people's true motivations. Remember that everything the customer says has the potential to make the difference between closing the sale and losing it. When you listen to the audience, you can better adapt to their communication style. Listen to learn.

11. Probe deeper: Do not rush into telling the customer how your solution meets one of their needs. First probe to understand the fuller picture. If you seek more information and listen to the answers, it empowers you to better position your product and shows that you are genuinely interested in understanding and addressing your customer's needs. Probe before you prove.

Probing is about listening to what the customer says, viewing that in relation to your offering, asking questions, and repeating. You never stop probing; you only do it less as you learn more. Probing distills information into knowledge and knowledge into insights. Here are some suggestions for probing:

Be patient. Do not move off a screen or slide before you have completed the conversation. Keep the prospect focused on the dialogue and not the display.

Start simply. Ask a simple question to get the customer talking. Use their answer to probe deeper and continue.

Know what is critical. Know the critical information that you require and listen for it. Use the customer's answers to steer the conversation to where you can get that information.

Discover the customer's motivation. Find out what drives a customer. What is their major pain point or real need?

Adapt your presentation. Know to adapt what you present to what is revealed by probing.

12. Discover "the" problem: A customer may have a litany of problems, but usually there is one hot button that underpins the need to buy. It can be a technical or a business issue. But it can also be an emotional need or a craving of the ego for recognition, control, or power. It is this real problem, frustration, or motivation that you need to discover and leverage. Great salespeople can identify their prospects' deepest pain points and offer a solution.

Make sure that your preconceived notions do not influence your interaction with a prospect. Do not assume the first problem your prospect mentions is the key issue they need to address. Probe further by asking insightful open-ended questions. Look for the root cause that is stirring the symptoms.

Then get the customer to articulate what the problem is costing them in the form of lost revenues or additional expenses. You can do this by asking the right questions. And if do it before you propose a solution, you have already created value for your product or service.

Also consider the personal motivations of the people involved. A key challenge is always one that makes your prospect's job or life more difficult or risky. This will help you understand their true motives, and you can better inspire them to invest in a solution.

13. Handle objections with empathy: No matter how well prepared your presentation is or how well you have rehearsed it, the prospect is still likely to throw you a curveball. A key component of your sales presentation is how well you can anticipate and handle the prospect's objections. When a prospect makes an objection, do not instantly leap in with a response. Instead, show understanding by saying, "Let's explore your concerns." Ask for more details so that you can understand and isolate the true objection.

You must have a deep reservoir of empathy as a salesperson. Customers want to know that you understand them and their situation and will make a recommendation that best serves their interests. When they make an objection, empathize and paraphrase what you think they mean. Then try to turn the objection into a question you can answer. For example, "Is it still a good buy despite the space it requires? Is that your question?" When you empathize and believe that your solution is the right one for them, you can answer that question in a convincing manner.

14. Quantify the benefits: Where possible, always attach a financial metric to a benefit or to whatever you are selling. For instance, an equipment salesperson could say that by installing their motors, the energy cost will drop by 24%, leading to a total saving of $9 million a year.

Generally, the benefit of your product or service consists in helping your customers do one of three things: make money, save cost, or mitigate risk. Ask the right questions to enumerate these benefits. Try to quantify using dollars rather than percentages or time, when possible. The ROI for your customer will be the money they spend on your solution against the money they save or make.

When your solution helps in sales growth, the benefit is the amount of revenue it helps generate in a certain time. On the other hand, your product or service can also help the customer do more with less, thus saving them money through reduced expenses, increased efficiency, or improved processes. Anything that helps your customer save time falls in this category and its monetary benefit can be calculated. Another scenario is when you offer a product or service to reduce the probability or impact of an unwanted occurrence. In such cases, weigh the cost of your solution against the probability plus the financial impact of the occurrence that your solution prevents or mitigates.

Also quantify the benefits of value-added services you provide or ripple effects that are related to the customer's needs: training, operational support, consulting services, personal services, promotional value, and so on. Not all value-added services or ripple effects have a tangible value or are worth quantifying, but when they are significant and tangible, do quantify them.

15. Get the commitment: The objective of every sales presentation is to either close the sale or elicit the commitment that is needed to move the discussion toward sale. Remember to ask for that commitment at the end of your presentation. Quite often the only reason customers do not commit is because salespeople do not ask for it. Ask for a commitment that will move the process forward toward a sale.

An effective close to a presentation is probably the most crucial aspect of making a sale. Always set a commitment objective before the presentation. It is not necessarily to get an order; it can be to schedule another appointment, to get an appointment with the real decision maker, or to get enlisted as a supplier. Look and listen for buying signals in the form of questions, statements, or body language. Ask for commitment in a straightforward manner.

AFTER THE PRESENTATION

Review in your head or with your colleagues to ascertain what went well and what went wrong, what you did well and what you did not do so well. Take everything into account from the physical setting, to your performance, to the customer's reactions. Where appropriate, seek feedback from the customer.

When you make a sales presentation, you can only control the conversation as long as you are in the room. Sometimes the sales presentation is just the first act of your selling story; most often the decisions are made after you leave. When you finish your presentation, you are not done. You always need to follow up. Invest as much time into your follow-up preparation as you put into your sales presentation. Put an effective follow-up strategy in place.

PART II

THE ART OF PERSONAL SELLING

In this section we will discuss how, as a salesperson, you can have honest discussions with your buyers and show that you care more about meeting their needs than making the sale. Practicing and paying attention to these aspects of personal selling contribute to a strong, trusting relationship between buyer and seller.

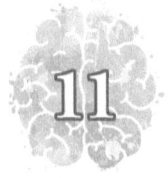

Using Metaphors

"The greatest thing by far is to be a master of metaphor. It is the one thing that cannot be learnt from others; and it is also a sign of genius."
Aristotle

Sales talk is laden with linguistic devices such as metaphor, simile, metonym, and analogy. For this reason, I will use the term *metaphor* in its broadest sense, that is, as a rhetorical figure of speech that employs association, comparison, or resemblance. So I am referring not only to an analogy between two things ("fear gnawed at his gut"), but also a simile ("the fear felt like a rat, gnawing his stomach") and a metonym ("the gnawing continued").

Personal selling engages social interactions that involve human sensations. Therefore, it uses language to stir, direct, or control those sensations. An effective sales message embodies an interactive blend of language, facts, numbers, and demonstration, each strand intertwined in a dynamic relationship.

When we argue, we view the other as an opponent. We defend or we attack, we gain ground or give it up, we win or we lose. Selling, though, is not an argument. It is a dialogue with a fine balance. Like a dance, we change rhythm, we follow a pattern, and we take turns leading. Keep this in mind while selling your product or your service. Metaphors will enable you to explain your offering more vividly and in fewer words than a full description. A car can be fast like a bullet train, sturdy like a tank, or sleek like a cobra. A house can be comfy like a sanctuary, imposing like a fort, or plush like a palace. For example, Skittles made their candies coveted by using the slogan "Taste the Rainbow" and General Motors described their Chevrolet truck as "The Truck Like a Rock."

Metaphors help your customers picture your offering without needing a detailed description. You can vary your metaphors for the same offering to suit each customer so that the image you use create connection at the deepest level. The more your customer makes positive associations to your product, the more likely they are to purchase. Metaphors generate links that resonate with the way our brain constantly arranges data. Our rational mind makes leaps of understanding because of its ability to associate.

Often, a prospect has difficulty understanding your message because they find it too technical, too complex, or too long. To penetrate that lack of understanding use a metaphor—a resemblance that makes the complex and unfamiliar simple and relevant. In our era of information overkill, a metaphor can distinguish you by making your message easy, vivid, and clear.

Although metaphors can be delivered concisely, they are rich with meaning. They connect with experiences that are often already wired into your customer. Through metaphors you make good use of the customer's attention, as they help you to cut through the clutter and get your point across effectively. While you may know a lot about your product or service, it can be a challenge to help the other person arrive at the same understanding. So you might ask yourself, "What metaphor or simile can I use to deliver a complex message in a simple way to this person? What examples can I use to help this person understand what I am saying?"

ADVANTAGES OF USING A METAPHOR

"I love metaphor. It provides two loaves where there seems to be one," wrote Bernard Malamud, author of *The Natural* and other novels. Here are some advantages of using a metaphor while selling.

1. It enhances the appeal: Imagine: the snow is a white blanket, the office was an oven, the sand is white milk powder. Salespeople are like poets, using metaphors to make things more attractive and beautiful. Metaphor is a powerful medium to describe meanings and emotions. Metaphor can be an effective tool for sellers to enhance their message by understanding the relationship between the buyer and the seller's product or service. They contribute a way of thinking. You can use a metaphor to express something that is unfamiliar in terms of something familiar, thus enhancing the meaningfulness of a product or service. Metaphor can create an emotional attachment between user and product or service by making it easy for the user to perceive and interpret.

2. It emphasizes a benefit: Metaphor uses drama to highlight a benefit. For example, a laser-sharp knife; an engine that purrs like a cat. You see how, in very few words, a metaphor brings out the signature benefit of what you are selling. When a truck is like a rock, it needs little further description of its toughness. Metaphors can express ideas for which singular words do not suffice. They can make the benefits of your offering more personal, memorable, and persuasive.

3. It simplifies: A good metaphor can capture everything you are trying to say in a single place—it is simplified and holistic. Metaphors give you the ability to relate to complex topics with something tangible and easily understood. When you get too complicated and want to teach your prospect all that you know, you fall into the expert's curse. When you are selling and want to lead your prospects into believing that they should buy your offering, the last thing in the world you want to do is to impress them with how much you know. Instead, learn how you can use metaphors to successfully convey messages and connect with your audience.

4. It makes your message memorable: The biggest challenge to selling is making your message stand out among many others. Often the differences between one solution and another are minuscule. In such cases a metaphor that resonates with your customer is highly effective; it is likely to stick in your customer's mind amid all the marketing clutter. By connecting your information with information already stored in their memory, metaphor makes it easier for customers to understand, retain, and later recall and use that information when it is needed.

5. It connects with an emotion: When Tim Hortons packaged itself to Canadians as a symbol of national taste as compared to myriad other coffee franchises, it became something essential in the mind of most

Canadians. By invoking an emotional need, a metaphor can serve as a useful tool to connect with a customer.

We all know how language works on the brain; therefore, how we choose our expressions can make a difference to our message. Research has shown that, while all stories activate brain regions associated with emotional responses, stories that use metaphors have much stronger effects on certain regions. They particularly affect the old brain (amygdala) that responds to emotional experiences, but other brain regions are also activated.

That is why using metaphors while selling hits home and elicits automatic emotional responses. Why does this happen? First, metaphors arouse more than one meaning—a literal one and an implied one—and our brain needs to evaluate both to decide which is more appropriate in a given context. This process may engage us more and activate an affective response, much as solving a puzzle gives us a sense of pleasure and reward. Second, metaphors link abstract concepts with more concrete ones. For example, a "bad day" can almost be perceived through touch if we describe it as a "hard day," which sets off the virtual experience of touching a hard surface. The audience imagines on a bodily level, and therefore on an emotional level too.

Effective imagery gets to heart of your customer experience. It can power a purchase decision by appealing to emotions. Quite often, salespeople miss the emotional pointer completely. Selling is rarely, if ever, devoid of human emotion. In business, people want to do good by their company. But they are also human. They want promotions. They want to look like stars. They want to earn more. You want to attract those emotions. Build your message on positive emotions that are genuinely associated with your product or service. Identify the feeling you want your metaphor to convey. Do not indulge in gross hyperboles; aim for authenticity.

6. It embodies the soul of the offering: A metaphor is effective because it can succinctly capture the ethos of a product or a brand. When Skittles likened candies to a rainbow, it represented their colorfulness. When Citibank said, "Citi Never Sleeps," it encapsulated reliability.

If you need to understand how a metaphor can encapsulate the soul of a message, imagine how the impact of poetry or figurative prose is lost in translation. A succinct and eloquent statement of the approach to follow is the following, from a 1989 study by George Lakoff and Mark Turner:

> Metaphor is a tool so ordinary that we use it unconsciously and automatically, with so little effort that we hardly notice it. It is omnipresent: metaphor suffuses our thoughts, no matter what we are thinking about. It is accessible to everyone: as children, we automatically, as a matter of course, acquire a mastery of everyday metaphor. It is conventional: metaphor is an integral part of our ordinary everyday thought and language. And it is irreplaceable: metaphor allows us to understand our selves and our world in ways that no other modes of thought can.
>
> Far from being merely a matter of words, metaphor is a matter of thought—all kinds of thought: thought about emotion, about society, about human character, about language, and about the nature of life and death. It is indispensable not only to our imagination but also to our reason.

Hence, metaphor has a significant impact on selling by offering customers an embodied experience of the seller's products and services, such as, "You will feel secure enough to sleep like a baby." Metaphor facilitates a meaningful relationship between the customer and the seller's offering. Metaphors particularly embody the soul of the sales message when conveying experiences most resistant to expression.

WHAT IS A GOOD METAPHOR?

You might ask, "What, then, makes for a good metaphor?" Even though there is no hard and fast rule to construct a good metaphor, here are some characteristics of an effective one.

1. It touches an emotional chord: In order to have a profound impact on your listener, you need to make an emotional connection with them. Know your customer and make your offering synonymous with something that deeply resonates with them. Buying is an emotional decision. Once you connect with their emotions, prospects will find their own justifications to buy your product or service.

2. It uses imagery: Use visuals or employ words that inspire a picture. People hear words but think in pictures, so visual metaphors are a good way to control the sales process. They make it much easier for the prospect to capture your message. Messages whose thought invokes an image in the mind are memorable and compelling.

3. It is simple and tangible: Do no indulge in telling a long-winded story where a metaphor can paint a quick picture. Lengthy stories and tedious explanations tend to lose your customer's interest. If you use a story, it has to be simple and tangible to successfully get your point across.

WHAT IS A POOR METAPHOR?

An ineffectively used metaphor can be counterproductive, diminishing your customer's interest in your message. Let's see what makes a metaphor unproductive.

1. It is a cliché: An effective metaphor is different from a stereotyped truism. More often than not, a cliché sounds unoriginal, worn out, and repetitive. If you want your message to stand out, avoid using clichés— such as "a force to be reckoned with."

2. It is irrelevant: To carry an impact, a metaphor has to be sharply on message. Irrelevant metaphors and stories do not connect and can be counterproductive. There has to be an unmistakable connection between the metaphor you use and the idea you want to convey.

Asking Questions

"If you do not know how to ask the right question, you discover nothing."
W. Edwards Deming

I f you are like most people, you will try to tell as much as you can as quickly as you can. You want to provide your listener with all the relevant information in the hope that something will trigger their interest. After all, you are the expert in your solution, have already resolved many similar problems, and boast stellar credentials. However, you may be burdening your prospect with more information than is necessary. Instead of making statements, try asking questions. Sales is more about listening than talking; by asking questions, you put yourself in a position where you have to listen. When something is imperative to talk about, turn it into a question.

Selling requires the knack of asking questions. If you do not ask the right questions, you will not be able to uncover the right needs and discover the problem to solve. Rather than going headfirst with your products or services, ask effective questions to understand your prospect's challenges and goals. By asking great questions, you can create great value in your prospect's eyes and astutely direct the course of a conversation.

THE ART OF QUESTIONS IN SALES

Asking sales questions is an art. Here are some tips for asking more effective questions while selling.

1. Understand the customer's emotions: Find out what motivates your prospect, what is their biggest concern, what they fear. Use questions to connect with your prospect's emotions. Emotion is a key element in the sales process. A major part of your customer's experience is emotional at both the conscious and subconscious levels. Throughout the conversation, your customer is having positive and negative emotions. Skillful questioning focuses on creating an experience where positive emotions outweigh the negative. Not only do you need to understand your customer's emotions, but you also need to make them feel self-assured, respected, and valued. Similarly, avoid emotions like annoyed, disillusioned, and frustrated.

2. Think outside the box: Consider how else the customer can solve their problem. This will help you disrupt the current perceptual frame when it becomes limiting.

Stop focusing on what you can sell the customer; start thinking about how you can help them reach their goals. When you think about how to help the customer, you will avoid getting trapped into a product or service mindset and optimize your creativity and flexibility. Focus on consultative interactions to create outcomes, and view your product or service as only one aspect of the value you can provide. Collaborate with customers and design customized solutions to deliver specific outcomes.

Understand your customer's genuine concerns, and do not rush to offer cookie-cutter solutions. The customer must feel comfortable throughout the sales process. They should not feel set up so that you can offer your preconceived solution without truly understanding their needs and desired outcomes. The customer is the expert on their own business needs. If you remain flexible, creative, and collaborative during the process of selling and ask the right questions, you can usually trust the customer to make the choice that works out best for both of you.

3. Induce reflection: Eugène Ionesco, the great playwright of the French avant-garde, once wrote, "It is not the answer that enlightens, but the question." How true! Make the prospect think of the consequences to their business if they do not act now. Buying decisions are often a game of consequences. Your prospect will be inclined to stick with the status quo unless the costs and risks of not changing are significantly higher than the costs and risks of change. You can ask questions to help your customer realize this.

Selling really boils down to three fundamental questions: why change, why now, and why us? Even if you have the best solution and you can establish a healthy ROI, you still will not win the sale unless the comparative benefits of addressing the problem are perceived to be higher than those of other competing demands on the prospect's resources.

4. Concentrate on the priority need: As Francis Bacon said, "A prudent question is one-half of wisdom." Understand your customer's priorities. Then, in order to cope with budgetary or timing constraints, you will know what the most critical component of your offering is.

In most practical business situations, your prospect will have more needs than they can afford to deal with. Their priorities will drive their behavior. The needs above the cut-off line will be addressed, and the rest will wait. If you do not probe, you will never know whether the issue you are attempting to solve is currently sitting above or below the cut-off point on your prospect's priority list. So, make sure that you are always pitching above your prospect's priority cut-off line.

The priority of an action is mostly governed by the impact that not solving the problem or not realizing the opportunity is likely to have on your contact and on their organization as a whole. Your proposal will then be reviewed by others in the approval cycle. They may have other priorities, and if you have not got their support already or coached your contact to get their support, they will also ask themselves, "How does this fit with my priorities?" And that is why, at every level, good salespeople focus on priorities, and not just on needs.

5. Ask permission: Seek permission to ask questions to gather information. This demonstrates respect. Asking tough questions is the heart of consultative selling. Doing anything less is just order-taking. The truly fulfilling stuff in sales is when a salesperson manages to change a prospect's point of view through questions, sometimes tough questions. The key to challenging a prospect on something is to get permission first. Preface the question by warning them of your intent and asking them if it is okay to proceed.

6. Listen actively and carefully: Good questioning involves deep listening. Listen carefully without interrupting until the prospect has a chance to fully answer the question. The prospect must feel heard and understood.

7. Be genuine: We have all experienced that fake "Great!" or "Awesome!" response to every answer. It is disingenuous, and prospects have particularly sharp sensors for sleaziness when dealing with salespeople. Ask questions to have a genuine conversation that helps you get to the heart of what the customer needs, what they think their problems are, and what their actual problem is, and see if you can help them. As you ask questions to discover, stay detached from the sale. Listen actively, not just hearing what they are saying but repeating their words back to them. Be transparent about how you work, what your exact steps are, and how your product or service is priced. If your service or product is not a good fit for them, be ready to say no.

8. Move from general to specific: Start with general, open-ended questions to gather information. They sound unintimidating and will put your prospect at ease. Listen carefully to what your prospect says. Then ask more specific questions to explore in greater depth.

9. Use the prospect's responses to probe further: As good interviewers know, the most obvious flow of questions comes from the interviewee's responses. Slot in your questions with the responses by paying attention to the key words.

10. Use familiar lingo: Where you can, use the prospect's industry or professional jargon. This helps your prospect relate to what you are saying. Do not bombard prospects with your own industry's technical language.

11. Keep it simple: The most useful answers are drawn by simple questions. Avoid lengthy or convoluted multi-part questions. It is better to ask questions that cover one topic at a time. Questions that ask for one answer elicit clear information.

12. Make your questions and answers personalized: Avoid being too general. People tend to chat more when answering personalized questions.

13. Follow a logical progression: When there is a sense of sequence to your questions, prospects know where you are leading. It builds trust when they can discern your intent. You will receive more undivided attention, it will spawn more action, and there will be a greater sense of urgency.

Quite often you lose sales because you are unable to uncover and link to your customer's real needs and motivations. The moment that linkage occurs, sales traction is born. Suddenly, you have a prospect that is very interested in what you are saying and what you can do for them and their company.

A tactful, logical progression results in fast-moving and successful sales cycles. To get to the core of what drives an individual, a salesperson needs to link to the personal agenda that is driving the professional agenda. Inside of each person these two intertwined incentives form the emotional motivation for advancing a sale. When you can build the sales interaction in consonance with its most logical course, you will be in position to craft a compelling value proposition that captures the prospect's interest.

14. Do not appear offensive: Start with general and non-threatening questions that do not touch on sensitive subjects. Build trust before asking any questions that may touch a raw nerve. Do your homework, and approach each prospect by striking the right balance between getting your point across and not offending them. Do not rush; take your time. Let your prospect do the talking by asking great questions. To make your prospect feel comfortable, smile and relax. Use humor to uplift the mood.

Focus on the prospect's problems and not on your product or service; they care about themselves and not about your company, product, or service. Show regard for the prospect's needs and pain points instead of coming across as someone who just wants to sell them something.

Avoid checklist-style interrogation. It is counterproductive to ask manipulative questions, because buyers will immediately put up their defenses and be skeptical of the seller's intentions. Shun negative conversational behaviors such as being too aggressive, not listening, and going on and on about your offering. Buyers can take offense to such conduct.

Avoid putting fake time pressure on buyers; they can read through such ploys. Urgency has to be backed by a reason; otherwise, it makes no sense. As you make progress, do not bully a customer into closing. Most customers will find this insulting and get turned off.

All this does not require you to be docile or gutless. Instead, be assertive but add a dash of humility and a lot of empathy into the mix. That combination will provide a great experience for your customers.

15. Interpret less, elicit more: A great mathematician like Georg Cantor knows this eternal wisdom: "The art of proposing a question must be held of higher value than solving it." Do not feel obliged to interpret every response from your prospect. The less you base your understanding on assumptions and the more information you elicit, the better aligned you will be with the prospect. Ask follow-up questions that explore things in more detail. If a prospect feels truly understood, they will trust you and feel better about you and your product or service.

Our brains are programmed to jump to outcomes, to look for shortcuts. Daniel Kahneman, the Nobel Prize–winning behavioral economist who was the first to highlight these biases, states, "Confirmation bias comes from when you have an interpretation, and you adopt it, and then, top down, you force everything to fit that interpretation." This bias can be ruinous for salespeople, as it can hinder their ability to understand customers and blindside them completely. Asking intelligent questions can help you sidestep this common error.

16. Explain before asking a sensitive question: It makes sense to first explain the relevance of a sensitive question you want to ask. Do not be afraid to ask your prospect tough questions, but acquire the knack of asking them well.

17. Focus on the benefits most relevant to the prospect: A prospect does not need to know all the benefits or features of your product or service. Focus on the benefits that best address their needs. Focus on what your product or service actually does for the prospect, which would be the basis for them to buy it. Extracting the most relevant benefits from features is what will get your prospect emotionally invested in your product or service.

18. Act like an advisor: Remember, the idea is to identify the problem and find the best solution to it in collaboration with your customer. Therefore, question your prospect in a way that will yield the maximum amount of information with the least friction. Use a relaxed tone of voice and allow time for answers.

This requires you to have the business acumen, experience, subject matter expertise, and integrity to be trusted to advise your customers well. When you are able to correctly identify your prospect's problems and then to recommend the right solution for them, you are more likely to negotiate deals that create value for all parties. When the customer sees you as a trusted advisor, you can be an agent of change. The customer can count on you to achieve the outcome that you have represented.

19. Do not ask yes or no questions: One-word responses kill a conversation. Frame your questions in a more exploratory, open-ended way. If you ask yes or no questions during sales, you will do all the talking, and prospects will quickly close out the conversation. Get the prospect talking by asking intelligent, open-ended questions that start with *who, what, where, why, when, how, which,* and so on.

20. Ask for a reason: When you do not get the information you want or do not fully understand, ask why or how. For example, "Why didn't it work?" or "How so?" Questions seeking a reason can transform simple answers into enriching conversations.

21. Ask who else you need to talk to: At the end of your questioning, ask your prospect if there is someone else in the organization you should speak with. If the prospect recommends that you speak to someone else too, ask them to introduce you. This allows you to understand and address the concerns of all the stakeholders.

22. Do not rush to pitch: You have one shot to make a great pitch. Do not blow it by rushing the process. It is tempting to pitch as soon as you feel that your prospect considers it a good fit. Make sure that your demo or strategy thoughtfully addresses their pain points and presents the solution in the best light.

When you rush the important early stages of the sales interaction, you risk starting on the wrong foot. Do not prematurely pitch your product or promote your company, or pass over critical qualification questions. Take your time and explore the situation thoughtfully. First be sure that a real issue exists and that the prospect understands the potential costs, risks, and consequences to their business of not dealing with the issue.

Before you pitch, you also need to identify who else is impacted and how, and if they are also likely to view the problem as worth solving. Once you have established that your prospect has the motivation to change, ascertain if the criteria they are likely to employ to appraise potential solutions play to your strengths and what you might do to influence the prospect's vision of your solution.

MAIN TYPES OF QUESTIONS

Here are some of the main types of questions you can ask your customers during the sale process.

1. Questions to build rapport: Good salespeople read a prospect's personality type at the beginning of their interaction. This allows them to determine the type of communication that will best suit the prospect and whether they should take time to build rapport first or get straight to the point of the meeting. Questions such as these help you build and strengthen genuine connections and trust with the buyer, setting the table for the rest of the conversation:

- What's going on in your business these days? How have things changed?
- What are your plans for this weekend?
- What's your story?
- You mentioned you want to retire in a few years. What are you thinking of doing then?
- What does success look like for you ... your business ... this project ... our work together?
- What will make this call worthwhile and successful for you?

2. Questions to uncover the problem: These questions are aimed at discovering the real challenge confronting the buyer. Questions such as these are best asked early in the sales process:

- Can you explain the problem you are trying to solve?
- What about this situation keeps you up at night?
- What difficulties have you faced in the past in trying to solve this problem?
- How much is this problem costing you?
- How does the issue cause problems that negatively affect your staff's motivation?
- How does the problem ultimately affect your current/prospective customers?
- If you were in your competitors' shoes, how would you take advantage of this situation?

3. Questions to find a solution: These questions are directed at helping the customer identify an appropriate solution to their problem. Ask questions such as these only after the problem has been clearly established:

- What is your biggest challenge with this?
- What would an ideal solution look like to you?
- What are the essential criteria for a solution to work for you?
- What is your timeline?
- What options are you currently looking at?
- What three key outcomes do you want from this?

4. Questions to navigate the buying process: These questions help salespeople ascertain what steps they must take in order to close the sale. Questions such as these are best asked after the problem is established and the desired solution is agreed upon:

- Who, besides you, is involved in the buying decision?
- Can you explain your decision-making process to me?
- How much time will it take to reach a decision?
- Do you require any other information in order to make your decision?
- What criteria are you basing your buying decision on?
- How much longer can you afford to let the problem go unresolved?
- What kind of return or payoff will you be looking for if you get a successful resolution of the problem?
- Have I covered everything? Is there anything I have overlooked?

5. Questions about the budget: These questions aim to ascertain the availability of budget and the sources of funding. Questions such as these are a part of the buying process questions:

- What budget do you have in mind for this?
- Where will the funds come from?
- Are there any other sources of funding that could be explored if necessary?

6. Questions that probe deeply: These questions help you uncover more detailed information and can be asked, as appropriate, at any time in the process. Probing questions ask for more detail on a particular matter. They are often follow-up questions meant to clarify a point or help you understand the root of a problem, so you know how best to move forward. A successful career in sales is dependent on your ability to ask good sales discovery questions, such as these:

- Can you tell me more about this?
- What does it matter to you?
- How does it impact you?
- How did you feel about that?
- How long has it been an issue/problem?
- How does this affect other parts of the business?

7. Provocative questions: Every prospect will turn up for a sales meeting carrying specific opinions and perspectives about their business. Often, as a salesperson, you need to ask questions that test those views and advance a different perspective. Provocative questions invite a prospect to think creatively and laterally. They can help to identify the real need and promote a level of creative thinking that may not be attained through merely straightforward questions. Provocative questions open up the scope of discussion and help to unearth ideas, values, constraints, and fears. Once these thoughts have been made explicit, they can be deliberated upon and reassessed. It is essential to build some rapport before asking a provocative question, such as these, so that it does not seem abrasive or presumptuous:

- If there were no budget or time constraints, what would your ideal solution look like?
- Imagine you do nothing about it, what would be the impact on your business over the next year?
- How do your competitors handle this problem? Do you want to be the same or different from them?
- What is the impact on your company if your new product/service is not successful in the projected timeframes?

Anchoring

"Confidence is a feeling, which reflects the coherence of the information and the cognitive ease of processing it. It is wise to take admissions of uncertainty seriously, but declarations of high confidence mainly tell you that an individual has constructed a coherent story in his mind, not necessarily that the story is true."
Daniel Kahneman

Anchoring is a cognitive bias that affects our decision-making. It occurs when we use an initial piece of information to make subsequent judgments. As T.S. Eliot, one of the 20th century's major literary figures, noted, "People exercise an unconscious selection in being influenced." Those objects near the anchor tend to be assimilated toward it, and those further away tend to be displaced in the other direction. Once the value of this anchor is set, future negotiations, arguments, estimates, and so on are discussed in relation to the anchor. When we interpret future information using this anchor, it may lead to bias. For example, the initial price offered for a used car, set either before or at the start of negotiations, sets an arbitrary focal point for all following discussions. Prices discussed in negotiations that are lower than the anchor may seem reasonable, perhaps even cheap to the buyer, even if those prices are still higher than the car's actual market value. Anchoring effects have been observed in a variety of domains, including pricing, negotiation, legal judgment, lotteries and gambling, probability estimates, and general knowledge.

This phenomenon was first discovered in 1902 by Edwin Burket Twitmyer director of the Psychological Laboratory and Clinic at the University of Pennsylvania, and was named "classical conditioning." At around the same time, the famous Russian physiologist, Ivan Pavlov, who in 1904 won the Nobel Prize for Physiology or Medicine, also independently discovered classical conditioning in 1903.

Twitmyer devised an apparatus that delivered a light tap below the knees of his research subjects. He used the sound of a bell to caution his subjects that the tap was about to be delivered. After repeating the experience a few times, the sound of the bell was accidentally presented to one of his subjects without the tap below the knee. Twitmyer realized that the auditory stimulus was sufficient to produce the now conditioned reflexive response. Twitmyer replicated the experiment with six more subjects and found that all of them learned to associate the bell with the hammer, and would produce the response to the sound of the bell alone. Following a sequence of several dozen trials, the conditioned response was not only unintentional, but several of his subjects also found themselves unable to prevent the response even when they attempted to do so.

The same phenomenon is at work when old photos take your feelings back to distant times or a perfume triggers memories of some special moments. In selling, you can engineer anchors intentionally by getting a customer into a specific mental state and creating an association to it, so that the state can be re-accessed at will. Let's say you are talking to a customer and you ask her about a photo on her side table. Her eyes light up and her tone of voice changes as she tells you this is her daughter. You may then ask a few questions that elicit her pride in her daughter, and every time you get a positive response anchor it to a sound or movement you make. You can also anchor someone to a feeling using your voice tone.

Anchoring also clarifies why, when asked to appraise something, our replies are influenced by how the question was framed. You can start anchoring well before you get to a price discussion with your customers by referencing what others have paid you. Anchoring is the reason car dealers still place price tags on cars, even though the internet has put all information in the hands of the buyer and we all know that the "dealer invoice" is not what the dealer paid and the MSRP (manufacturer's suggested retail price) is an artificially inflated number. Hard to believe, but it does work.

However, in many conditions you cannot just artificially inflate your price and let the anchoring effect work its magic. There is a counterweighing sales principle called "price integrity," which is vital for building trust and enduring business relationships. In order to demand a higher price, you must demonstrate more benefit; do not lower the price without a reduction in benefit. The customer must be able to see integrity in your price.

Also, as sellers of value, do not inflate prices. Instead use the anchoring effect to help you deliver the highest level of benefit for which your customer is willing to pay. Your best solution that provides the most benefit to your customer and has the highest price is your anchor. It allows you to establish a point of reference for both benefit and price. From there you can provide solutions at several levels, from best to good, for a particular need. The customer is likely to buy the highest level of benefit possible at the highest acceptable price.

As you talk to a customer, watch them as they access their memories. The best time to anchor the state is exactly as they access the state linked to the memory. Observe their eyes and watch for any subtle body movements. If they suddenly change their voice tone or become relaxed or more alert and excited, then this is the time to set the anchor by bringing up a particular topic or adjusting your tone of voice.

Anchoring effects have conventionally been understood as a result of inadequate adjustment from an irrelevant value, but new evidence suggests otherwise. Anchoring effects appear to be produced by the increased accessibility of information that is consistent with the anchor. The confirmation heuristic and the limitations of the mind explain why anchoring is so powerful. We tend to privilege hypothesis-consistent information without realizing it. Nobel laureate Daniel Kahneman thus wrote, "A compelling narrative fosters an illusion of inevitability."

Availability also plays a role in anchoring. To examine this heuristic, in 1974 psychologists Amos Tversky and Daniel Kahneman developed a paradigm in which participants are given an irrelevant number and asked if the answer to the question is greater or less than that value. Countless experiments have shown that people's absolute answers are influenced by initial comparison with the irrelevant anchor. For example, in one such experiment, people estimate that Gandhi lived to be roughly 67 years old, if they were first asked to decide whether he died before or after the age of 140, but only 50 years old if they first had to decide whether he died before or after the age of 9.

Reframing

"Between stimulus and response there is a space. In that space is our power to choose our response. In our response lies our growth and our freedom."
Viktor E. Frankl

Reframing is the art of changing outlooks; it is an essential skill in any area that entails guiding people's perceptions. We all live in our own reality, constructed by our minds, which can often resemble a tunnel. The mind works more like a paintbrush than a camera. It is not so much recording reality as creating it, thus making it look better or worse than it actually is. Once we realize the made-up nature of our personal reality, we know it can be framed differently in any moment without compromising authenticity. The idea of reframing is to raise our consciousness to the level where we can see something from a different perspective. This teaches us to regard our opinions and thoughts less rigidly as we become aware of their imperfection.

Persuasive and refined reframing happens when we rehash behavior, experience, or emotion in such a way that it sounds even more straightforward, and leads to more effective thinking and decision-making. Reframing is about setting or resetting frames of focus. Whoever calibrates the frame controls the ensuing experience. Every frame of focus determines how we order our attention and what we pay attention to. This in turn controls how we feel, talk, and decide.

In sales, reframing helps you to use an objection as an opportunity to do a better selling act. The pivotal point in resolving customer objections is paraphrasing the objection as a need—the need that the customer feels is not adequately addressed by your proposal. Once that need is uncovered and agreed upon, you can then focus on moving toward a solution. Remember, you are not ready to reframe unless you identify the need that prompted the objection. A general reframing format to discover the customer's unaddressed need could be: "If I understand you correctly, you need to … Is that correct?"

Reframing aims to take the objection and transform the situation into a positive in the mind of the prospect. A positive frame of mind makes it easier for people to change or to make a purchase. Keep your focus on the person you are selling to and not on yourself or on your company. To be able to effectively reframe their objection, you must understand your customer's motivations.

An effective way to handle objections is to reframe the conversation in a manner that helps the buyer understand why your solution will create value for them. Remember, an objection is not a rejection; it is a concern expressed by the buyer. Be prepared to address the concern in a way that helps change the buyer's view. Most salespeople learn the art of reframing by trial and error. Let's discuss some of the common types of objections and see how you can reframe the conversation to help buyers look at the same thing from a different angle.

1. Price objections: Some of the most common objections you will hear as a salesperson are related to price or availability of budget. Sometimes it is a genuine concern and a true blocker, but the customer may also be using it as an excuse to wriggle out. Most genuine price objections are about the relative value of your solution and not about its cost in absolute terms. In order to buy, the business has to be convinced that your solution offers a good investment. Your prospect needs to know that the solution you propose will create more value than it costs to buy. When you encounter an objection like "We can't afford to spend that much," you know that the value proposition does not make sense to the prospect. Reframe the problem by explaining the value your solution can create for them. It is not only about the price; it is also about efficiency, expense reduction, higher revenue, time saved, and so on.

2. Satisfaction objections: Another common type of objection is when the customer is satisfied with the existing supplier and sees little reason to switch. These objections sound somewhat like "We already work with A for this" or "There is no reason for us to incur costs switching from A to you." In such cases, reframe the discussion to make it about your relative strengths and then focus on them. Provide specific comparisons to explain how your offering is a superior overall solution and addresses the prospect's needs better.

3. Buying authority objections: This objection occurs when a prospective buyer does not have the authority to pull the trigger on the purchase. You will hear something like "I have to run this by the rest of the team and decide if it is the right fit." When this happens, your objective is to turn the person you are speaking to into an ally, an internal advocate for you and your company. Gain understanding and insight of their needs and pain points. Use this information to create leverage with others in the organization, and to be fully prepared when you meet with the person who does have the authority to make the decision.

4. Best fit objections: Some objections focus on the specific fit or need for the product or service. Of course, your product or service cannot be the right fit for everyone. Listen carefully to these objections to truly understand your customer's needs. While sometimes you may really not be the right fit for the customer, often these objections emanate from a lack of understanding or from a feeling that the prospect's needs are not being addressed. These objections come across as something like "We really need feature X and your product doesn't offer that." Reframe the conversation to get to the root of these objections. Then seek to understand the needs of the customer to be able to assess whether they are true mismatches or simply minor barriers to purchase. Next, explain how you can help address their reservations.

You can use reframing at any stage of the sales process in handling and overcoming objections, and in closing. Your skill lies in setting the belief or thinking pattern of the buyer in the context you desire. It often pays to frame the selling process when you start. When you use reframing while trying to identify the buyer's needs, to get to the buyer's beliefs, it helps you influence them more effectively in the later stages of the selling process. Let's say a prospect wants to move to a bigger house. You can readily ask, "To understand what you are looking for, may I ask why buying a new house is important to you?" If the customer answers that now their grandchildren often come and stay with them, you can use this information later in the process when you pitch a suitable house.

Sometimes, just one word will suffice to change a customer's perspective. For example, it can happen when you start referring to the price as an investment or when you highlight the distinction between the price and the cost. The secret is to reframe the decision the customer has to make. Focus their mind on the basis on which they can decide to buy. Then you can hurry the customer into buying by playing as if the customer has already decided to buy. For instance, you can ask whether they want to pay by check or with a credit card.

Reframing is not difficult to use, but you have to be able to come up with creative tactics. Do not use ready-made or trite scripts; come up with the reframing on the spot so it looks fresh and spontaneous.

Mirroring

"Acting is not about being someone different. It's finding the similarity in what is apparently different, then finding myself in there."
Meryl Streep

Mirroring is behavior that imitates someone else during interaction with them—exhibiting similar postures, gestures, or tone of voice. It may include copying gestures, movements, body language, muscle tensions, expressions, tones, eye movements, breathing, pace of delivery, accent, attitude, choice of words, metaphors, or other features of interpersonal communication.

Mirroring is hardwired into the human brain. It is called "limbic synchrony." During pregnancy, babies' heartbeats and body functions tend to adopt a tempo that matches that of their mothers. As adults when we are talking to someone and feel engaged and connected, our body subconsciously tends to mirror that person's nonverbal behavior. Limbic synchrony was scientifically recognized with the discovery of mirror neurons and how empathy develops in the brain. Mirror neurons are a type of brain cell that respond equally when we perform an action and when we witness someone else perform the same action.

In the early 1990s, researchers led by neuroscientist Giacomo Rizzolatti at the University of Parma, Italy, found individual neurons in the brains of macaque monkeys that fired both when the monkeys grabbed an object and when the monkeys watched another primate grab the same object. In terms of motor cell activity, the monkey's brain could not tell the difference between actually doing something and seeing it done. Scientists thought that if watching an action and performing that action can activate the same parts of the brain in monkeys—down to a single neuron—then it makes sense that watching an action and performing an action could also elicit the same feelings in people.

The researchers then found that in human beings, mirror neurons are far smarter, more flexible, and more highly evolved than any of those found in monkeys. They not only simulate actions, but they also reflect intentions and feelings. In the findings, published in 1996, Rizzolatti said, "We are exquisitely social creatures, our survival depends on understanding the actions, intentions and emotions of others. Mirror neurons allow us to grasp the minds of others not through conceptual reasoning but through direct simulation. By feeling, not by thinking." Therefore, mirror neurons play a key role in our ability to socialize and empathize with others. By observing body language signals and instinctively inferring the emotion behind them, we get an intuitive sense without having to think about it. Being on the same wavelength is no longer an imaginative expression; it is a biological reality.

Mirroring can be used as an important tool in selling to build rapport or to increase the other person's comfort. Begin by observing a person's body posture and then subtly let your body reflect their position. Some salespeople can even match their customers' breathing patterns—inhaling and exhaling in sync with them. Similarly, when your prospect begins to subconsciously mirror you in a business setting, it is a sign of rapport and trust.

Analyses have revealed that salespeople skilled in mirroring find greater success in getting prospects to buy than those who do not use mirroring. For instance, a research team led by psychologist William Maddux—a professor of organizational behavior at INSEAD and the University of North Carolina—performed several experiments to study the effects of mirroring in business situations. In one of their experiments, the scientists got MBA students to partake in negotiation exercises. Some of these students were instructed that during the negotiation they should subtly mirror the verbal and nonverbal behaviors of those whom they were negotiating with. The findings were quite revealing. The students who had not mirrored arrived at a negotiated settlement 12% of the time. In contrast, the students who had mirrored the behaviors were able to successfully reach an agreement 67% of the time.

MIRRORING IS USEFUL IN SALES

Mirroring is a potent strategy for salespeople because it helps you promote two vital elements of influence.

1. Rapport: Mirroring verbal and nonverbal behavior improves rapport because stimulation of the mirror neurons strengthens the feelings of rapport that one has with the other person. Mirroring also increases rapport because it produces the perception of similarity, and people instinctively feel amplified levels of rapport with those whom they view as similar to themselves.

It has been borne out by research, especially in social psychology, that imitating the words and gestures of the person you are interacting with will increase goodwill between you. Some mirroring happens naturally when people are speaking; it is a behavior we learn from a very early age. Infants and children learn by copying adults, much to the adults' delight. It is a bit like dancing, where people try to match one another. When you mirror, you do not only listen with your ears; you listen with your entire body. You are fully present to the other person.

Any friendly chat offers plentiful proof of this intuitive social tango. Smiles are contagious, and nodding is infectious. The idea is to be a mirror but a slow, imperfect one. Follow too closely, and most people catch it and regard it as fake. Skilled salespeople focus on physical cues and respond to them without thinking much about it.

Neuroscientists have shown that mirroring, if done sincerely, is a powerful way to establish and strengthen rapport. In several studies, Jean Decety, a neuroscientist at the University of Chicago, has established that some of the same brain regions that are active when we feel pain are also triggered when we envision someone else, like a loved one, feeling the same pain. A similar process almost definitely occurs when we feel happy about the good fortune of a friend or the apparent enjoyment of a conversation partner. Dr. Decety says, "When you're being mimicked in a good way, it communicates a kind of pleasure, a social high you're getting from the other person, and I suspect it activates the areas of the brain involved in sensing reward."

Author Benedict Carey has reported on experiments indicating the efficacy of mirroring. In one such experiment—conducted by Rick van Baaren, a psychologist at Nijmegen University in the Netherlands—participants were asked to provide their opinion about a series of advertisements they were shown. A researcher mirrored half the participants as they spoke, imitating their posture and body language. Minutes later, the researcher dropped six pens on the floor, making it look like an accident.

In quite a few versions of this simple experiment, participants who had been mirrored were two to three times as likely to pick up the pens compared to those who had not been mirrored. The mirroring had not only augmented goodwill toward the researcher within minutes, the study determined, but it also encouraged "an increased pro-social orientation in general."

In another study, Robin Tanner and Tanya Chartrand, psychologists at Duke University, led a research team that tested how being mimicked might affect the behavior of a potential customer or investor. The team had 37 Duke students try a new sports drink, Vigor, and answer a few questions about it. The interviewer mirrored the posture and movements of half the participants. None of the participants who had been mimicked realized that mirroring had taken place. The researchers set up the interviews so that each student's experience was virtually identical, except for the mimicking. At the end of the interview they were significantly more likely than the others to try the drink, to say they would buy it, and to predict the drink's success in the marketplace.

In another run of the experiment, the psychologists discovered that this was especially true if the participants knew that the interviewer, the mimic, had a stake in the product's success. "This is somewhat counterintuitive," Dr. Chartrand said in an interview. "Normally, you'd expect when people realize that someone was invested in a product and trying to sell it to them, their reaction would be attenuated. They would be less enthusiastic. But we found that people who were mimicked actually felt more strongly about the product when they knew the other person was invested in it."

Jeremy Bailenson, a Stanford psychologist who has researched mirroring, has found that his subjects pick up the mimicry when it is immediate and precise. However, if it is vague and done with a delay of a few seconds, then the mimicking goes unnoticed and is effective in building goodwill and rapport. "The point is it's a delicate balance to get it right, and I suspect that people who are good at this know how to do it intuitively," says Dr. Bailenson.

2. Empathy: Empathy is an important element of social behavior and interpersonal selling. The neural processes of empathy had been largely unidentified until recently. The discovery of a special class of cells in the monkey brain has inspired a series of recent imaging studies that have revealed a large-scale neural network for empathy in the human brain. This neural system seems a robust biomarker of the human capacity to empathize with others. Suffice it to say for our purpose here that it is now scientifically established that a congruence between the observed action and executed action it triggers creates empathy between both parties.

Therefore, another essential element of influencing that mirroring empowers is empathy. Empathy is the emotional sensor that enables a salesperson to gain awareness of the thoughts or feelings that trigger the prospect's verbal or physical signals. Empathy boosts a salesperson's efficacy, because it helps the salesperson gain better understanding of the prospect to more precisely address the prospect's needs.

One example of the empathic power of mirroring was demonstrated by a study undertaken at Dartmouth College where participating students were instructed to watch a person who was administered an electric shock. Some of these students were told to make a pained expression whenever the person received the shock. The researchers supposed, as Freud and others had believed, that expressing an emotion would lead to catharsis. So, by making a pained expression whenever the subject received a shock, the student watching it was expected to discharge any anxiety and immediately feel better. However, the opposite transpired. The students who acted pained when the person was given the shock sweated and had faster heart rates than other students who were not told to express visible emotion. The result of this experiment established that mirroring another person actually provides a pointer into that person's world and, thus, builds empathy.

PUTTING MIRRORING TO USE

Here are some suggestions of how to approach mirroring.

1. Look natural: Mirroring works best when it becomes a skill that can be performed unconsciously, like driving on a familiar route. Stick to behaviors that come naturally.

2. Build some rapport first: First make a connection. Mirroring cannot supersede the priority of listening and understanding the other person.

3. Make eye contact: Face the person squarely and make frequent eye contact.

4. Start subtly: Begin by nodding and moving your head as you listen.

5. Mirror speech: Try matching the other person's vocal tone, pace, and vocabulary.

6. Mirror behavior: If mirroring their speech works, move on to mirroring body postures, energy level, and language.

7. Be genuine: Be genuinely interested in the other person and what they are saying.

Here are some pitfalls to avoid while mirroring.

1. Do not fake interest: Pretending to be interested when you are not can be counterproductive.

2. Focus on the positive: Do not mirror negative body language or tone.

3. Do not be a monkey: Do not try to precisely imitate the person's body language and expressions.

4. Do not be self-conscious: Do not invest so much attention in mirroring that it makes you self-conscious or removes your attention from more important details of the meeting.

Storytelling

"Humans are not ideally set up to understand logic; they are ideally set up to understand stories."
Roger C. Schank

Selling is never about pushing information down people's throats. For you to sell, your customer must want to listen to you. Not just listen—but want to listen. Especially when you are selling high-value or long-term solutions, dry pitches enumerating a solution's benefits without context or any attempt to connect will not make you successful. That is where storytelling comes into the picture.

Since long before the advent of recorded history, the art of storytelling has been a means to pass and store information. People are hardwired to listen to stories and relate them to their own lives. Religions understood this a long time ago; they use stories to great success. Almost every world religion has its holy book (Bible, Koran, Vedas) that communicates its lessons through stories. A story is not just pieces of fact, it is a narrative—the most effective way to transmit information into someone's mind and make it memorable.

Great salespeople have known, often intuitively, that stories, not facts, have the most dominant influence on how people feel. Stories can therefore lead the path to closed deals. Successful salespeople know how to use available information to weave engaging stories. There is no shortage of narratives in your company, in your prospect's business, and in the industry. Develop a keen eye for information that can provide the elements to create a story.

WHY STORIES HELP IN SALES

Here are some of the reasons why a good salesperson has to be a good storyteller.

1. Stories stimulate retention of information: An ancient Native American adage beautifully captures this eternal truth about humans: "Tell me the facts and I'll learn. Tell me the truth and I'll believe. But tell me a story and it will live in my heart forever." People cognitively retain information more completely and efficiently when taught in story form rather than as cold facts. When facts and data are woven into an interesting narrative, your story will command the listener's attention and help them connect the information to their context. Later, if the prospect is in a similar context, your story will spring to their mind rather than a dry pitch from your competition.

2. Stories help you connect with the audience: Storytelling is a respected technique in any field that requires connecting with people—sales, politics, religion, and so on. As the sales process is usually not a single-meeting situation, the connections that stories build help you stay on your prospect's mind. Stories humanize your message by acting as conversation catalysts that spark thoughts, imagination, discussions, and emotional engagement.

3. Stories exert a pull on both emotions and reason: It is common to think that emotions and rational thinking interfere with each other. Plato described emotion and reason as two horses pulling us in opposite directions. When you tell a good story to explain why your solution is the most logical one for the prospect, your pitch carries a lot of impact. A story rich with imagery and meaning stimulates the brain as a whole. You can link the features and benefits of your solution with the everyday situations your prospect experiences.

4. Stories inspire imagination: Stories help customers imagine your solution in the context of their operations. Their imagination forms an immediate connection between the need and its solution. Stories are the wings both the intellect and the imagination fly on. There is nothing like a story to train the mind to take off from immediate reality and return to it with new understanding and new strength. "There's always room for a story that can transport people to another place," remarked best-selling author J.K. Rowling. This is as true for selling as for anything else human.

5. Stories invoke action: Once you manage to tell a good story that is relevant to a prospect's situation and you have their full attention, you are in a strong position to get them to decide to buy. Make your call to action strong and confident.

TYPES OF STORIES IN SALES

There are two kinds of stories you can frequently use while selling.

1. Success stories: Present your case studies in story form. Narrate the experiences of similar customers to show how your proposed solution helped them. Tell how a customer was suffering and how your solution helped them, or how a customer had initial doubts and their experience of your solution dispelled all their misgivings. Let the details talk: how your customer's experience improved, how much they saved, how their business grew, how their efficiency increased. Inspire the desire in your prospect to be your next success story.

2. Your solution in action: Be imaginative and show simulations of situations where your solution will help the prospect. Do your research to help them visualize the practicability of your solution in their own operations. Stick to realistic scenarios and cover all relevant details.

INGREDIENTS OF A STORY

Every great story has a structure. A basic story has a beginning, a middle, and an end. A good sales story has five essential components.

1. The hero: A good story needs to have a main character that the prospect can relate to. The hero should invoke the prospect's experience by sharing some of their traits or situations. When salespeople realize that the prospect is the hero and they are assisting in the hero's success, it becomes clear that they need to incessantly learn about the prospect's outlook, pain points, and needs.

2. The impetus: A story includes a cause for action that propels the hero toward solving the problem.

3. The plot: The main components of the plot are difficulties, struggles, pains, and hazards that the hero has to overcome.

4. The climax: This is the crossroads where the hero needs to make a choice to arrive at the solution. Here you spur your customer into making the choice to buy.

5. The ending: The hero has resolved the problem by taking the path they chose to take.

CREATING A PERSUASIVE STORY

Here are six suggestions for creating a persuasive story.

1. The story should be about the prospect: Even when you are talking about other customers, narrate it so that the prospect can see themselves in the story.

2. The story should be straightforward: Keep it simple; do not overcomplicate. You are not a Cicero in action. Get your points across in simple language and an understandable manner.

3. The story should provoke the imagination: Paint scenarios and provide details of the settings to stimulate the audience's imagination.

4. The story should include humor: People like some humor, even in dry business stories. If you have a sense of humor, do not be afraid to make your prospect laugh. Do not overdo it, though; it is a sideshow.

5. The story should highlight your difference: Your story must differentiate your company or your solution from the competition that offers a similar product or service.

6. The story should transmit a lesson: The story needs to show the negative situation and then the positive outcome of following the course you are suggesting.

Active Listening

"When people talk, listen completely.
Most people never listen."
Ernest Hemingway

The foundation of successful selling is how well you listen. In this age, when so much information is freely accessible, it is increasingly difficult for salespeople to demonstrate their expertise as a way to build credibility and establish trust. Without credibility, you are not likely to hold your prospect's interest. So, what is the antidote? Invest in listening.

Listening well is the key to building rapport, gaining trust, and uncovering buyer needs. Neuroscience research has established that people's brains generate oxytocin, the social bonding chemical, when they feel they are being listened to. The production of oxytocin can lead to more trust between you and your prospect, and it increases the ability to anchor and remember details about others.

Morgan Scott Peck, an American psychiatrist and author, makes an important point: "You cannot truly listen to anyone and do anything else at the same time." Yes. Listening effectively is not as easy as it sounds; it requires discipline and training. Do you consider listening as a passive skill? Quite the opposite—listening is an active process. Often, while we think we are listening, our mind is actually working on what to say next and simply waiting for our turn to speak. To sidestep this trap, we need to learn to listen actively.

Active listening will enable you to learn things about your buyer that will lead to more sales. Improve your listening skills by focusing totally on the buyer's perspective, taking notes, and using active listening techniques to ensure you completely understand their point of view. Active listening helps increase empathy and rapport between a speaker and a listener. It is an essential communication technique for all salespeople. When salespeople demonstrate they respect the prospect's opinions, it is far easier to develop trust and make sure that the conversation produces a mutually beneficial experience.

LEARNING ACTIVE LISTENING

"When listening to another person, don't just listen with your mind, listen with your whole body. You are giving the other person space— space to be. It is the most precious gift you can give," teaches Eckhart Tolle, a spiritual teacher and author of *The Power of Now*. Here are some suggestions to learn and practice active listening.

1. Pay undiluted attention as the prospect speaks: Even when they are attentive, salespeople are often listening for a word or a tip that will indicate whether the prospect needs their product. Prospects can sense such an attitude and then feel that all the salesperson is interested in is making the sale and not in understanding them. The right way to listen is to be fully present with a blank mind. Forget about the script or your own agenda, and pay attention to the prospect's words and feelings. Note their language, tone of voice, speed, facial expressions, and body language. Look for auditory, visual, and kinesthetic clues.

2. Disengage from distractions: Turn off all distractions including cellphones, extra tabs in your browser, your email, and chat customers. If you feel yourself losing attention, do something—like tapping the desk or making a little note—to get back into the moment. If a question comes to your mind, write it down so that it does not weigh on your mind and you can ask it at the right time. Do not allow background noise or your environment to hinder your ability to listen.

3. Listen to understand: Active listening involves listening with a genuine intent to understand. It could not be more straightforward; it begins with intention.

A study at Princeton University, "Speaker-Listener Neural Coupling Underlies Successful Communication" by Charles G. Gross, discovered that there is a lag between what you hear and what you understand. It could be between a few seconds to up to a minute, depending upon the person and the situation. This is the trouble spot; during that lag time, we start to listen to ourselves and not to the other person. More often than not, this lag time is caused by our own thoughts.

Confirmation bias drives us to pick out facts or aspects of a conversation that corroborate our opinions. Confirmation bias is also fed by the difference between the speeds at which we speak and listen. Research shows that most individuals speak at a rate of 175 to 200 words per minute, whereas people are generally capable of listening and processing words at a rate of 600 to 1,000 per minute. Because it is not using its full capacity when listening, the brain drifts off to other things.

Therefore, as a salesperson, you have to discipline yourself to listen to completely understand what the other person is saying. Pay attention and do not assume you know what they have to say. Respond by repeating before commenting to make sure that you have understood correctly.

4. Observe the nonverbals: Active listening includes listening with your eyes as well as your ears. Carefully watch the prospect's body language to discern their personality, emotional state, and underlying meaning.

Awareness of what the customer is really feeling, and responding effectively, is an essential skill for a good salesperson. When you interact with a customer, you both communicate on two levels—verbal and nonverbal. Nonverbal communication is critical in understanding subtle complexities of personality.

In sales the most revealing body language signals are your customer's engagement and disengagement behaviors. The former convey interest and receptivity to what you are saying; the latter betray resistance, disagreement, or antagonism. Take conscious note of nonverbal signals that convey these feelings:

The eyes. Observe the eyes; our eyes often betray us when we are hiding what we really feel. Our gaze lingers longer at texts, objects, or people they are drawn to. When people like you or agree with you, they tend to increase their eye contact. Less than normal eye contact, on the other hand, reflects disengagement. Avoiding eye contact by frequently gazing past you shows boredom. Eye pupil size is a sign of a person's emotional response. Eyes that are interested are likely to be wide open, whereas eyes exhibiting disengagement narrow somewhat.

The face. Someone in agreement is likely to smile and nod as you speak. Tightly compressed lips, lowered eyebrows, a tense mouth, clenched jaw muscles, a frowning face, or a head turned away show disagreement or annoyance. However, do not put much reliance into face reading. Facial muscles respond well to voluntary control. Therefore, people can often mislead by hiding their feelings behind a friendly mask.

Hands and arms. An open position of the arms shows receptiveness. Gestures that flow naturally show that the person is relaxed and at ease. Folded arms or clenched fists betray defensiveness or anger. Also observe how the arms and hand movements change as the negotiation progresses. For example, if your prospect's arms that had been resting openly on the table are withdrawn to under the table, it is a signal worth noting. It might indicate that something unsettling has just happened. Self-touching gestures show stress, fists reflect aggression, and clasped hands indicate guardedness.

Shoulders and torso. When a customer leans toward you frequently, they probably like you. When someone disagrees with what you are saying or doing, they tend to create additional space from you. Shoulders turned away show a lack of interest. When people are engaged they are likely to face you openly with their torso pointed toward you. An attempt to shield the torso with an object—a bag or a file—reveals defensiveness.

Feet and legs. In a fight, flight, or freeze situation, our feet and legs are wired by the limbic brain system to respond faster than the speed of thought. Ankles crossed and legs stretched forward show the person is feeling positive about you. Feet locked in a tight ankle clasp or enfolded around the legs of a chair likely indicate disengagement or retraction. High-energy heel bouncing or rocking back on heels and raising the toes are strong signs that your prospect is feeling pretty good about the proceedings. Bouncing legs that suddenly go still show sharp anticipation. When the legs are crossed and the foot of the leg on top is pointing toward you, the person is likely engaged. If the legs are crossed so that the top foot is pointing away from you, it shows withdrawal.

Finally, the key to understanding the buyer lies in understanding your own nonverbal expressions. Salespeople who are unmindful of how their own body language contradicts what they say often do a poor job in reading their buyers. Cultivate a sharp awareness of your nonverbal expressions before you can hope to decipher others' nonverbal expressions with any degree of accuracy.

5. Listen to the emotions: Regardless of what you are selling—from perfumes to cars—people buy based on emotions, making the decision to purchase because of certain feelings they experience about a product or service and the person offering it. Focus not just on the words being spoken but also on the emotions that lie behind what is said. Reflect the feeling when you rephrase the content or ask questions. In order to build a connection and a relationship with customers, listen for their underlying emotions. By listening for and acknowledging their emotions, you demonstrate to the customer that you care.

Ask the right questions to discover emotions; questions are key to personalizing any sales conversation. Regrettably, most salespeople only ask elementary questions intended to learn what a customer wants from their product or service, rather than what is important to them about having it. Instead, it is important to observe the customer's emotions and to ask them emotional needs questions.

When you describe your offer, focus on your buyer's emotional needs, using their words. These words are stored in their emotions, and when you use them you will tap into their emotions. Once you attend to their emotional needs, your prospect will feel trust, confidence, and care at a level well beyond a typical sales conversation.

6. Do not interrupt: Even if you interrupt in a polite manner, you can still miss out on something that your prospect would have said if you had not interrupted. Do not break their train of thought when they are speaking. Also, if you pause for a couple of seconds after your prospect is done speaking, they might often add something to what they said.

Interrupting also likely impairs the rest of the conversation, as the interrupter has exercised dominance. If the customer is not able to complete what they wanted to say, they may feel offended, engendering resentment and a disinclination to be open. That will hinder real communication.

7. Repeat the important points you hear: When a prospect reveals a pain or explains what they are looking for, repeat it so that they hear it back from you. Make sure that your understanding of the matter is accurate. Depending on the situation, you can repeat what you heard verbatim, paraphrase what the prospect said, or repeat in your own words what you heard. Reassure your prospect that you understand them.

Try to adopt the words your customer uses. Good salespeople often make good use of repeating back the words they hear from the customers they are speaking with. When you use the same vocabulary as a customer, it bridges the social distance between you and makes the customer see you as more similar.

Restating the customer's message also helps them find a way to simplify or clarify what they said if you have misheard or misunderstood. Here are a few introductory phrases that you can use to indicate what you heard:

- Let me see if I understood correctly.
- Can I just check what I got from that?
- I would just like to confirm that I got that right.
- My understanding of what you said is … Is that what you meant?
- So, what you are saying is … Does that sound right?
- You mean that we should … Is that right?
- Am I reading your suggestion right, when you said …?
- You mean …?

Not only is it polite to use an introductory phrase, but by highlighting that you are repeating their ideas to validate your understanding, you also show that you take accuracy seriously and convey a sense of importance to the customer. Ending with a question empowers the other person to clarify any confusion or provide additional details they feel are pertinent.

8. Ask follow-up questions: Your next step is to ask relevant follow-up questions. Ask an open-ended question that encourages your prospect to communicate more about their objectives, challenges, and business plans. When you ask the right question, the prospect might themselves come to the conclusion that your solution is the right one. If you do not ask questions whenever there is a doubt, you run the risk of making assumptions that may not correspond to what the buyer intended.

9. Listen for what is not said: What is implied can be more important than what is said. If you perceive that the customer is vague or is articulating conflicting messages, ask a question to explore the meaning behind the words and the message that you think the customer is trying to convey. This requires you to be totally focused, completely mindful, and perceptive of the conversation, both spoken and unspoken.

"The most important thing in communication is to hear what isn't being said," says management guru Peter Drucker. How often do we miss something that was not spoken? Quite often. We walk away from a conversation, thinking we listened and understood all that was said. Yet, when we continue the dialogue, we feel like we really missed something earlier.

Sometimes what is not being said is more important than what is. This is as much true for sales calls as it is for literature or clinical interviews. Writer Ernest Hemingway used the metaphor of an iceberg to explain his own legendarily frugal short stories: "The dignity of movement of an iceberg is due to only one-eighth of it being above water. If a writer of prose knows enough about what he is writing about he may omit things that he knows and the reader, if the writer is writing truly enough, will have a feeling of those things as strongly as though the writer had stated them."

Let's take Hemingway's short story "Hills Like White Elephants" to briefly illustrate what this means. A couple at an alfresco café have a vague conversation about the shape of clouds, their drink orders, and the possibility of an unspecified but "awfully simple operation." This rather enigmatic discussion is the one-eighth of the iceberg noticeable above the water. By paying close attention to what is and is not said, the reader comes to understand that the woman is pregnant and the man wants her to have an abortion, though neither the word "pregnancy" nor "abortion" appears in the story.

The reader also understands that the discussion has been going on for some time and is straining the couple's relationship, because the woman keeps asking her partner to stop talking about the operation. The man disregards her appeal to stop talking about it four times, even after she has implored him, and instead repetitively insists "but I don't want you to do it unless you really want to." This helps the reader understand that the man very much desires her to have the abortion, but is not prepared to fully own his desire not to be a father. Perhaps he does not want to see himself as a man who has bullied his partner into having an abortion and, thus, wants to make it emotionally easier for himself by making her take the responsibility for the decision.

Noting carefully what is not being uttered orally, but is being said in a customer's body, behavior, silence, or insinuation, can deepen your understanding and ability to help. Here are some things that can help you listen to what is not being said:

Guard against personal bias. Be aware of your personal bias in a matter and stop it from affecting your interpretation.

Use all of your faculties. Do not merely use your ears to hear what is being said. Observe carefully, especially when someone's words do not match their body language. Get out of your head and also heed the signals from your intuition, gut instinct, and sensations.

Do not worry about your response. Concentrate on the speaker and the message. Do not fret over how you will reply.

Maintain eye contact. Put away anything that could distract. Do not stare around; look at the speaker.

Imagine yourself in your customer's place. Put yourself in your customer's shoes and try to understand the situation from their point of view, concerns, and experiences.

Listen for emotions. Volume and tone can give you important clues. Go past the facts to decipher the underlying emotion.

Be open-minded. Do not assume; be curious to know what they have to share.

HOW ACTIVE LISTENING HELPS

Here some of the ways in which active listening is helpful.

1. It softens resistance at the beginning: Active listening tells the prospect that you are there to listen and to help, and not just to sell.

2. It builds trust: Active listening communicates respect for your prospect and is helpful in building rapport and trust. One key element in earning trust is that the customer must believe that you understand them, you care, and you are capable of helping them. In the sales process, when you speak, you merely deliver information, but when you genuinely listen, you exhibit respect, generate trust, and develop rapport.

Where salespeople are poor listeners, mistakes occur, relationships fail, and opportunities to make the sale are missed. On the other hand, when you take the time to listen and really seek to understand your customer's opinion, you are demonstrating respect and acknowledging their perspective. You foster trust by nurturing a mutual understanding of what is being discussed.

3. It helps identify the problem: When a prospect sees you listening with a genuine intent to help, they will be more willing to share emotions about their challenges. With active listening, you can help your customer perceive you as their advisor. You also get valuable information to inspire your own imagination and creativity.

4. It enables you to proactively address objections: When you listen carefully, you can often anticipate an objection and address it proactively.

5. It helps in smooth closing: When you listen carefully and confirm your understanding with the customer, closing should just happen as the logical denouement. Taking a cue from your buyer's signals, push for forward progress when it counts most. Active listening makes you receptive to signs that tell you when the buyer's mood swings in your favor and enables you to seize the right closing moments.

6. It prevents miscommunication: Active listening is a great way to prevent miscommunication, because the salesperson recaps the conversation and reconfirms the key points, and the prospect gets the opportunity to clarify anything that was not well understood.

Likability

"It is better to be likable than to be talented."
Utah Phillips

If several competitors are equal in capability and quality, that is, if everyone is equally good, you might think that the buyer will decide to choose the lowest-cost provider. Not necessarily! Even when the buyer perceives the offering as a commodity, the seller's interaction with the buyer has a lot of influence on their choice. That is where likability makes a real difference. It is very human: we like to do business with people we like. Yes, a seller has to bring a value proposition, listen, understand needs, offer the right solution, and so on—but if the buyer likes you, it makes things much easier.

The salesperson, then, is a key factor in the buyer's decision. Personalities and personal interaction can either abet or hamper getting business and growing customer relations. Before you sell anything to the customer, you have to make the first sale—yourself. They have to like you.

WHY LIKABILITY WORKS

Emotions always play a part in our decisions. We try to mitigate any lack of information and misgivings by working with people we like.

1. Information about a purchase is never perfect: When someone buys something, it always involves a leap of faith. Irrespective of how many meetings they attend or demos they watch, they never have perfect information to buy.

2. Mutual liking: People tend to better like those who like them. They feel better about themselves and enjoy the company of those who give them positive feelings.

3. Support: When customers like you, they are more optimistic about getting support after the sale that they might need if anything does not work out the way it should.

4. Elevating effect: We feel elevated in the company of people we like. Likable people elevate others by sharing credit and enjoying the success of others. That is why people feel relaxed in the company of the people they like.

BENEFITS OF LIKABILITY

Here are some of the advantages when your customer likes you.

1. Discovering needs is easier: When a buyer likes you, they are more likely to share information. That makes it easier for you to probe deeply and ask challenging questions.

2. The buyer takes your expertise seriously: Likability fosters trust and the buyer will accord more credibility to your insights. When buyers take you seriously, they are more willing to take your advice and buy into your ideas.

3. Access to the buyer is easier: People are likelier to say yes to meeting people they like. Therefore, it becomes easier for you to get meetings. In today's world of information parity, buyers have more resources, information, and options than ever before. Therefore, personal access to a buyer is a distinct advantage for a salesperson.

4. Referrals: When buyers like you, they are more willing to introduce you to others in your target market and to provide referrals to their network.

5. More room to negotiate on price: Buyers are often willing to pay a premium to work with suppliers they like.

HOW DO YOU BECOME MORE LIKABLE?

Likability is not a fixed or inborn thing that we cannot control. Instead, we all have the ability to become more likable. Here are a few suggestions on how you can increase your likability.

1. Nurture positive personality traits: The best qualities in a person will vary, based on who is assessing or being assessed. But there is no denying that there are certain qualities that are common across the board. Be enthusiastic in what you do. Smile. Learn to be patient. Be happy; everyone likes happy people. Be interested in others. Ignore the negative. Be flexible in your thinking.

We have already discussed a salesperson's best quality traits at length. We can all work to develop positive character traits. There is a simple, three-step process to assimilate a new positive trait into your life: First, notice what you want to change or learn. Second, decide on one positive character trait to focus on building. Finally, practice it. Be aware of your thoughts and behavior as you move throughout the day. Act according to your new choice and guard against slipping back into old habits.

2. Do your homework: Do your research before meeting the customer; learn everything you can about them. When a customer sees that you have done thorough homework, they will feel more comfortable with your professional knowledge and will take you more seriously. The more you know about a customer, the better you can help them out. Research each customer thoroughly, and when you meet, ask questions that deepen your understanding.

3. Focus on the buyer: A sales call is not for blabbering on about yourself. It is for listening to your prospect and asking questions to fully understand their needs. Instead of delivering a canned pitch, look for an enriching interaction with the buyer to learn how you can address their problems.

A focus on the customer and empathy for their needs, backed with good judgment and agility, will go a long way in ensuring your success as a salesperson. Get as close as you can to the market and customer. Have the discipline to stay focused on your key target prospects and informed about their needs. Align your behavior with your goals for engagement and penetration of your targeted customers.

To fashion a deep-rooted relationship with your customers, show them how your corporate strategy interconnects with theirs. Instead of just selling your product or service, sell them on the idea that you can help them sell to their own customers.

4. Listen more, talk less: Do not try to control the conversation by talking too much. Master the art of listening—listen to learn and listen to ask. When you listen and learn about people, you can ask them intelligent questions to inspire them into giving more information that you need. Be patient when they are talking about their favorite subject—themselves.

Ask them questions about themselves. Where you lose them is by not sharing the stage. Even when they are nodding and smiling, most people know what you are up to. They know when you are interested and when you are trying to impress. They know when you are trying to solve their problem and when you are just trying to push a sale. If you really want to build a relationship and get your customer to like you, do it by talking less and listening more.

5. Keep your word: Make sure you deliver on any promise you make to the customer—be it making a follow-up call, sending more information, or making an introduction. As a salesperson you are working to create a belief in you that has lasting value for your customers. That is why successful sales professionals keep their word, no matter how difficult or problematic some promises are to keep.

6. Find common ground: Commonality builds friendships. When we find things in common, we tend to like each other more. The more unique a commonality is, the more it is likely to click. For example, two owners of dogs of a very rare breed share a more resounding commonality than two owners of German shepherds.

The sale process is likely to flow more smoothly when your customer learns that they have something in common with you. So, part of your job early on is to learn something about your customer that you have in common and talk about it briefly to demonstrate that commonality.

7. Think win-win: Win-win selling is about designing a relationship that is highly beneficial to both the buyer and the seller. Healthy relationships must have balance. The best relationships are those in which both parties share the benefits. Asking a customer for help can also deepen your relationship.

Win-win selling is not always about dropping the price. It is about understanding your customer's needs, solving those needs, keeping your word, and ensuring a decent ROI for both parties. Typical win-win relationships in business have a spirit of partnership, where two companies buy from each other and refer business to each other regularly.

In order to build a win-win perspective, you have to understand your customer's goals and how they measure those goals. Use follow-up questions to gain clarity. Unless you understand your customer's goals well, you cannot really help them change course in their own interest. Be genuine and maintain a helpful, positive attitude.

Win-win selling is about your customer as much as it is about you. When you focus your sales approach on helping your customer win, you position yourself to win at the same time. Instead of explaining your product or service first up, say you might be able to help and then ask the customer to elucidate their needs first. Sell only when you have the right solution. A win-win approach is to position yourself in selling so that they feel good long after the transaction.

8. Maintain contact: The "mere exposure effect," or the "familiarity principle," is a psychological phenomenon by which people tend to develop a preference for people or things simply because they are familiar. Just because we see a stranger occasionally does not make them any more trustworthy—we just feel like they are because we are familiar with them. Stay top of mind with a customer by staying in touch with a certain frequency.

If you neglect a customer who trusts you as a salesperson and as a company, that customer may be won over by a competitor who perhaps calls regularly to get their business. So, make sure you keep regular contact with your customer relationships. Make sure they have several methods available to reach you.

Keep multiple communication channels open. Pick up the phone and enquire after their wellbeing from time to time. Call on them in person. Write a business blog. Send regular newsletters about the industry, case studies, or your work. Leave comments on their blogs. Connect on Twitter, Facebook, LinkedIn, and so on. Take every real opportunity to thank them. Send out greetings and giveaways.

9. Mirror the buyer's communication style: Match how your customer communicates. If they speak slowly, talk slowly. If they like using examples, respond with examples.

Do not undervalue the influence of communication styles on selling. A style that works well for selling to one customer can cause a deadlock with another.

Look at things from the customer's perspective and match your sales approach with the way they like to be sold to. Know your own negotiating style as well as your prospect's preferred style, and use this knowledge to build a stronger relationship. Know when you need to be flexible. Mindfully adapt your communication and behavior to help the prospect feel more comfortable.

10. Nurture a sense of humor: Humor is a great leveler. The ability to make people laugh or to laugh at their jokes makes you more likable. A self-deprecating sense of humor is a key that unlocks many doors, likability being one of them. When in doubt, do not make a joke about the other person. Instead, make jokes about yourself. Do not take yourself too seriously.

When you use humor, you encourage your customers to warm up. Humor shows you are friendly, creative, and intelligent, and that makes you vulnerable. Being vulnerable often makes us more endearing, and you can also cart off some of the vulnerability the customer feels. Humor levels the playing field to help people be fully present, feel comfortable, and focus on finding a solution with you.

The latest brain research reasserts that genuine humor lights up multiple areas of the brain. Our frontal lobe processes the information, and that information travels as an electrical wave through the cerebral cortex. Laughter supplies dopamine and endorphins, which make us feel good, relaxed, and inspired to accomplish tasks. So, use self-effacing humor to appear humble and consider humor as a tool to build strong relationships. The more they laugh with you, the more they are likely to like you and buy from you.

However, as a salesperson, be mindful of the fine line between being funny and being offensive. Stay away from sensitive topics—avoid any racist, sexist, or religious jokes. Sarcasm is also out of bounds. Salespeople are not supposed to be sarcastic.

11. Be humble and well-mannered: Being respectful and polite enhances your likability. Good manners will get you a lot further than you might think. Be genuinely humble; it is okay to be imperfect. Do not try to impress anyone. Get sincerely interested in your customer—their life, passions, goals, and all that they share with you. Remember the important details. Be kind; kindness is not the same as niceness, it means having empathy for others. Be constructive, and not critical, in your feedback and comments. Acknowledge kindness and express gratitude. Do not come across as a whiner.

12. Be authentic: A fake smile plastered across your face or an inflated sense of self-importance will not endear you to people. Authenticity does. Be yourself. It takes tremendous ego strength to be authentic; become comfortable with authenticity. Look in earnest to find a solution rather than selling. Where possible, try to sit next to the customer instead of across from them.

Selling on Value

"Price is what you pay. Value is what you get."
Warren Buffett

Value is a highly overused, and often misused, term in business and pricing. For instance, "value pricing" is frequently misused to mean low or bargain prices. The real definition of value is the surplus of the benefits a customer receives from a solution over the price they pay for it. Customers do not buy solely on low price. They buy according to customer value.

Customer value equals the customer's perception of benefits minus the customer's perception of price. So, the higher the excess of the perceived benefit over the perceived price of a product or service, the higher the customer's perception of value and the greater the likelihood that they will choose that product. Hence, a business and its salespeople must understand the customer-perceived benefits that drive customer choice. The key to adding value consists in gaining a clear understanding of the factors that drive that choice and of their relative importance.

Great salespeople sell on value and not on price. People are willing to pay more for a product or a service if they attach a special value to it. Selling on value, not price, requires a blend of expertise, quality, confidence, personal rapport, and a thorough understanding of the customer's need. It has become more challenging as technology gives consumers easy access to information about price, specifications, and competition. In value selling you do not sell your offering; you sell the outcome the customer is looking for.

When you do not focus on value, the only thing you sell on is price. The objective of focusing on value is to take price out of the equation as much as possible. Selling on value rather than selling on price will also get you a more loyal cadre of customers—ones less likely to dump you the moment they come across a lower price. Differentiate your offering on results and ROI.

HOW TO SELL ON VALUE

Here are some suggestions about how to make your solution stand out in a world of ubiquitous information.

1. Choose your target market carefully: Narrow down your target market to who your product or service is meant for. That will help you focus on customers who are good candidates to meet your price benchmarking, instead of wasting your time talking to customers who want to buy solely on price. The right target market will be receptive to hearing why they should pay more for your proposition over the competition's. Deselect customers or segments that will not provide you with the margin you require. Identifying the target market is a vital step in the development of products and services, and the marketing efforts to promote them. Here are some steps you can use in determining your target market:

Analyze your offering. Define the features of your product or service. Identify the benefits each feature provides. Identify the industries, businesses, and people that those benefits serve. Focus on your primary value proposition.

Identify the problems that you can solve. Start with the end result you want to create. Understand clearly the problems that your product or service solves. Once you know that, you can identify who is likely to benefit from these solutions. Define what outcomes you provide to your customers.

Study the competition. Which customers are your competitors targeting? What can be your niche?

Decide on target market criteria. Refine your target market by employing qualitative and quantitative criteria to define which players in the target market are the right fit for you. These criteria can include management experience, shareholding, industry, location, size, profitability, and so on.

Evaluate your target market. Make sure that your target market has the critical mass to be of interest to you. If it is too small, you might need to revisit your criteria. Understand what drives your target market's need for your offering and their decision to purchase it. Consider how they can best be approached.

2. Identify your customer's problem: Fully understand the scope and nature of your prospect's problem before rushing in to propose a solution. When the customer feels you have a thorough understanding of their problem and are the right fit, they will be happy to pay you to solve it.

Albert Einstein is reported to have said, "If I were given one hour to save the planet, I would spend 59 minutes defining the problem and one minute resolving it." Probably not Einstein's, but still, wise words. Unfortunately, not everybody heeds them. Many businesses are not adequately rigorous in defining the problems they are endeavoring to solve and articulating why those issues are important. The result is wasted resources, missed opportunities, or both.

I am sure you have seen a sales team deliver an apparently great solution only to find out that it addressed the wrong problem. Salespeople need to ask the right questions so that they can address the right problem. Ask questions until you get to the root cause of a problem. Here are some questions or steps that may be useful:

What is the basic need? Try to articulate the problem in the simplest terms, clearly and succinctly. Focus on the need at the heart of the problem instead of jumping to a solution. Define the scope of the need.

Is the problem actually many problems? Drill down to root causes. Break complex issues into separate elements.

What is the desired outcome? Understand the perspective of the customer and other stakeholders. Address this question both quantitatively and qualitatively. Define a high-level but specific goal.

Is this the right fit for us? Consider why your organization should attempt to solve this problem. Is it aligned with your strategy? Also consider whether the problem fits with your firm's priorities.

Who stands to benefit, what benefits does the customer desire, and how will they be measured? For whom in your customer's organization are you solving the problem? The definitions of success from different perspectives may vary considerably. Consider how the customer will evaluate the solutions they receive.

What approaches has the customer tried? It is crucial to understand why the competition or the market has failed to address the need. Examining past efforts to find a solution can save time and resources and stimulate innovative thinking.

What requirements must a solution meet? Think about the resources a solution might require, and what resources your organization is prepared to dedicate to assessing solutions and then implementing the best one. Consider who in your organization will be responsible for the solution's successful implementation.

What are the internal and external limitations? It is time to re-examine the matter of resources and organizational commitment. Do you have the necessary support, resources, and expertise? Also consider external constraints such as legal issues or regulatory or environmental constraints.

Finally, write down a problem statement. Your problem statement is the bedrock of the proposal that you will make to the customer. Describe the problem you are seeking to solve, what a viable solution would be, and what resources would be required to achieve it. A full, clear description is particularly important in the case of complex problems whose solutions often involve experts in other fields. In such cases a problem statement must be extremely specific without being unnecessarily technical.

3. Sell outcomes and not features: Focus on the outcome your offering achieves for the customer. People will buy based on the outcome to them rather than the features of your product or service. Firms that used to sell athletic wear now sell dreams of success or better wellbeing; perfume companies sell romance, sophistication, or both; drill-machine manufacturers sell the impeccable hole in the wall. Companies do not sell televisions; they sell family closeness or enjoyment on game day.

Consumers' emotions resonate with these outcomes far more than with the actual products.

A buyer of industrial equipment might require reduced labor charges; a buyer of financial services technology may actually be looking to ensure enhanced efficiency. Selling enterprises know to quantify the economic value of these outcomes, and their sales teams communicate that value to the buyer. Good salespeople sell outcomes rather than products or services and their features.

Features and benefits are important, but they are focused on your product or service and not on the customer—their problems, their goals, their desires, and their imperatives for ROI. Becoming an outcome-centric organization requires a business to design every major function to define, produce, and sell value propositions tailored to deliver an outcome.

As a salesperson, you must know the customer well enough to understand the specific outcome they seek. Business intelligence is a strong competency in a company focused on outcomes. In an outcome-centric sales ecology, salespeople help their organization collate and analyze customer data to identify and make improvements.

Today, simply explaining the details of your product and service capabilities is not of much value. The customer already knows most of that through the internet. Instead, the customer expects you to proffer a specific perspective based on your expertise and industry know-how and then explain how your offering can improve their business results. They want you to help them quantify outcomes.

To focus on outcomes, you need to see the situation from your customer's eyes and think like them. This is the outlook you must employ in your customer interactions to focus on the business value your solution delivers.

4. Differentiate your offering: Customers are often willing to pay a premium for solutions that provide an edge. Those same customers will push you to sell below market price if you cannot distinguish yourself from providers with similar, commoditized business solutions. Selling coffee is a commodity; Starbucks made it into "The Coffee Experience Journey." Careful positioning and changing the market perception along with top-quality salesmanship can turn a highly commoditized product into a sought-after brand—thus differentiating a non-differentiated product.

If you are unable to make your offering distinctive, you will compete only on price. It is important to find something unique to your product or service that customers value. Know your strengths and communicate them to your target audience in a way that gets them to notice you above others. Incorporate your differentiation into your messages everywhere. Here are some ways to differentiate your offering:

Focus on one thing. One method of differentiation is to focus on one aspect of your product or service and make it the best in the market. Focus on one thing you think others are not doing well, or not doing at all, and demonstrate how you are bucking the trend. Show how you stand out from similar companies.

Use customer feedback. Look for what customers say and determine the strengths and weaknesses of each competitor. Then use your creativity to differentiate based on the solutions customers are seeking.

Espouse a core value. For example, be the only one that employs solely green technology. Find and champion a value—environment, health, charity, education—that your customers will identify with. Understand the difference between selling the "what and how" and selling the "why." Ask yourself why your company does what it does to serve its customers. Why are your values better than those of your competitors?

Make your packaging or presentation stand out. Ask yourself if there is a way to alter your packaging or presentation to make your offering stand out from the competition. For example, while so many of their competitors are selling their product in a bottle, Pet Naturals of Vermont decided to package theirs in a bag. Not only did it make them look different from their competition, but it also comes across as more biodegradable and eco-friendly.

Add a simple element. Where possible, you may be able to differentiate your offering by adding one feature or ingredient. A simple addition can sometimes be a great contrast from others.

Expose the competition's weaknesses. Keep an eye on your competition's customer reviews. See if you can find any consistent weakness in their offering that you can capitalize on.

Narrow your target market. Differentiate yourself by specializing in a specific customer niche, being the best to provide a solution to their unique situation.

Offer superior processes. Offer a guarantee or a refund policy or a bonus. Ensure superior customer service. Make your delivery better and faster. Offer larger coverage, quicker access, and greater ease of ordering.

Be known as a specialist. Build a reputation as an expert in your field through books, media, training, and so on. Use your expertise as the foundation upon which to build your capacity to create value for others. Remember, in today's world you are a bigger part of the sale than at any time before; your customers are, more than ever, buying you.

Offer price differentiation. The value of your offering is subjective. Offer every customer a different price by targeting each segment with a differentiated product or service at a price they are willing to pay.

5. Understand the buyer's emotions: Even though large corporate customers are inclined to be less whimsical than smaller consumers, emotions play a huge part in all purchase decisions. Risk aversion, respect, a future together, and patriotism can weigh heavily even on large, impersonal buyers. They represent an emotional need for reassurance that the seller shares similar values and that the buyer is making the right decision. Survey after survey shows the relationship with the account manager as one of the main drivers of both supplier choice and customer satisfaction.

Despite millions of years of evolution and the development of abstract thought and critical thinking, we still rely heavily on our emotions when making decisions. Our decision to buy is largely influenced by one of the more primal brain areas, the amygdala. Therefore, as a salesperson, you need to be good at connecting emotionally with customers. As Benjamin Franklin said, "If you would persuade, appeal to interest and not to reason."

A professor of neuroscience at the University of Southern California and the author of *Descartes' Error*, Antonio Damasio says that emotion is required in almost all decisions. Damasio performed research on people with emotional loss, but whose thinking areas of the brain were unaffected. These people were able to process information and think critically, but they found it very challenging to make decisions because they lacked any sense of how they felt about their choices. While they were able to describe what they ought to do and why, they found it difficult to arrive at a final choice even in simple decisions like what to eat.

It has been studied over and over. Tests using fMRI show that when people evaluate buying options, their limbic systems light up, whereas the data processing and analyzing parts of their brain remain quite unstimulated. Emotions are unique to each stakeholder. Emotions unrelated to the decision, called "incidental emotions," also play a role in buying. Studies reveal that positive emotions toward a brand have far greater influence on customer loyalty than trust and other judgments based on a brand's characteristics.

Emotions that play a role in buying decisions are influenced by one of the two main drivers—fear of loss and motivation for gain. To identify which of these two drivers dictates a situation you must be familiar with the set of facts, effects, and situations that contribute to the decision to buy or not. These buying factors are interrelated and continue to evolve through the customer's buying journey. These are some of the buying factors:

The case for change. The customer needs to be certain that they have a valid business case to support their buying decision. The case for change is fueled by a problem or an opportunity that warrants a change. Help the customer compare their options and evaluate value versus risk. Fear often suppresses the desire for change.

Stakeholder buy-in. The buyer has to get their own stakeholders committed. Identify the different stakeholders involved, their differing needs, and the power structure in which they operate.

Buying process. Varying priorities and timelines might pull different stakeholders in different directions. You must know how to manage this process.

Dislike of disappointment. Fear of regret is a powerful inhibition. Psychological studies have found that the fear of regret is often more powerful than the odds for regret in a situation.

Sunk cost fallacy. This happens when a buying decision necessitates accepting that the money previously spent has been lost.

Choice overkill. Excess of choice can be a burden for the customer's attention, especially as they have other job responsibilities too. Try to limit the choices for your customer. Simplicity sells.

Comfort zone. After a while we tend to become comfortable with the status quo. Upsetting the status quo can be stressful. You must know how to move customers frozen by the status quo forward.

6. Be a storyteller: To buy for outcomes, customers require a persuasive, complex, and multilayered proposal encompassing benefits, features, products, and services, as well as emotional satisfaction. Salespeople need to interweave these elements of the proposal together seamlessly in order to make the outcome look plausible and compelling. The same gripping story must be told to different parties involved in decision-making in a way that engages each of them. Touch the hot buttons of both the technical buyer and the commercial buyer, while preserving coherence from start to finish. Rather than attacking customers with a price/quality message, indulge in storytelling to clearly communicate complex proposals to multi-part decision-making units. Flexibly package critical information into storytelling.

Good salespeople make their point through stories and anecdotes that the prospect can relate to. Build your story collection and have a pool of anecdotes that you can draw upon in any situation. The timing of a story is important for it to be effective; a misplaced story could seem forced and awkward.

7. Go for the highest decision maker possible: Before selling on value, gain a thorough understanding of the customer's decision-making unit and determine the most senior person who will place value on the offering. Targeting high enhances the likelihood of making a sale, particularly a large sale. Decision makers in strategic positions are most likely to think strategically about the offering and see value in it.

Do everything in your power to get access to the decision makers. Do not rely solely on your contacts in the organization; take charge of moving the deal forward. It is your responsibility to make the sale happen, and you have to be proactive. No one can do it as well as you can. The most efficient way of communicating the value of your product or service is by talking to the real decision maker.

In order to develop connections with the most senior people in your target companies, you need to connect with them before you sell to them.

Find a suitable way to do it, depending on the situation. Here are some examples:

- Interview them as a guest journalist for a newsletter or publication.
- Seek their advice on some important industry matter, like a new regulation.
- Ask them to participate in a panel discussion.
- Share your research with them.
- Ask them to contribute an article to a publication.

The real decision maker is typically the person who allocates the budget and approves the expense. Decision makers are interested in how your product will help the company increase market share and achieve its long-term goals. When selling to them, sell the big picture and be sure to demonstrate the ROI.

8. Forget about selling: Do not appear eager to sell from the very first conversation. Just talk and listen and ask the right the questions to understand their problem and determine that you are the right fit. There is a lot of clamor in the market over fad terms like solution-selling, strategic-selling, and social-selling. The truth is every time you act purely in your own interests, you erode trust. If you can approach every interaction with your customers with the aim of trying to provide value, by helping them and leaving your interests back at your office, then you are a long way down the road to selling on value.

9. Educate to elevate: Educate your customer beyond what your competition provides. Your buyer will quickly begin to see the value-add of having you as a growth partner. Focus on adding value to the relationship first, before looking to sell.

Value-based selling involves educating customers on many subjects such as technology, case studies, the marketplace, industry information, and competitive analysis. The process leads to perfect solutions based on the customer's needs, challenges, and goals. As Russian playwright Anton Chekhov said, "Knowledge is of no value unless you put it into practice."

Buyers increasingly expect to be educated and not sold to. They use the internet to glean most of the basic information and have their own questions based on that research. Forget about what you want them to buy; instead, focus on understanding what your customer is looking for. Help facilitate an educated decision, instead of presenting features and benefits.

Educating your audience is a non-intrusive way to get your messages across and create a perception of value in your offering. Apple is an example of a business that has focused on educating its customers and has prospered substantially in the bargain. Apple stores have a variety of products that visitors can try, and employees are constantly moving around to educate potential buyers about how the product on display works.

Apple has some of the most ardent customer evangelists in the world. No wonder, love them or hate them, that Apple is the company that others in the industry seem to be measured against. And you do not have to be a tech genius to do so. Amazon is another such company, with a much easier to understand business. There are ample examples to show that the more knowledgeable and empowered customers are, the more fulfilled and confident they are with their choices.

10. Ascertain what constitutes value: Sales teams often operate under the delusion that product quality and price are all that matter, conduct no systematic research into customer requirements, and may even fail to consider that customer needs change over time. Before you rave to your customer about the value you offer, ask the right questions to understand what represents value to them. Then tell them how you will add value to solve their problem. They will then see your solution as relevant, interesting, and of value.

An understanding of customer drivers is becoming more and more important, as customers increasingly have more choices than before. To win in the market, a business needs to find the means to capture customer needs, to measure how well it is fulfilling those needs compared to the competition, and to have an effective action plan founded on what customers value.

Only when you know what customers value can you deliver this value better than the competition. Ask your target customers what they value, find out how they rate the value you deliver compared to the competition, and use your understanding of the customer drivers to forge and present the right value proposition to the right customer at the right time.

11. Add value in your conversation: When the conversations you have with your prospect include value, they will feel happy talking to you and be amenable to more conversations. Adding clarity to their thinking and providing them with useful information is a great way of bringing value to the conversation. Start off by adding to customer's knowledge and perspective. From there you can build trust and go to a solution when you sense the customer is ready to spend money to solve their problem.

As commerce in general moves online, only salespeople who add value and act as a strategic partner will remain important. Their success will be buoyed by the strength of their customer relationships—built over shared successes from season to season and solution to solution. The emotional element and persuasive power of a person-to-person conversation that brings value still has an edge over the digital experience.

To be successful in personal selling, you have to be good at the art of conversation. Having engaging sales conversations, however, requires skill and practice. Here are some things that might help you have conversations that add value for your customers:

There is no single prototype. There is no one formula for becoming a great sales conversationalist. You do not need to have the "gift of the gab." A good conversation consists in two-way spontaneity. Do not get stuck on transmitting a set message; keep your prospect involved by asking good questions, actively listening to what they say, and responding suitably.

Be relaxed. Do not try to impress. Put yourself in the other person's shoes. The last thing they want you to do is to try to impress them and force your product or service upon them. Start gently, find some common ground, ask a question, encourage a response, and steer the conversation around to proceed in the direction you desire.

Reflect your customer. Connect with the other person's energy and pace. Match their style of communication. You will build a better conversation when they feel you are on their wavelength.

Show genuine interest in them. Be genuinely interested in understanding what they value. The more you understand what they place value on, the better you will be able to guide the conversation.

Tell real stories. Use stories to inspire and persuade and to add value. Real stories of how you added value in similar cases, woven into a genuine conversation, are more powerful than any data.

Show passion. Let others see your passion and your belief. Demonstrating that you find true pleasure in adding value is the quickest way to form a connection that the customer will resonate with when the conversation deepens.

Exhibit trust. Trust in the value of what you offer and show it. Sincere confidence is contagious.

12. Quantify your value and the customer's ROI: Where possible, show the prospect the economic benefit of your value. For example, their product gets better to command a higher price, your solution brings increased revenue, they save money because of higher efficiency, they save money because of the longer life of your offering, your offering is less expensive to use, and so on. The key to value selling is driving the discussion away from the transaction price. In addition to articulating the outcomes and benefits of the offering, also talk about ROI. Most business purchases are made with ROI in mind. Communicate your offering in terms of quantifiable units and, wherever possible, in financial terms. And be absolutely credible in doing so.

Quantifying your value involves communicating a lucid, persuasive picture of how your solution will drive business results for the customer. Translate the benefits of your solution into measurable outcomes. Demonstrate the competitive advantages that distinguish you from your competition. Here are some fundamentals for quantifying the value your solution brings to a customer:

Sell the idea first. Even a great set of numbers may not serve the purpose if you do not first establish a foundational level of understanding of your solution and a high level of trust. This will prevent your quantitative analysis from being viewed as a selling ploy and, thus, being discounted.

Identify value drivers. Identify what really drives value for the customer by reducing costs, enhancing revenues, or offering an intangible benefit. Sometimes, a customer may not even know they have this need, but by linking it directly to your value, you can convince them that they do. These are some of the value drivers you can quantify:

- Salary or HR cost savings
- Savings because of improved processes

- Savings brought in by superior efficiency
- Risk avoidance
- Increase in market share
- Increase in price or margin
- Gains in productivity
- New revenue streams
- Higher creativity
- Superior integration
- Improvement in cashflow

Identify how your solution ties in with those drivers to create value. Explain your solution's benefits to the customer and compare them with the benefits in the next best solution they have identified.

Understand the customer metrics. Fully understand the metrics that will demonstrate the impact of the business outcomes your solution will enable the customer to achieve.

Take into account the knock-on effect. Often in addition to the primary benefit of the solution, there are ancillary benefits. These might occur in a different department, for an alternative set of players in the organization, or in a different timeframe. Make sure that you have uncovered and quantified the payoffs of the knock-on effect.

Develop a value algorithm. Correlate the value you are offering the customer to numbers that can be readily analyzed and calculated in dollars. Highlight the quantifiable facets of your customer's operations, and the status quo, that impact the value drivers you have identified.

Estimate the dollar value. Show the estimate of the dollar amount your solution would put in the customer's pocket in a certain timeframe.

Keep your message simple and uncluttered. Do not bury the impact in complex detail. Identify the most compelling anchors. First mention the final figures before taking the customer through calculations. Be verifiable and quote only from authentic sources.

13. Present social proof: Customer testimonials, scientific data, market research, case studies, and product reviews are all great ways to prove your value. Testimonials that tell a story of someone in your prospect's situation who benefited from having your product or service are a highly effective social proof. Where possible, you can arrange for your prospect to speak with one of your current customers, preferably someone in a similar industry or life situation as your prospect.

14. Offer a trial before sale: An effective way to diminish your prospect's perception of risk and to provide concrete proof of your solution's value is to give them a chance to try your offering before purchasing it. If the nature of your offering makes a free trial difficult, see if you can make a demo.

15. Offer a guarantee: Customers value reducing the risks they incur, and some form of money-back guarantee or service-level agreement that reduces risk is the obvious expression of a value proposition. When you are confident of the quality of your product, find ways to offer warranties to reduce the customer's perception of risk. A post-sale maintenance service can also help.

Whatever guarantee you choose to offer should do four things: It should comfort your customer that you are completely confident of the quality of your offering. It should clearly explain your terms and conditions. It should specify a time period for its validity. And it should unambiguously state the action you will take if the guarantee is invoked.

16. Highlight the personal benefit: It is important to remember that, regardless of what you sell, you are still dealing with people who are making a decision on what to buy and from whom. Understand how your solution will help the buyer in achieving their own goals or enhancing their personal performance within their company. This appeals to the buyer's emotions. It can be done in a number of ways; your solution can make them look better in the eyes of their bosses, it can increase their productivity, it can add to their achievements, it can boost their confidence or happiness, and so on.

17. Do not bargain: You cannot expect to sell on value if you keep succumbing to attempts to bargain. Readiness to bargain on price diminishes the perceived value of your offering in the customer's eyes. For example, if you are a service provider, bargaining on hourly rates surely detracts from the value of your proposition. Value selling is effective when a compelling package of benefits is conveyed. Deconstructing this package into its constituent parts decreases the coherence of the offer and eliminates the synergies achieved by putting together a package of complementary benefits. Losing these synergies diminishes the value in the eyes of the potential customer.

In order to sell on value, stop training buyers that price concessions are obtainable on demand. Show confidence that what you are doing is delivering value, and sell that way. This requires selling right through the sales cycle, not presenting and bargaining. For example, Apple does not bargain; you pay what is on the ticket. Sales are at their discretion, not on demand. The company's approach has trained its buyers to pay the stated price.

Selling to The Old Brain

"When dealing with people, remember you are not dealing with creatures of logic, but with creatures of emotion."
Dale Carnegie

Successful salespeople know that they are not selling to robots that logically process and rationally justify everything, and have no capacity for emotion. Prospects are human. Your prospective buyers make decisions to change and buy based on emotion, while justifying them with facts. The real decision maker is not the person; it is an organ—the brain. We see and experience the world as the brain interprets it. It is 2% of our body mass but it still burns up 20% of our energy. You are really speaking to people's brains, not to them.

The brain is divided into three primary areas. The neocortex is the brain's newest part. It is the brain's analytical computer, which processes data. It is the slowest part of the brain. It can read or see, but it does not understand what it is reading or seeing. This is "system two," as described by Nobel laureate Daniel Kahneman. It is slow but clever, has an on/off facet, comprehends and deals in past, present, and future, entails attention, makes effort, and is aware and manageable. We could not speak or operate our bodies in the way we do without this lobe.

The middle brain is the emotional brain, also known as the "mammalian brain" or the "limbic brain." The limbic system in the middle part is where all emotions reside.

The brain stem and other brain structures are responsible for our survival. This part of the brain is described as the "old brain" or the "reptilian brain." Evolution has programmed the old brain to rapidly assess conditions to establish if we are at risk or in danger. When it senses danger to our wellbeing, it triggers a reaction to save us from the potential threat. According to Kahneman, this is "system one." This part of the brain is fast but limited. It operates in immediate experience and only functions in the now; it does not know or understand the past, present, or future. It is always on and is automatic, effortless, unconscious, and uncontrollable—because it cannot be controlled. It prefers certainty to uncertainty. System one has a dominance on our ability to come to a different decision. Our old brain chooses what we notice and what merits our attention. The old brain decides—it takes input from both systems and makes the call. Whenever there is a conflict between the two systems, system one will always win. Therefore, in order to sell, you have to appeal to your prospect's old brain.

HOW TO SELL TO THE OLD BRAIN

The author and motivational speaker Zig Ziglar said, "Selling is essentially a transfer of feelings." The old brain is where our feelings reside. Here are a few suggestions for reaching out to the old brain while you are selling.

1. Be visual: Language is a new development in the evolution of the brain. Hence, when you try to influence people's decisions with language and logic, you are selling to the new brain and not the final decision maker. The old brain is visual. Out of all the senses, the old brain responds most strongly to the visual sense. Almost half of our brain's resources are deployed in processing what we see; the other half is devoted to everything else. Use big images, videos, and props to make your case to a prospect. Through the old brain, we are hardwired to make decisions that are mostly informed by visual input. By using visual stimuli, you tap into the processing method that the brain has learned over thousands of years.

2. Use contrast: The old brain loves contrast. Use contrast to show your prospect how the change you propose is better than the status quo. The old brain is responsive to clear contrast, such as late/early, heavy/light, bright/dark, fast/slow, in/out, with/without, or risky/safe. This concept is not at all novel. Direct marketers have used it for years. One way, for instance, is to state a comparison with a competitor, typically to show a contrast between a competitor's weakness and your own strength. Success is often determined by your ability to establish the uniqueness of your product or service. Show the contrast and make it easy for the reptilian brain to make the decision.

3. Make strong beginnings and endings: The old brain is powerfully swayed by firsts and lasts; it enjoys openings and endings and often overlooks what is in between. This has huge implications on how to construct and deliver your messages as a seller. The old brain constantly watches out for the unexpected, things that break the pattern that it is used to. Therefore, it always pays attention at the beginning of your message, and it is up to you to take advantage of that. Ending is also an opportunity to close with a grabber. Be direct and make your ending stick. For example, "You have seen that only with us can you get what you really need. So, what is our next step?" Place the most important content at the beginning, and repeat it at the end.

4. Appeal to emotion: The old brain is only triggered by emotion. It uses emotion to remember things that it considers important. Studies show that emotions create electrochemical reactions in our brain. These reactions directly influence the way we treat and remember information. Triggering an emotion makes memories stronger while they are being shaped by the brain. However, in order to have an effect, the nature of emotional persuasion must be contextual to your own audience.

5. Keep it simple: Do not overload your prospect with information or complexity. The old brain does not like to get bogged down by details. Keep your message simple, focus on things that are relevant to your solution for the prospect, and elucidate by using metaphors and analogies.

6. Keep it concrete: The old brain prefers concrete language to abstract notions. If you have no difficulty imagining an orange, it is because you have seen and experienced an orange physically. An abstract idea such as increased productivity or enhanced efficiency is easier to understand when it is demonstrated through tangible figures or case illustration. It is not enough for the prospect to intellectually understand a benefit. Explain it in concrete terms. Get to understanding quickly; make it real so that it can be felt.

7. Personalize: The old brain merely cares about its own survival and is programmed to classify others as either part of its tribe or not. Use "you" in your message as often as possible to stimulate your subject's engagement. Make it personal to show to the customer's old brain that you are a part of its tribe. Think of the old brain as the center of "I," with no patience or empathy for anything that does not immediately concern its own wellbeing and survival. That is why 100% of your message as a seller should focus on your audience, not on you. When you present a feature, the old brain only wants to see a benefit for itself in it.

MISTAKES TO AVOID IN SELLING TO THE OLD BRAIN

Here are some common mistakes that salespeople make that trigger the fight, flight, or freeze mode of the old brain.

1. Always looking to close: A salesperson might ask questions, which they hope will lead to a sale, without caring whether the buyer is ready to buy. Such an approach usually does not result in a sale because the prospect senses they are being rushed and does not feel safe. Rather than hustling the prospect, make them feel in control and able to choose.

2. Being overzealous: If you are selling to a prospect who is a little subdued or quiet, watch and adjust your energy level to that of your prospect. The old brain encourages us to buy from people who are like us and whom we like. After the meeting, try to connect with your prospect on WhatsApp, Twitter, or LinkedIn so that you can continue the conversation on a low-key note—as they might now be comfortable with it.

3. Seeking to conquer objections: Instead of overcoming objections during a sales meeting, paraphrase and bring the objections up. Use an objection to have an objective discussion around the potential challenges of implementing your solution. Your candor builds trust with the prospect and keeps the discussion pleasant and open.

4. Being too logical: We all come across sales emails or messages that are impersonal, robotic, and flat. The old brain is programmed for security and comfort, and is not comfortable opening up to a salesperson who has not instituted a relationship or a connection in the conversation. Do your research to know about your prospect, and then invest some time to build the necessary rapport.

Networking

*"The thing that I learned as a diplomat is that human
relations ultimately make a huge difference."*
Madeleine Albright

Human relations make a huge difference in business, just as they do in diplomacy. Networking is a great way to increase your brand awareness and credibility in the market. Success in any field, but especially in sales, consists in working with people and not against them. Sales is about relationships, though not just with customers. Your long-term success as a salesperson depends on your ability to work together with others. In sales, networking is an essential skill for finding new customers and centers of influence and building a strong pipeline. Bringing the element of face-to-face credibility and trust, it is a beneficial strategy to open doors and build powerful relationships.

Sales is a human enterprise, propelled and controlled by people. Networking is actually a way of seeing the world. Other people and how you relate to them is the common denominator of your work happiness and your life happiness. After decades of experience in sales around the world, I fully believe that connecting is one of the most important sales skills you can learn. And real networking is about finding ways to make other people more successful.

Effective and fulfilling networking draws on two broad psychological processes: differentiation and integration. A self that is only differentiated—not integrated—may attain a huge network, but risks being mired in selfishness. By the same token, a self that is based exclusively on integration will be connected and secure, but may lack individuality. Only when you invest psychic energy in both of these processes, and avoid both selfishness and conformity, are you likely to use networking optimally. Proper networking can make an instance of personal connection more enjoyable, as well as build self-confidence that allows you to develop skills and make significant progress in sales.

When you understand how networking works, you can use it to build business success, create more harmony in your life, and release psychic energy that would otherwise be wasted in tedium and worry. Unless the rest of the world is familiar with how good you are, you are only selling up to a part of your potential. Your sales vocation gives you a perspective in which to employ the purpose and utility of networking. It is so much easier to reach out to your audience when you are tethered to a real community, a community that is both your anchor and your sail.

The very successful salespeople I have seen are not necessarily incredibly talented, educated, or charming. But they generally have a circle of trustworthy, talented, and inspired people upon whom they can call for support and connections.

PROVEN NETWORKING TECHNIQUES

Here are some suggestions for networking effectively.

1. Focus on the target market: Your target market determines who and what kind of people you should be meeting. Find the organizations and activities in which such people are involved. Going to networking events where your target market is not present is a waste of time. You want to mingle with people who are interested in what you bring to the table, in what you have to say.

As we have discussed, a target market is the people or sector you serve best. Hence, first define your target market to develop a focused strategy about where you frequent, what you say, and whom you network with. This ensures the most productive use of your time. Develop a strategic plan, identify the types of people who epitomize your target market, and research networking avenues offering access to these people.

2. Find ways to stand out: When you network in a group frequented by your target market, do not become lost in the group. See how you can be visible. Seek a leadership position, or volunteer for a prominent cause. Become known as someone more important and involved than the many other people that participate in an organization. Here are some suggestions to set yourself apart while networking:

Make personal connections. Effective networking is all about building new relationships, not desperately exchanging business cards with loads of people who will not remember you. Take the time to connect with two or three key people on a personal level. Try having a genuine conversation and make sure you ask questions and listen well. Use any interests and experiences you have in common to deepen the connection. If you know you will meet specific people at an event, do some research on them ahead of time.

Transform connections into relationships. Once you have made a personal connection, continue to foster it. Find a suitable way to follow up your meeting—a thank-you note, a piece relevant to the conversation you had, a referral, and so on. If you can help in some way, be a genuine giver without conveying the impression that you want something in return. Make a point of staying in touch.

Be interested in what they do. A good way to connect with people is to engage with the work they do. People are more willing to engage with you when they feel that you are sincerely interested, and you care about what they do—as their work or their passion.

Exhibit positive body language. Put away your phone, be attentive, and smile. Make eye contact, give the person you meet your complete attention, and do not look around. Stand confidently with your feet pointing toward the person you are talking to and keep your arms open.

Find a way to be memorable. Mention some unique, relatable fact about yourself or your professional career. Think of something unique in your experience or life story.

Be a team player. Networking is a team sport. Show the ability to work and communicate well with others and be a team player in a group, in a club, or at an event.

Practice. Practice your conversation skills and body language in situations where you feel comfortable. That will give you will greater confidence when you network in situations that can make you anxious.

3. Add value: Focus first on how you can help others make the connections they want to make. It will come back to you. Being of service to others, even in small ways, is a great way to connect. Find ways to make yourself of service and people will appreciate you. Start offering something for free to people, such as introductions or ideas for success in their undertakings.

Adding value is a key element in successful relationship building. While it can mean different things to different people or in different contexts, in simplest terms adding value is the commitment to invest in others. When you use your words or deeds to demonstrate that commitment, people see you as an ally in their life. Here are some ways to add value in your network:

Offer encouragement. Take every opportunity to encourage those around you. Wish them luck before an important undertaking. Praise them for their achievements. Offer support when they encounter a setback.

Contribute to their success. Help people succeed in something that they value. Collaborate directly, offer your expertise, or find them the right help. For example, you can share their articles or social media posts with your social network or write a review of their book on Amazon or of their podcast on iTunes.

Be a connector. Find it intrinsically fulfilling to connect people who can add to one another's lives and businesses. Support your own success by creating connections for the people around you to be successful as well.

Be thankful. Show gratitude when it is due; expressing gratitude builds relationships. When someone does something or shares something that is meaningful to you, be sure to express gratitude.

Offer knowledge. One effective way to help those around you is to teach them something or offer guidance. For example, mentoring someone to bring the person closer to their goals. Taking the time to help educate someone in your network in your area of excellence shows that you are investing in others around you.

Make referrals. Refer potential customers to people in your network.

4. Follow up: French philosopher Albert Camus wrote, "Human relationships always help us to carry on because they always presuppose a future." Help build that future. If you connect with someone good, follow up with a kind email or handwritten note expressing gratitude for their time. It will make you memorable. Humility and gratitude are qualities of a successful sales professional. However, do not use this as a license to start sending unsolicited emails. Here are ten suggestions to build on the initial interaction you have had with someone:

Tell them how you will follow up. Will you call them in a few days? Will you share some valuable content? Will you call to set up a one-on-one? Will you connect on social media? Where possible, let the person know how you will follow up. When they are expecting it, that makes it more real for them. You are also more likely to make it a point to follow up because you have already promised.

Give them a call. Take the scenic route and give your new contact a phone call; it is more personal than an email. If you leave a message, keep it brief, remind them of where you met, leave a number to call back, and do remember to thank them.

Send an email. Send a simple email, saying that you enjoyed meeting and, where appropriate, use a point from the conversation to deepen the discussion.

Connect on LinkedIn. If your contact is present on LinkedIn, try to connect with them. Once you are connected on LinkedIn, the platform offers many ways for you to remain in touch with your contacts.

Set up a one-on-one meeting. Ask for a one-on-one meeting, ideally somewhere convenient for the other party. Use the first meeting to further develop your rapport with the person instead of forcing your agenda on them.

Take the opportunity to be of assistance. If during your meeting your contact indicated a need where you can be of help, do so. For example, if they mentioned someone close to them is looking for a job, reach out and pass on some useful connections or information.

Remember birthdays. Facebook and LinkedIn make it easy for you to send birthday wishes to your contacts.

Reach out on important occasions. A surgery? A child? Whenever your contact has an important occasion, reach out and extend your support or good wishes.

Create a database to stay in touch. Create a brief database to remind yourself to connect with your important contacts periodically.

Send a handwritten message. Send your contact a handwritten card or a note. As handwritten notes are becoming rare, people deeply appreciate receiving them.

5. Do not sell: People who brag and boast at networking events stick out like a sore thumb. Do not sell at networking events; they are simply to make connections and find opportunities for your selling activity elsewhere.

Networking is an opportunity to meet new people, establish rapport, and begin to build a relationship. It is not an occasion to talk to people just to sell. The last thing you should be thinking about when attending a networking event is hard selling. The event is an occasion for you to have conversations with other professionals and entrepreneurs and decide how you would want to further some of those conversations after the event.

It is about the quality interactions that you make, not about how many cards you distribute. Spend time determining who among the people you meet are a good fit for you. When you meet such people, develop your relationship by finding out as much as possible about them. Follow up after the meeting and then take it from there.

6. Be a good listener: The easiest way to underline your interest in someone is by listening to them. You can break down walls by hearing what someone else has to say. Always be receptive to people's ideas and stories. Listen carefully and use open-ended questions to draw people out in conversations. The more you listen, the more you will learn about new leads, prospect needs, and changes in your industry or your customers' businesses. Also, the attention and concern you show for others enhances your image as a genuine and trustworthy person.

Think of networking as being a good listener rather than agonizing over what to say. Just stay in the moment and let your interaction be all about the other person. It is just as effective to be interested as to be interesting. Ask questions to learn and to show your interest. If you are joining a conversation, be polite and start by listening.

Most people approach networking events with a view to promote themselves and talk a lot. Therefore, it is not very probable that you can talk your way into win-win relationships. However, if you listen to others and make them feel valued, they are more likely to remember you.

7. Take every opportunity: You do not have to be at a networking meeting or at work to network. Good contacts can happen anywhere: on public transportation, children's school meetings, health clubs, and so on. Be fully present wherever you are, pay attention to those around you, and watch for opportunities to meet people who can help make things happen for you.

The power of networking lies not so much in learning about your own craft as in learning about other people's craft. That makes you more interesting, secure, strategic, and insightful. Be genuinely interested in the people you meet. Take advantage of chance encounters. Air travel, for instance, can offer a good opportunity to make connections.

8. Treat everyone with respect: Great salespeople know that it pays to stay in people's good graces. Show good manners and attention to everyone you meet. When you treat your customers fairly and with respect, they will be more likely to come back and more willing to recommend you to others. Treat your colleagues right and they will be motivated to look after your customers.

As a professional and as a salesperson, your reputation is your most prized possession. Guard it by being upright and respectful in your dealings with everyone. Remember, it is an increasingly small world. No matter who you are, where you live, or what you do for a living, the world that envelopes your existence is much smaller than you think.

One way to genuinely respect others is to see things from their perspective. People feel valued when they sense that you can put yourself in their shoes. Henry Ford is quoted as having said, "If there is any one secret of success, it lies in the ability to get the other person's point of view and see things from that person's angle as well as from your own."

Look for the good in everyone you meet. While it may not always be obvious, everyone offers some value. Remember, nothing in life is equally distributed; everyone has a different journey and they all bring special experiences and wisdom with them. Everyone knows something that you do not and, for that alone, they deserve respect. Respect diversity, difference, and divergence. Give people the benefit of the doubt.

9. Show gratitude: Be genuine and show empathy. Show your gratitude to others by saying thank you and being grateful to those who help you. When someone offers you a referral, useful information, or sincere advice, tell people how they have helped you; everyone likes to feel helpful.

Studies have established that we hear and feel the negative more powerfully than the positive. Therefore, even a small bit of criticism can often overshadow substantial praise. However, we usually tend to give more negative feedback than positive feedback. That is why a disposition that bends toward gratitude is a huge plus in life.

Luckily, it is easier to be grateful than to provide any kind of feedback. It costs us nothing and empowers those around us. Do not wait for Thanksgiving; show gratitude throughout the year to those who influence your life. And instill gratitude into your networking.

Increasing your ability to feel and express gratitude is one of the most significant ways you can bolster your network and relationships. How you give and receive that gratitude matters. The key to effective gratitude lies in the details. Be very specific when thanking someone. Describe why you are thanking them and how their deed made a difference for you.

Today there are so many ways to express gratitude or appreciation. Here are some examples:

Thank in person. Make it a point to meet up to personally express your gratitude.

Make a phone call. Just call up and say thank you.

Send a message. Write a handwritten note, an email, a text message, or a WhatsApp message.

Provide a referral. A business referral is the greatest thank you because it helps pay the bills. Make a connection or send a qualified lead.

Share. In your networks share something good that someone has done.

Comment. Leave a comment on a recent post from someone you are grateful to and share it.

Endorse on LinkedIn. Say thanks and endorse people on LinkedIn for the skill that has been of use to you.

Recommend on LinkedIn. Better still, write a recommendation on their LinkedIn profile. This is a powerful way to give thanks.

Make an introduction. There is no better way to thank someone than to provide a good connection.

Send a gift. Give a thoughtful thank-you gift, within the applicable professional norms.

Provide reviews. Write reviews on the social media and websites they use. For example, review their podcast on iTunes or their book on Amazon, review their business on Yelp, Quora, or Reddit, and so on.

Write a testimonial. Write a testimonial that they can use.

10. Pay attention: You can learn so much about someone just by noticing their verbal and nonverbal communication. Make eye contact. Ask questions. Focus on getting to know the other person, even if you only have limited time to talk.

11. Make a good first impression: Most people decide if they like you within the first few seconds. They then spend the rest of the conversation internally justifying their initial reaction. You can take advantage of this by making a strong first impression. Body language is intimately tied to how others perceive you and their first impressions of you. How you hold yourself, your posture, and your facial expressions are cues others will look at to appraise what type of person you are and whether you are approachable and likable. Therefore, how you interact with someone in the first few minutes has a huge bearing on how your relationship with them pans out. Here are some suggestions on making a positive first impression:

Dress appropriately. Dress for the occasion you are attending. Do not wear something or use accessories that make you look out of place.

Be well groomed. Pay attention to your appearance. Make your hair look good and make sure you are clean and smell nice.

Be on time. Do not rely on a "good excuse" for running late; arrive on time.

Manage your body language. Your body language is more important than you might think. Give a good handshake. Make eye contact. Adopt a positive posture and gestures.

Smile. Obvious as it may seem, it is worth repeating here. A genuine and hearty smile goes a long way in creating a good first impression. It will put both you and the other person at ease.

Make a good introduction. Introduce yourself properly to let the other person know what you and your business are all about, without coming across as arrogant or self-promoting.

Intonate your delivery. Make sure to vary your tone and inflection while speaking. How you say it is as important as what you say. Speaking in a monotone may lessen the impact of your words.

Choose your words. For example, trustworthiness matters more than confidence in the first impression. Therefore, it is more important to use words that present you as a trustworthy person than words that project confidence. Do not use unnecessarily complicated words.

Look interested. Settle down and look focused right away instead of appearing to overcome distractions. Do not indulge in just talking about yourself or your business. Make the person feel that you are genuinely interested in them. Ask questions and understand what other people do.

Be yourself. Be natural. Do not pretend to be what you are not. The finest way to create a good first impression is by being your authentic self. Doing this will make you feel more self-assured and help you to build trust and gain respect from the people you meet.

Come prepared. Turn up for the meeting or event prepared. Have some knowledge of who is attending and why. Be prepared with questions that help you learn about others and hold mutually interesting conversations.

Find common ground. Discovering and underlining a similarity with the other person early in the interaction will have a positive impact on the impression you make.

Be positive. Do not come across as a whiner. A positive attitude shines even brighter in the early stages of a human interaction. Project a positive attitude in an upbeat manner.

Make people laugh. If you can introduce laughter early in the interaction, you will engender positive feelings.

Ask for stories and not answers. Elicit stories from people you are meeting. For example, instead of asking "What do you do?" try "What are you working on these days?" Or instead of "Where are you from?" you can ask "What was the town like where you grew up?"

Follow up. Note down significant details while things are still fresh in your head. Follow up as required and promptly.

12. Use names: Remembering names and being able to address people directly will instantly make them feel acknowledged and welcomed. Ask people about themselves. What are their hobbies or passions? Find something that will help lock their name into your memory bank.

Remembering people's names is one of the elementary rules of networking. Dale Carnegie once said, "A person's name is to that person the sweetest and most important sound in any language." The simple act of making the effort to remember someone's name is a subtle way to show that you care. However, much as we try, we often struggle to remember the names of the people we meet. Here are some suggestions for remembering names more easily:

Pay attention to the introduction. Do not treat introductions as a mere formality. Be fully engaged, listen for the name, blank out other distractions, and concentrate on the person to whom you are being introduced. Being fully present and aware at the moment of introduction can make a vast difference in remembering people's names.

Repeat the name in your mind. When you hear someone's name, mentally repeat it to yourself a few times while looking at their face. This enables your brain to establish a connection between the face and the name.

Repeat it in conversation. Repeat a person's name you want to remember as often as appropriate during the conversation or event. One way to do this could be to repeat the name to someone else after the conversation.

Look for patterns. Use the brain's penchant for finding patterns. Play with the sound of the name to see if it rhymes with something that reminds you of the person. For example: Peter, sells heater. Oscar from Ottawa. Mike, loves bike. With every new name you hear, repeat the previous names you have learned while imagining their faces. This also plays into the brain's love for finding patterns and connections.

Learn the spellings. Making sure that you have the correct spelling and pronunciation of someone's name enhances the likelihood that you will remember it. Understanding how a name is spelled or pronounced gives your brain one more connection to save.

Note it down. Write down the name as soon as possible after meeting the person. If pen and paper are not practical, use your phone.

13. Have a connection story: Make yourself memorable by having a story about yourself that gives insight into who you are and what you are about. It will also make others feel comfortable to share their stories with you.

All of us have stories to tell, stories that define us. Every person is a story. To know someone well is to know their story—the life experiences that have forged them into what they are. The story of their childhood, their family, their education years, their career, their love life, their political views, and so on. Telling a compelling story while networking with colleagues, customers, acquaintances, or strangers inspires belief in your motives and your ability.

An effective connection story is not an embellished narrative. Instead it is a sincere account of your life that is deeply true and so engaging that listeners feel they have a stake in your success. Creating and telling a story that can move others also reinforces your self-confidence.

Many people are reluctant to include their stories in their communication because they feel that, in order to be appealing, a story has to have a complex plot. This is not true. In fact, an effective story is a simple one; just narrate where you were, what happened, and what the takeaway is.

Do not make the story any longer than necessary. Prune out superfluous details but give people enough information to visualize the context so they can experience the story and see what you see. Make sure you include dialogue instead of telling the story in the third person. Narrate the actual words the characters spoke. Dialogue infuses life into your story and makes it easier to relate to.

To get better at telling your story, practice it in different ways and places. The content depends on the situation, but the goal is always to make a connection when you tell your story. There is no substitute for practicing in front of a live audience. Tell and retell your story to rework it, like the manuscript of an epic novel. Any context where you are likely to be asked, "What can you tell me about yourself?" or "What are you looking for?" invites you to tell your connection story.

Your stories evolve with time, with the seasons of your life. You have to connect with your reality at a given point in your life. Be self-reflective and ask yourself questions that lead you to a deep understanding of yourself, of who you are and what is important to you. Be mindful of the stories you tell yourself. This will help you bring authenticity to the stories you tell others—stories about your experiences in life, your struggles, your personal transformation, and the lessons you have learned.

The connection story you tell depends on the context, on the message you want to convey. Here are some suggestions for crafting compelling personal stories:

Talk about a difficult moment in your life and how you faced it. Find a challenging time in your life and how you managed to get past those challenges, including your successful and unsuccessful attempts to meet them.

Talk about a moment that transformed your thinking. Find stories in the moments that taught you to think creatively or differently, stories that demonstrate simple life lessons leading to deeper understanding.

Talk about something that transformed your career. Most people's career path is not a straight line. Twists and turns and learnings of a person's career usually make an engaging story.

Talk about how you learned from others. Chances are you have had colleagues or mentors in your career that you have looked up to and learned from. Tell a story about how your career was influenced by a mentor.

Talk about success after failures. Crises or misfortunes often lead to struggle and change in direction. Stories of struggle and eventual redemption have a universal appeal.

Talk about how you have changed. Take a look back at yourself and see how you have changed as a person and as a professional. Explain what triggered those changes, sharing the process you went through as well as the results.

14. Do your homework: Do a little groundwork ahead of time. Thinking through some thought-provoking questions to ask people will help put your mind at ease and keep your conversation moving.

If you are attending an event, find out who else will be attending ahead of time. Some invitations come with a registration list. If the list is not available, try checking the event site. If there are many people, identify who you want to focus on and develop some opening ideas of how you can provide value to them. Once you have an idea of the people you will meet, research their background. Learn a little about who they are—their qualifications, career, current position, or job title. Have they been in the news? If so, read the article or watch the video clip. Find out if they are active on LinkedIn and perhaps already share connections with you. Do they like to post opinions and successes on Facebook?

15. Reveal yourself: If you really want to connect with somebody, try upping the ante and revealing the real you. You do not need to get too personal, but reveal what you are passionate about. People will find you more interesting and memorable if they know more about your experiences and what makes you tick. Most of the time, if you open up, the other person will follow your lead and do the same.

Different people will identify with different parts of you; in order to appeal to more identities, you need to be elastic. Think of yourself as a glitter ball with lots of different faces. When we talk about our identity, we think of faces that are quite evident—color of skin, gender, profession. But you have other faces too; to reveal them, rotate that glitter ball so that people can see different facets of you and likely find a piece of themselves represented in you.

You will not make real connections by being artificial and scripted. You will make them by being yourself. People will remember you and want to stay in touch because you have opened the door to future conversations. To connect deeply, be more personable. Reveal more about yourself and not just to be the persona that is obvious. Do not be afraid to open up to people a little bit and to be vulnerable.

16. Look to learn: Be keen to learn from the person you are meeting with. It will make them feel more important, will strengthen the bond, and may also teach you something useful.

That wise man Ralph Waldo Emerson wrote: "Shall I tell you the secret of the true scholar? It is this: Every man I meet is my master in some point, and in that I learn of him." How true. I have never met a person who was not my superior in some way. Learning from everyone around me is a passion that has brought me valuable knowledge.

As you sit down with other people, talking with them and learning their stories, you learn about the world and how other people experience it. You learn to be an entrepreneur through the stories of others' successes and failures. You learn to sell through conversations with prospects about how they work and think and what is important to them.

Dale Carnegie is best known for his work on the basic, yet vital, principles for dealing with people successfully. As a salesman at one point, Carnegie made his sales territory the national leader for the firm he worked for. Even Warren Buffett, one of the most successful investors of the 20th century, took Carnegie's course at age 20. Carnegie's common-sense advice included letting the other person do a great deal of talking to tell you their stories and teach you about the world.

Dale Carnegie also wrote: "You can make more friends in two months by becoming interested in other people than you can in two years by trying to get other people interested in you." Of course, you cannot be genuinely interested in a person unless you are open to learning from what they have to say.

When you want to learn from someone's life, get them to tell you a story, not a quote. It is a lot more powerful to discover how someone learned a lesson than to have them just straight up tell you their conclusion.

As Ralph Waldo Emerson said: "The enthusiast always finds the master, the masters, whom he seeks. Always genius seeks genius, desires nothing so much as to be a pupil and to find those who can lend it aid to perfect itself."

17. Do not judge: Even if you do not agree with someone, do not judge them. Empathize with their approach to life, and then reciprocate by revealing more about yourself.

Brazilian novelist Paulo Coelho wrote: "We can never judge the lives of others, because each person knows only their pain and renunciation. It's one thing to feel that you are on the right path; but it's another to think that yours is the only path."

So, judge less and accept more to be able to connect better and sell. The less judging you do, the better off you are. Here are some reasons why you should not judge other people:

Their journey is different. You do not know all the facts about the other person. Different people's approaches to different contexts are largely influenced by their life's journey. Even in a specific situation, it is important to hold off your judgment until you know all the facts.

They are different from you. Each person is different from the other. Cherish similarities and respect differences. Do not judge people based on your preferences. You have no reason to make others see the world as you do; yours is not the only valid perspective.

Treat people as you would like to be treated. "Do unto others as you would have them do unto you" is a command based on the authority of Jesus. In fact, it is often called the golden rule, and has a parallel in many religious traditions. Instead of judging someone, try placing yourself in their shoes. Ask yourself if you would like to be judged.

Connecting is accepting. You cannot build genuine connections without true acceptance. Learn to be wise and accepting.

Be wary of first impressions. Do not rush into making judgments about people. Such judgments will almost always be based on superficial things like appearance.

When you judge, you define yourself. Author Wayne Dyer says, "When you judge another, you do not define them, you define yourself." How you react to or judge other people will always define you.

18. Do not be self-conscious: Turn off that chatter in your head. Do not seek to impress. It keeps you focused on yourself when you should be trying to learn about the other person and to find common ground.

Business is conducted with people, and building face-to-face relationships is still key. As a salesperson, the better you are able to leverage contacts through networking, the better you are able to sell. Here are some suggestions for overcoming self-consciousness during business networking:

Approach it with a purpose. Being focused on the outcome and not the process helps shift the attention away from the self and quietens the chatter in the mind.

Feed your curiosity. Being curious opens up your mind and takes self-conscious attention off yourself. Approach people, places, and conversations with curiosity to learn and to bring value to them. When you talk to someone, think what you can learn from the person.

Take initiative. Quell the unease and take action; standing self-consciously in a corner will not bring people to you. Make eye contact with a smile and start talking to people. Do not worry about what others might think about you; focus on what you think about them.

Think of what you enjoy. Keep self-consciousness at bay by focusing on what you like about an event or a meeting. Think of the last useful connection you made or the value you can leverage from the person you are talking to. Think what you find endearing about that person.

Take genuine interest in the other person. Forget about yourself. Get interested in what makes the other tick. Discover their passions by asking questions. Listen carefully without thinking about yourself. What about that person is interesting to you?

Consider how you can help. Your desire to help will make you feel more confident and able to add value to the conversation. It will also help other people find you more endearing. Even the smallest of selfless gestures matters. When you are genuinely trying to help someone, you have no time to be self-conscious.

Do not try to impress. Do not try too hard to impress or conjure up something amusing to say. Just smile, be friendly, stay in the moment, and enjoy the proceedings. Ask questions, listen carefully, and show interest in anyone you speak to.

Come prepared. Do some research on the people you are likely to meet. Have discussion points in mind, including questions or stories of interest to share with them. The better prepared you are, the more confident you will feel.

Arrive early. It helps to show up early. When it is a meeting, you can get comfortable with the venue and use the time to rehearse the important things in your mind. If it is an event, it is better to arrive early than to walk into a room already full of people, many of whom might be strangers. It is easier to start a conversation with people you are targeting before they have established themselves in a large group. While there are fewer people, other people are also more likely to approach you.

Act confident. Look the part and act confident and composed, regardless of how you feel inside. If there is alcohol at the event, drink sparingly. You can swig the rest of what you allow yourself to drink when you get home. Above all, do not depend on alcohol to feel composed. If you do, you might begin to do so at every event you attend. Not a good recipe, by any means. Also, drunkenness shows.

Reflect and learn. After each event or meeting, reflect on what worked well and what did not and why. Be positive and learn from your insights for the next time.

TIME MANAGEMENT FOR EFFECTIVE NETWORKING

Meeting people and building relationships can be extremely time consuming, especially in the face of other demands. Here are some ways from my experience to improve your time management while networking.

1. Be discerning: Do not just join any group or attend every event that comes up in an effort to meet as many people as possible. Pick those that connect to your goals. Identify the sources that provide the most productive contacts to you; focus on specific people or certain events. Do some research to determine the optimal networks for your business and focus your efforts there.

2. Target: Be proactive. Identify specific people you want to meet. Use LinkedIn to explore introductions or cold email. Attend events where your target individuals are likely to participate. Try as you may, it is not possible to network with everyone in your niche. Examine your contacts to see who is worth establishing a relationship with. Ask yourself whether or not you are the right fit for each other. Present yourself as a problem solver and not just another name in their address book.

3. Schedule back-to-back meetings: Make your schedule more productive by planning consecutive meetings. This helps divide your time into clear blocks and prevents meetings from running too long. Schedule your meetings in one area so that you do not waste time traveling. I try to hold most of my meetings near where I already am, so I do not waste time commuting. Though I rarely do back-to-back meetings in the exact same location, I try to choose spots near each other for consecutive meetings.

4. Make use of breaks: Schedule meetings during breakfast or over coffee and lunch breaks to make the best use of your breaktime.

5. Meet in groups: Where you have to meet multiple people for the same purpose, try to organize a group meeting.

6. Meet remotely: Where a meeting by phone or video can suffice, it can make the interaction easier and save a lot of time. However, for the first meeting where a main objective is to build a connection, it is always better to meet in person.

7. Leverage: Having a strong online presence, connecting with connectors, and speaking engagements are nice ways of leveraging the time you allocate to networking.

8. Be willing to say no: Do not be afraid to say no where a meeting or a networking event is not a good use of your time. The more successful you are, the more likely you will be to get requests seeking "an hour of your time," a chance to "pick your brain," or an offer to "buy you lunch." However, you cannot meet everyone—the time is just not there. Networking is about give and take, and you must be strategic. Of course, often it is difficult to say no outright. Here are some suggestions for deflecting a networking request where it is difficult to plainly say no:

Request more information. Some people might seek to meet you just because they think it is a good idea. Such meetings often wind up in rambling, aimless chatter that is a waste of your time. Unless someone can clearly articulate why they want to meet with you, you are better off saying no. Write back to ask what they want to discuss. Many will not respond at all. For those who do, you can decide whether it is worth your time to meet them or if you can help them by referring them to someone else.

Refer the person to pertinent resources. Once you know what information the other person is interested in, you can refer them to content or people that can provide the information they seek. Those who are worth your time will first make use of these already available resources before they write back to you with targeted, specific questions.

Invite them to a group gathering. A good way to save time is to invite the person to a group gathering that you are already planning to attend. You can also organize your own event to invite and meet with several people at the same time.

Delay your acceptance. Another way to guard your time is to delay the invitations you accept, corralling them into a time period when you have greater flexibility.

9. Optimize time for different types of meetings: Ten-minute calls are a great way to initially connect or to give someone quick advice. You can do a video call—using Google Hangouts, Skype, or Zoom. That is efficient because people get to the point right away. You can also do these calls while working from home.

Introductory coffee meetings, lunches, or dinners are usually not a good idea. Coffee or meals are a better use of time to meet with people you already know. It is more productive to do a 30-minute meeting in the office when you are meeting someone the first time.

Whatever meetings you hold, group them into blocks depending on your particular schedule and allot them a time duration. When you feel like a meeting needs more or less time, you can adjust your schedule accordingly, but always start with a goal in mind.

SEVEN SINS OF NETWORKING

When done right, networking is an extremely valuable investment of every salesperson's time and energy. It helps you establish useful business connections, get feedback, and advance your business and career. And best of all, it pays dividends that continue to accumulate over time. However, in addition to the obvious lack of etiquette or professionalism, like bad behavior or not dressing the part, there are a few pitfalls you should avoid while networking. Here are some common networking mistakes.

1. Not listening well: Taking time to listen instead of talking too much helps build rapport. Listening helps you understand people and find common ground and ways to work together. Find the appropriate balance between talking and listening for the person you are meeting.

As civilization becomes busier, our listening skills have been much blighted by our compulsion to shut out the opus of sound in which the living world is dunked. For example, before connecting different names with distinct people, children have to be able to distinguish between the sounds of those names; between Jenny and Kenny, Tim and Kim. That is one of the first steps we take in making sense of the world. Plus, hearing is the most social of the senses after touching. It is actually quite hard to really know a person by sight alone, without listening to them. And it is not just the words that inform. The tone and rhythm of voice and movements also reveal intent, character, and variations of mood.

Remember, there is wisdom in listening. When we are not listening, we can miss much that could give us insight and information.

2. Being overly humble: Being utterly humble may work quite well in a social setting; however, a business setting requires you to underline your strengths and achievements without sounding arrogant. In business, relationships are mostly driven by the value on offer. People have to see how you can be of value to them. Hence, it is important to let people know that you are someone they will benefit from knowing or working with. Being humble may take you places, but being too humble will not get you anywhere. Here are some reasons why:

Humility means different things to different people. Different people have different perceptions of humility. While meeting other people, be aware of how they perceive humility. For some people, too much humility may mean that you are timid or a pushover. Beware of people looking to take advantage of your humility. Humility should be conditioned to suit different situations and people.

Other people may not know your value. If you are too humble, then people who do not know you or your achievements well may not know what real value you possess. Sometimes you need to use words to create opportunities for your actions.

You may not realize your value. Being too humble will stop you from truly expressing the skills and qualities that make you unique and thus may blunt the realization of your potential. Often, you have to assert your way to the opportunity to use your skills.

You may be viewed as a follower. Too much humility in a networking milieu may make people view you as someone not ready to lead.

You may leave money on the table. In situations that require negotiations, too much humility can thwart you from asking for the maximum gain. You may accept a lower reward out of humility.

You will lose leadership to others. When you are too humble, you can be surpassed by people with lesser credentials than you who can talk their way into becoming a leader.

3. Not staying connected: Meeting someone once is not enough; building a strong professional network requires building relationships. And building relationships requires interacting multiple times. Find ways to regularly communicate with people you want to build relationships with.

Networking is not just about continually meeting new people and enhancing your Rolodex. You should also not forget people you have already connected with. Positive relationships are like plants; they require nurturing. You cannot close your eyes to someone for months or years and then reach out to them to seek a favor. Building enduring business relationships requires taking the time to check in with people, to see how they are doing, to show an interest in their goals and ambitions, and to see if you can be of help to them.

4. Not following up: People can miss emails or get too busy to respond. Do not assume no response as a no; follow up on unanswered emails. The person may feel more inclined to respond if you follow up.

Not following up after connecting with someone is the most common networking sin. We are all prone to this mistake as we get caught up with other demands on our time. However, it is a mistake. You are better off not networking in the first place than not following up with the people you meet. Following up is the key to networking; without it, meeting people and developing connections may be a waste of time.

5. Excessive networking: Spending more time networking than carrying out selling can be counterproductive. Networking must be aimed at building a reputation as being productive.

6. Not backing your personal brand: When you interest new people you meet, they are most likely going to look you up online to know more about you or your deal. You should have an active, interesting, and thoughtful online presence—LinkedIn, Twitter, website, blog—for them to browse.

7. Not asking for anything at all or asking for too much: It is more productive to network with a goal in mind. Once you have a goal, you must know to let the other person know about it without coming off as manipulating. Many people just talk without making an ask. You will never get what you want unless you clearly indicate what it is. It is fine to have an ask when you are networking; it helps move the relationship and provides a context for the conversation. However, be reasonable and do not make the mistake of asking too much or too soon.

Using Voicemail

"The human voice is the most perfect instrument of all."
Arvo Pärt

An essential requisite of personal selling is to be able to get through to
decision makers. One skill needed is effectively using voicemail to
cultivate sales opportunities. A major portion of prospecting calls will go
to voicemail. Like all sales tools, voicemail can be a double-edged sword.
But if you know how to manage it, it can be a formidable ally. To get the
best results, you need solid voicemail techniques.

Checking voicemail is a tedious task. If you require someone to do it,
be sure to leave them an interesting message. Use voicemail to arouse your
sales prospect's curiosity. Put yourself in the prospect's shoes and think
about what would interest you the most, if you were in their position. Too
many voicemails left by salespeople are dull and uninteresting. Do not
forget a voicemail is not about you; it is about the person you are calling.

IS IT WORTH LEAVING A VOICEMAIL?

Yes, voicemail is worth it. "The tongue can paint what the eyes can't
see," goes a Chinese proverb. Of course, it is hard to leave a good voicemail,
and even if you do leave an effective message there is a significant chance
that the prospect may not listen to it. If the prospect does listen to your

voicemail, there is every possibility that they may not call you back. However, it is worth leaving a well-crafted voicemail. Although you might get a higher response rate from an email or another type of message, responses to voicemails are generally richer and reveal a greater level of interest. So, what you lose in quantity, you gain in quality.

HOW TO LEAVE AN EFFECTIVE VOICEMAIL

"Words mean more than what is set down on paper. It takes the human voice to infuse them with deeper meaning," said poet and civil rights activist Maya Angelou. Here are some suggestions for leaving an effective voicemail.

1. Make sure the recipient listens to the voicemail: Find out that the person you are trying to reach listens to their voicemail. Before you let the receptionist or another gatekeeper transfer you, ask if the person actually listens to their voicemail. If the answer is not an emphatic yes, then inquire what could be a better way to make contact.

2. Keep it short: An effective sales voicemail should be 20–30 seconds and not much longer or shorter. Longer messages tend to lose the recipient's interest. Plus, most phones show the number and voicemail duration. If the recipient sees the message is from an unknown number and only a few seconds long, they are likely to think it is not important. If it is too long, it may be daunting. Experience has shown that 20–30 seconds is the optimal length for listening. A voicemail in this range spurs curiosity without demanding too much time.

3. Be very specific: Be even more specific than you would be in an email. Do not leave a generic message. The story you tell or the questions you ask in a voicemail should be so specific that they could never be intended for another listener. The more personal the question, the more likely you are to get a response. The more specific the question, the more responsibility the person feels to answer you.

4. Do not disconnect without leaving a voicemail: When you call a prospect, you have to leave a message. Do not think that your number will pop up as a missed call and the prospect will call you back. If there is no accompanying voicemail, your chances of getting a response are minimal. If you do this two or three times in a row, you further diminish your chances of connecting. Since the prospect has now seen your number come up multiple times without receiving a voicemail, they will think that this is not a call they need to take and may not pick up the next time you call. One the other hand, if you record a few messages with a highly specific question, the prospect may feel a pang of guilt each time you call back because they feel they owe you an answer.

5. Speak in your normal tone: Do not fake enthusiasm in an unnatural tone. Such a tone of voice makes it clear to the listener that this is a generic call. They imagine you hanging up, calling another prospect, and leaving an identical voicemail in the same high pitch. When they feel that you are making a number of similar calls, they do not feel responsible to respond. Remember, the more the listener feels the message is meant for them and only them, the more likely it is that they will respond.

6. Do not sound salesy: Make your message stand out by staying away from sales talk. Do not use clichés or buzzwords—*cheap, once in a lifetime opportunity, incredible, cutting-edge, most, customer-oriented,* and so on. Instead tell about the outcome you can help them achieve or mention a unique fact about your prospect's company or objectives.

7. Do not talk about what you sell: In your voicemail, do not wax eloquent about your product, services, and company. Your objective is to provoke interest in a discussion. Rather than talking about what you sell, talk about the problems you fix, outcomes you help achieve, stories of how you helped, how you are different, the ROI you delivered, and so on.

8. Do not mention failed attempts: Never leave a voicemail that starts like this: "Hi Jane, this is Peter from ABC company. I have left you a few messages and am trying to reconnect to see if you would be interested in…." If the prospect did not care the first few times, why should they care now? By saying this, you are actually spurring the prospect to delete your message without listening to the rest of it.

9. Vary your messages: If you leave more than one voicemail to a prospect, leave a different message every time. Share a different anecdote, a new fact, or a new theme.

SCRIPT FOR AN EFFECTIVE VOICEMAIL

Here are some suggestions for voicemail.

1. Lead with relevance: First up, make the prospect realize that the voicemail is about them. Lead with something relevant to the prospect, such as a thought-provoking question. If it is a referral, state the name of the person who has referred you.

2. Identify yourself: Say your name, your firm, and your telephone number in a clear and easy-to-understand manner. If your name is difficult or unfamiliar to the recipient, spell it slowly.

3. Give the reason for the call: Explain why you are calling in a short statement about the value, benefits, and outcome that you are offering. This should include a quantifiable benefit that captures the prospect's attention.

4. Add social proof: To show that you can deliver, provide a one-sentence story about a similar company that has benefited from the solution you are offering.

5. Call for action: Do you want your prospect to call you back, read an email you have sent, or expect you to call again? Whatever it is that you want them to do, make it clear. Also give them a reason for taking the action you are requesting by telling them what is in it for them.

6. Repeat your identity: Do not expect your prospect to replay the message. Instead, make it easy for them to call you back. Identify yourself again by saying your name and number once more at the end of the message.

Handling Rejection

"Dear to us are those who love us but dearer are those who reject us as unworthy, for they add another life; they build a heaven before us whereof we had not dreamed, and thereby supply to us new powers out of the recesses of the spirit."
Ralph Waldo Emerson

G ood salespeople know the value of rejection in the process of developing customers. That they do not mind rejection helps them enjoy contacting prospective customers. Instead of taking rejection personally, they take a positive attitude and reaction to rejection. You must relish transforming resistance into receptiveness, leading to relationships that ensure success.

Fear of disappointment and rejection can cause salespeople to lose their eagerness, their assurance, and their enterprise. Rejection can be damaging to your ego. The secret is to not to take it personally. When you do not take rejection personally, you can react with aplomb and humor without getting disappointed and defensive.

To stay unperturbed in the face of rejection, you need to understand that, in the broadest sense, you will come across two types of rejection—valid and invalid. When you know which of the two types you are confronting, you can react objectively without it affecting your self-esteem. If the rejection is valid, then try to find out what you did to irk your prospect. Their critical comments may help you improve your approach.

If the rejection is invalid and the prospect is just venting their frustration, then instead of taking their behavior personally, try to find out what is causing the anger.

If your self-image is nourished by acceptance by others, then failure and rejection will make you feel bad. When your self-esteem is based on your own sense of worth, you will thrive on failure and rejection. You will take them as opportunities to learn. More importantly, you will always feel good about yourself regardless of failure or success and rejection or acceptance.

NURTURE RIGHT BELIEFS ABOUT REJECTION

Our beliefs determine our attitude toward failure and rejection. Winston Churchill once said, "Success is not final, failure is not fatal: it is the courage to continue that counts." You can nurture a similar attitude that overrides any self-limiting assumptions. Negative reactions to rejection can be divided into two categories. One, avoiding the situation, backing off, and retreating. Two, counterattacking, overreacting, and becoming aggressive. If you understand which of these reactions you are more prone to using, you can work on developing a positive approach to handle such situations.

This understanding will also help you improve your selling skills. If you are the withdrawing type, then it is likely that for fear of rejection you avoid situations of potential conflict, for example, confronting objections or making a case for closing. That causes you to sell at a level below your potential. If you are the second type, then you are likely a strong, assertive person who quickly establishes authority. But you may need to ask yourself if you have a tendency to become too aggressive, upset people, and damage the relationship.

Here are some beliefs and attitudes that can help you handle rejection more positively:

- Rejection is an essential part of selling. The more I fail, the more I try and the more I succeed.
- The only two ways of failing are not trying and quitting.

- Rejection gives me insight into where there is a need to improve or change.
- Rejection gives me an opportunity to try new ideas.
- If the rejection is invalid, then I must be stupid to take it personally.
- Rejection reinforces my humility.
- My self-esteem is not based on the other's personality.
- Rejection reminds me not to take myself too seriously.
- Rejection helps me reinforce my self-image and fly above the storm.
- Negative feedback fuels my energy.
- Hostile people amuse me.
- Rejection helps me decimate my fears.
- Rejection is an opportunity to become more persevering and resilient.
- Rejection challenges me to do better.
- Fear of rejection is worse than rejection itself.

HOW TO HANDLE REJECTION

Here are some suggestions for handling rejection productively.

1. Expect rejection and do not take it seriously: Hollywood actor and producer Sylvester Stallone states, "I take rejection as someone blowing a bugle in my ear to wake me up and get going, rather than retreat." Rejection happens; it is a natural and common part of sales. Challenge it when you can, learn from it every time, and move on to the next opportunity. Train yourself to accept it. Do your best to avoid it, but do not be surprised by rejection. Rejection is a reality of your profession that needs to be taken in stride.

2. Deliver a good response: Since rejection is a part of selling, be prepared with good responses for when you hear no. Practice to construct words, phrases, and responses to redirect or reframe the conversation.

Try converting the objection into a question in your mind so that you can respond as a helpful advisor, rather than defensively. Identify the concern behind the rejection and then empathize, for example, "I understand how that might concern you." Agreeing with the concern shows that you are sincere in understanding the person's perspective, and it can open doors for a deeper dialogue.

When someone expresses doubt, they probably need more information to be able to borrow your perspective. Probe gently to see where you missed the mark. When you have a convincing response, calmly state your case. Use the word *because* to explain the reason behind it. Be specific and make sure that your reasoning is calibrated to the doubter's concerns.

When you do not have an honest answer right away, do not bluff and do not fake a response. Let the prospect know you appreciate their concern and will think it through and get back to them.

3. Keep emotions out of it: Choose not to focus on your feelings or allow others to command your self-image. Have the emotional strength to be inured against others' opinions, whims, and biases. Focus on the objective of each step of the sales process and not on yourself or the difficultness of others.

4. Within rejections lie opportunities: The more valuable contacts you make in your target market, the bigger a pipeline you have. In many cases, rejection is purely because of timing. A prospect who says no today can become a valuable customer tomorrow when the conditions have changed.

View a rejection as no more than a stepping stone toward the success you want. It is simple arithmetic. The more often you put yourself out there, the better your odds of achieving what you want. By declining to get sucked into negative comparisons, resentment, and self-pity, you can transform your rejections into footholds that help you climb closer to your goals. Stay open-minded, act on feedback, and shun self-rebuke, and you will eventually know that it pays to risk rejection.

5. Do not take rejection personally: Usually, a rejection in sales just means that your product or service was not what the prospect needed. It is not about you. To the prospect, it could be anyone. Rejection can stem from numerous reasons that have nothing to do with you. Smile and get on with your job, or move on to the next prospect.

Remember, rejection is just part of the process. When people say no to your offer to sell, it can mean one of the several things:

- They are not ready for what you offer.
- They are confused or overwhelmed for now.
- What you offer is not right for them.
- An unseen influencer killed the purchase.
- Their priorities have changed.
- They do not see the value of what you offer.
- They do not have enough information to feel confident enough to buy your solution.
- You rubbed them the wrong way.

So, it can be any of various reasons, many of which you cannot control. Your prospects have their own issues. Reflect on what you could do differently the next time and wish them well.

6. Focus on your own process: Your job is to execute the sales process at a high level, and not to worry about someone's reaction to you. Rejection is simply an element of the sales process; factor it into the equation. Stay focused on your process, and do not allow yourself to be derailed by someone's words.

7. Stay optimistic: Be confident that there are businesses that need what you offer. Make timing, mastery, and execution your vehicle to success. Keep plowing; a certain percentage of the contacts you make will eventually become customers.

Rejection in sales is inevitable. No matter how good your offering, some prospects are just not likely to buy. Stay optimistic and persevere. Retrace and think how you can add more value to your proposition the next time. Overcoming rejection through the power of positive thinking is an essential skill for a salesperson. Remember American philosopher, political theorist, and revolutionary Thomas Paine's words, "The real man smiles in trouble, gathers strength from distress, and grows brave by reflection."

8. Learn from rejection: Every sales rejection is a learning opportunity. Examine each transaction in detail to identify what went wrong and what went right. Sometimes your competition beat you to the punch or offered a better deal. Sometimes your product is just not the right fit.

You cannot improve your sales if you do not meticulously examine each rejection. Do not be afraid to ask the prospect for the feedback. Keep your self-examination critical yet positive. Constructive thinking is productive and keeps you on task. Think of the sales you do make, and learn what distinguishes them from the ones that are rejected.

Remember, rejection is not about everything being offered; it is usually a small part your customer does not like. When a prospect says no, break down the no to clarify what exactly your prospect is rejecting.

Stay in control and identify the areas where you could have handled the sale better. Often there are some things you could have done better to increase the likelihood of the sale. Figuring out what you could have done better will boost your confidence and your chances the next time.

Focus on what you want to accomplish in the long-term instead of being consumed by short-term wins and losses. Keeping long-term goals in mind will help you keep things in perspective. The goals shift your focus from any immediate losses to the bigger picture of your progress over time.

9. Keep in touch: Do not cross the prospect off your list forever. They may not be interested now, but that does not mean they will never be. Many sales opportunities fall through the cracks due to lack of follow-through. Do not quit too soon. Stay in touch and check in from time to time.

In order to stay in the reckoning over the long-term, it is crucial to stay top of your prospect's mind, including prospects who have rejected you in the past. You have nothing to lose by checking in with them every few months to see how things are going. Work to position or maintain yourself as a valuable resource for them.

10. Be professional: Remain polite and courteous in the face of rejection. If you take the rejection well and remain professional, your prospect will remember that. If they need your offering in the future, they may remember your good attitude and approach you.

11. Remember what you love: Do not focus on making the sale; think of what makes you passionate about your business. Revisit what you like best about what you sell.

Sales, after all, is the lifeblood of the business you love. Thrive on the challenge of fulfilling your customers' needs. There are a lot of things that successful, satisfied, and happy salespeople love about their jobs. Here are some:

Contributing to people's lives. Whether personally or for business, people buy to resolve a problem or to enhance their experience. Both of these are ways to improve their lives. You are the enabler of that life improvement. When you make a sale that is the right fit, you are making someone's life a little or a lot better.

Problem solving. Making a sale is a motivation to find a solution to a problem. Most sales may not relieve a breakdown or a disaster, but they still solve a problem by replacing one or more pieces of the picture with a better fit.

Enjoying partnerships. Collaborating with people to achieve a win-win result is an incredibly rewarding aspect of sales. When a mutual purpose is established with honesty and open communication, the salesperson is more like a partner for the customer.

Performance-based rewards. Sales is less about politics and connections and more about results achieved. When you do well, your achievements and work pay off in tangible rewards. The potential for growth in sales is directly related to real performance.

Relationships. You meet a lot of people. When you help people in a way that is better than others do, you build relationships. Satisfied customers work as your ambassadors. Over time, you will acquire a team of mavens who bring you more business.

Self-management. Sales teaches you to manage yourself and allows you relative liberty to do so. You set goals, create a game plan, and achieve your targets. Even in large corporations, you are minimally constrained by traditional corporate and institutional obstacles. You also better manage your time as you can set your own schedule.

Learning about the world. You handle different types of people and have a continuous opportunity to learn from colleagues, customers, prospects, and connections. Whether you travel locally or internationally, you have the opportunity to see and experience the real world.

Independent thinking. In order to make things happen each day, constantly envision the possibilities and think for yourself. Goals that occupy your mind push you to think and look ahead. Such compulsory reasoning and awareness are healthy and motivating.

Never being bored. Sales can be lot of things, but it is never boring. No two days are the same in a sales job. You are always juggling diverse prospects, changing demands, emerging technologies, economic conditions, competition, and so on.

Learning to handle rejection. Most people, including those with otherwise healthy self-esteem, find it difficult to handle rejection. The profession of sales fills that void in human character. You learn that rejection is a part of trying, and handling rejection successfully is an important life skill. As the influential German philosopher Friedrich Nietzsche points out, "That which does not kill us makes us stronger."

Other Books by the Author

The Stuff of Life: An absorbing compendium of deep thoughts on a variety of subjects that are important to our life's thought process, this book has attracted rave reviews and is a must-read for inquisitive, intelligent minds. The book presents a completely cosmopolitan outlook with diverse influences and an expression borrowing freely from Western literature and philosophy and Oriental liturgy. It attempts to see the problems of life in the light of human reasoning. Anyone reading this masterclass in how to think freely and why will notice not only its enormous sweep but also the author's conscientious fairness.

Face Time: Event Planning for Business Success: A concise, practical book that is a complete guide for designing, planning, marketing, and staging any event. *Face Time* covers the basics of organizing a successful event of any type and offers a step-by-step guide to visualize and execute an event with clearly measurable results. This book will help you understand all aspects of event management from huge conferences to small dinners and manage the financial, marketing, and operational functions of your events. A must-have for entrepreneurs, executives, and homemakers alike.

Happiness: A Way of Life: A wondrous amalgam of wisdom from the East and evidence from the West, this book lays out a path to lowered anxiety, better health, sharper focus, and enhanced performance. All of that distills into a life of happiness. As we liberate our minds from the tyranny of external factors, happiness becomes our authentic state of being rather than a reassurance or a mere external performance. We then realize that happiness is not something we acquire; it is our natural state of being that arises when we stop creating chaos. This book, based on deep research, talks about how happiness relates to almost every aspect of life. It is an open invitation to create a life in which happiness plays the central role, a life worth living.

www.ingramcontent.com/pod-product-compliance
Lightning Source LLC
Chambersburg PA
CBHW020734180526
45163CB00001B/229